7

39936

Psychology's
Scientific
Endeavor

Psychology's Scientific Endeavor

Christopher F. Monte

PRAEGER PUBLISHERS
New York • Washington

Published in the United States of America in 1975
by Praeger Publishers, Inc.
111 Fourth Avenue, New York, N.Y. 10003

Library of Congress Cataloging in Publication Data

Monte, Christopher F.
   Psychology's scientific endeavor.

   Bibliography: p.
   1. Psychology, Experimental.   2. Psychology—Methodology.
   3. Science—Methodology.   I. Title.
   [DNLM: 1. Psychology.   BG38.5   M772p]
   BF181.M66   150'.1'8   73-15179
   ISBN 0-275-51790-X
   ISBN 0-275-84990-2 (pbk.)

Grateful acknowledgment is extended to the following for permission to quote passages from their works. Additional specific citations are made throughout the book.

AMERICAN PSYCHOLOGICAL ASSOCIATION for permission to quote in Chapter 4 several passages from Stanley Milgram, "Behavioral Studies of Obedience," *The Journal of Abnormal and Social Psychology*, 1963, *67*, pp. 371–78; BASIC BOOKS, INC. and ROUTLEDGE & KEGAN PAUL, LTD. for permission to quote in Chapter 1 from Jean Piaget, *The Construction of Reality in the Child*, (translated by Margaret Cook), copyright © Basic Books, Inc., 1954, (Ballantine Books paperback edition, 1971); JONATHAN CLOWES, LTD., JONATHAN CAPE LDT./JOHN MURRAY (PUBLISHERS) LTD., BASKERVILLES INVESTMENTS LTD., for permission to quote in

Chapter 4 passages from *The Valley of Fear* and from "The Adventure of the Abbey Grange," *The Complete Sherlock Holmes,* Garden City Press Edition, 1930; HOLT, RINEHART & WINSTON for permission to quote and to adapt figures in Chapter 4 from Eugene Galanter, "Contemporary Psychophysics," *New Directions in Psychology* (edited by Theodore Newcomb), *I,* 1962; HOUGHTON MIF-FLIN COMPANY and COLLINS PUBLISHERS, LTD. for permission to quote in Chapter 2 Jane van Lawick-Goodall, *In the Shadow of Man,* copyright © 1971 by Hugo and Jane van Lawick-Goodall, (Dell paperback edition, 1971); GUSTAV JAHODA and PENGUIN BOOKS, LTD. for permission to quote in Chapter 1 from Gustav Jahoda, *The Psychology of Superstition,* copyright © Gustav Jahoda, 1969. (First published by Allen Lane, the Penguin Press, 1969); THOMAS S. KUHN and THE UNIVERSITY OF CHICAGO PRESS for permission to quote in Chapter 4 passages from Thomas S. Kuhn, *The Structure of Scientific Revolutions* (Second Edition, Enlarged), copyright © 1970 University of Chicago Press; WILLIAM J. MCGUIRE and ACADEMIC PRESS, INC. for permission to quote in Chapter 4 from "Suspiciousness of Experimenter's Intent," from *Artifact in Behavioral Research,* edited by Robert Rosenthal and Ralph L. Rosnow; copyright © Academic Press, Inc., 1969; MARTIN T. ORNE and ACADEMIC PRESS, INC. for permission to quote in Chapter 4 from "Demand Characteristics and the Concept of Quasi-Controls," from *Artifact in Behavioral Research,* edited by Robert Rosenthal and Ralph L. Rosnow, copyright © Academic Press, Inc., 1969; RANDOM HOUSE, INC. for permission to quote in Chapter 1 a passage from James A. Michener, *The Source,* copyright © 1965 Random House, Inc.; MILTON J. ROSENBERG and ACADEMIC PRESS, INC. for permission to quote in Chapter 4 from "The Conditions and Consequences of Evaluation Apprehension," from *Artifact in Behavioral Research,* edited by Robert Rosenthal and Ralph L. Rosnow, copyright © Academic Press, Inc. 1969; ROBERT ROSENTHAL, RALPH L. ROSNOW, and ACADEMIC PRESS, INC. for permission to quote in Chapter 4 from "The Volunteer Subject," from *Artifact in Behavioral Research,* edited by Robert Rosenthal and Ralph L. Rosnow, copyright © Academic Press, Inc., 1969; ST. MARTIN'S PRESS, INC. and MACMILLAN PUBLISHING CO., INC. for permission to quote in Chapter 1 passages from Sir James George Frazer, *The Golden Bough,* copyright © 1922 by Macmillan Publishing Co., Inc., renewed 1950 by Barclays Bank, Ltd.

Printed in the United States of America

*For the three people
to whom this book
will bring the most pleasure,
and
for Jean-Mary.*

Contents

Acknowledgments

I would like to extend special thanks to the following individuals: Professor Frank R. Lifrieri and Dr. Eleanor Boll, both of Post Junior College, for their reading of an earlier version of the manuscript and for their valuable suggestions and timely encouragement; and, most particularly, to my wife, Regina, whose sensitivity, wisdom, and never-failing sense of wonder are responsible for what is of value in this book.

CHRISTOPHER F. MONTE
January, 1975

Introduction

This book is about scientific thinking and theory in psychology. It emphasizes the motives that impel scientific psychologists to do what they do, but it is not a book on how to do it. It provides no formulas, recipes, or statistical techniques for doing research. Instead, the primary purpose of this text is to help both the sophisticated and the not-so-sophisticated student understand what a behavioral scientist does when *he* attempts to understand. This text, therefore, is intended not for the casual reader, but for undergraduate or graduate students of psychology who desire, or are required to have, some knowledge of the rationale for scientific method in behavioral study. If his study focuses on the social and biological sciences, the student of the philosophy of science may also find some value in these pages.

In organizing the material for this book, emphasis has been placed on two central assumptions: first, that the construction and use of empirical theories are the most fundamental and important scientific processes of which a student can acquire knowledge and, second, that most important of all, as far as scientific theories go, is understanding. A logically constructed and empirically testable theory *is* a scientist's understanding of nature. The attempt at theoretical understanding of behavior is not new to psychology, but it is rapidly becoming the primary goal of scientific psychologists working in such diverse areas as cognition, learning, and developmental and physiological psychology.

An Overview of the Book

Our study of psychology's scientific endeavor will take us through four chapters and four major themes. These major ideas, in order of presentation, are:

CHAPTER 1 Man, since earliest times, has been motivated by a fortuitous combination of necessity and curiosity to explore his universe and to understand its workings in a *reliable* way. Toward this end, he has employed magic, religion, art, and science.

CHAPTER 2 Scientific method involves the capacity to ask questions of carefully made observations and to test *tentative* explanations under controlled conditions (such tests are called experiments). This was not always the rationale for scientific explanation, however, as demonstrated by some early Greek scientists. For some of these early thinkers, observations were not to be explained but to be explained away.

CHAPTER 3 Science, as one of the tools man uses to understand his universe, involves constructing theories that are refutable and testable. Such theories are attempts to provide a conceptual *summary* of many diverse observations and to *predict* new observations. As such, a scientific theory *is* a scientist's understanding.

CHAPTER 4 Theories are modified or abandoned only when they no longer serve adequately the functions of summary and prediction, but the rate of change may well depend on the readiness of the scientific community for scientific revolution. In psychology, a revolution of method has been realized: Subjects in experimental investigations are no longer conceived of as passive, inert particles, but as *human* responders who possess expectations, interpretations, and hypotheses of their own.

Suggestions for Reading This Book

The reader will find interspersed in several places throughout each chapter—typically after a major section—several questions or problems based on the material just read. These are called *Implications* for reasons that will become obvious as the reader progresses. In many cases, the answers or solutions to the problems are indefinite. That is, there is no sure "right" or "wrong," "yes" or "no." Rather, the purpose of these problems is to help the reader gain some mastery of the ideas presented in the text by posing these ideas in a new frame of reference that requires more than passive reader participation. The reader can benefit most from these sections by pausing at each one in order to formulate a thoughtful solution to the problem or to discover why a solution would be difficult or impossible to obtain. Either of these alternatives will ensure maximum understanding and enjoyment of this exploration of the work of scientific psychologists. The reader will find that these problems are designed to encourage the jotting down of ideas, objections, counterarguments, or summaries in the working of the problem. Whatever has been said about the destructive habit of writing in books does not apply here. Some of the most fruitful thinking takes place with pencil in hand, not to mention the benefits derived when preparing for a quiz or test.

Also interspersed throughout the text is a series of boxed summaries.

Called *Key Concepts,* these presentations are more than a mere rehash of what has gone before, but less than a new collection of ideas. In most cases, a Key Concepts section pulls together a series of important conclusions or facts just presented in the text. However, each pulling together is an attempt to present concepts in a new light as well as to summarize them concisely in one central place. Thus Key Concepts aid the reader by utilizing central ideas from the text as an aid to studying the book for tests. The sophisticated student will enjoy the opportunity to consider main ideas from alternate viewpoints, while the less sophisticated student will appreciate the chance to review the discussion.

Another suggestion to both teachers and students is that this book be read in one-chapter segments, rather than in a single large, indigestible gulp. Unlike the approach of some books on psychology (an introductory survey text, for example), the order and sequence of the chapters in this book make a substantial difference to the reader attempting to acquire a fundamental understanding of the subject matter. The sequence of chapters is cumulative so that Chapter 2 makes little sense without first having read Chapter 1, Chapter 3 will make infinitely less sense without the advantage of having read the two preceding chapters, and, needless to say, Chapter 4 will be all but unbearable if the first three chapters have not been read in sequence. Therefore, professors are encouraged to assign one chapter at a time for reading, discussion, and study, maintaining the sequence presented here, as appropriate for their courses and subject matter. My own practice is to assign the first two chapters at the beginning and at the end of the first semester, respectively; in the second semester, the same procedure is followed with the last two chapters. However, in one-semester courses, I have assigned all four chapters successively at various points in the semester with equal success. The essential point remains that the chapters should be read in order, unless the reader already has a sound knowledge of basic psychology and its methods.

Why Teach Scientific Thinking?

I should like, lastly, to make a personal plea for the teaching of scientific method and theory use to psychology students. These remarks are addressed to both colleagues and students.

It has often been my experience in the teaching of psychology and biology that students who come to these subjects with a firm distaste for, or shallow background in, things scientific do not come away from these courses any more tolerant, concerned, or sophisticated for the experience. It was rather a grim discovery that my students had gained not so much as a glimmer of what I considered most important: a sense of the scientific endeavor. Mere exposure to the data and theories of

biology or psychology in no way assured them of a concomitant grasp of
scientific thinking or discovery. The delight in the elegance of a well-
constructed theory or the pleasure of following with full understanding
the thread of a scientific argument lost out to the temporary acquisition
of facts without organization, pat answers without questioning, and
puzzlement without concern or direction.

It is at times like these that a teacher finds himself compulsively
engaged in one of two behaviors: Either he berates his students for their
genetic, cultural, and compound-psychological deficiencies as evidenced
by their inability to decipher the brilliance, logic, and grandeur of his
discipline as he has just skillfully presented it, or he berates himself for
his inability to communicate with, inspire, or instruct the culturally,
genetically, and psychologically deficient organisms the admissions com-
mittee calls students. All of this grousing is done over coffee with
colleagues or wife.

Neither of these teacher-protective strategies is likely to lead to productive communication, inspiration, or instruction. The problem of
imbuing students with the excitement of intellectual mastery is old,
widespread, and unsolved. It is likely to remain unsolved for some time
to come, but, while we are wrestling with the nonsolutions devised to
date, we might temporarily recast the problem in the form of a question.
Mary Henle, in her lectures on cognitive processes at the New School
for Social Research, asks, "How do we teach students the body of facts
of our subject when that body of facts is perpetually, and with increasing momentum, made obsolescent, revised, and then made obsolescent again?" In answer to her own question, Professor Henle suggests that it might be possible to teach students to run in two directions
at once: to teach them not only subject matter but also the process of
discovery. For psychology instructors this means not only that we must
teach students what is momentarily "relevant" or what is immediately
palatable, but also that we must teach them about the nature of scientific
endeavor in an attempt to make them part of this ongoing enterprise.
This is the fundamental purpose of this book, which is a partial pallia-
tive to the "facts-versus-process" predicament facing teachers of psychology just as it is a text about psychology's endeavor to be scientific.

Psychology's
Scientific
Endeavor

1

The Origin of Scientific Thinking: The Need to Understand in Magic and Science

Men are ever engaged in the dual activity of making observations and then seeking explanations of the resulting revelations. All normal men in all times have observed the rising and setting of the sun and the several phases of the moon. The more thoughtful among them have then proceeded to ask the question, "Why? Why does the moon wax and wane? Why does the sun rise and set, and where does it go when it sets?" Here we have the two essential elements of modern science: the making of observations constitutes the empirical or factual component, and the systematic attempt to explain these facts constitutes the theoretical component. As science has developed, specialization, or division of labor, has occurred; some men have devoted their time mainly to the making of observations, while a smaller number have occupied themselves largely with the problems of explanation.

CLARK L. HULL
Principles of Behavior

Prospectus

In this chapter, Lewis Carroll's poem "Jabberwocky," a nonsensical journey through whimsy, sets the stage, by way of analogy, for an overview of scientific thinking and method. Observation, proposing tentative explanations, testing the explanations, and predicting new phenomena can all be attempted by the unabashedly curious reader who will not hesitate to admit that he sees spots over the words.

The absolute necessity of survival in a world little understood by early man probably provided the motive underlying early magic and religious ritual. When his magic proved unreliable, a new necessity began to exert control over man. The need to know his world and to understand its workings was now satisfied only with difficulty as he was forced to realize that it was not he who was *being* observed, but he who *must engage in* observation.

Little Laurent, delighted by the sound of a moving chain of crib rattles, does not yet comprehend at his innocent age of three months that a waving hand that does not hold the chain cannot shake it. Laurent's magical thinking will pass into more causal thought as he grows older, but personality theorist Carl Jung's quasi-magical principle of "synchronicity" is likely to haunt scientific thinkers indefinitely. One of Jung's patients in psychotherapy reported a dream of a golden beetle only to have the dream come true in Jung's office. Coincidence? Accident? Magic? Synchronicity?

Basic Processes of Scientific Thinking

"Beware the Jabberwock, my son! The Jaws that bite, the claws that catch!/Beware the Jubjub bird, and shun the frumious Bandersnatch!" Thus read two of the lines of a famous, whimsical poem by Lewis Carroll. On initial reading, the reader is probably a bit taken aback at the content, or seeming content, of these lines. His surprise is all the more disconcerting because he has settled down to what he expects will be a treatise on psychology and scientific method and theory. By now, he is also wondering about the purpose of the oddly assorted dots that appear over certain of the words in the first two lines. Furthermore, the reader has probably taken closer notice of the dots than of the nonsensical content of the sentences. On closer inspection, the consistency in the use of the dots over various words becomes apparent. If the use of the dots is orderly and consistent, and the reader is able to decipher the order, he should be able to predict where dots must fall in a similar sentence when presented with one: "And as in uffish thought he stood, the Jabberwock, with eyes of flame,/Came whiffling through the tulgey wood, and burbled as it came!"

Looking closely at the sentences that began the preceding paragraph, it seems likely that the common denominator for the occurrence of dots is the presence of the letter *b*. So the reader would have put a dot over each *b* in the sentence that ended the paragraph. However, it should be noted that there seems to be an annoying exception to this prediction. Notice that in the second sentence of the preceding paragraph the *u*'s in "frumious" are dotted, but the *u*'s in "Jubjub" and "shun" are *not* dotted. These vowels are exceptions to the generalization that only all *b*'s are dotted, and might be the result of a typographical error. This would mean that the *u*'s in "frumious" and in no other word were accidentally dotted, or that the exception might be a one-of-a-kind occurrence so that, wherever the word "frumious" appears, it and only it has dotted *u*'s, or, lastly, that this exception of the dotted *u*'s might be a special case of the general dotted-*b*'s dictum: "Any word that has more than one vowel should have its *b*'s dotted, and, in the absence of any *b*'s, dot the *u*'s instead. Amen." All of these *possible*—and sometimes outlandish—explanations or hypotheses that arose from our attention being directed to a peculiar circumstance can be checked by anyone interested in this phenomenon, provided there are more occurrences of nonsense sentences. It is an open and public phenomenon, accessible to anyone who can read.

These processes of (1) *observation of occurrences* (reading the various words in the nonsense sentences), (2) *discovering similarities* among your observations (looking for regularity in the placement of dots, finding all *b*'s dotted), (3) *noting the exceptions* among your observations of the phenomenon (discovering dotted letters that are *not b*'s), (4) *offering a tentative explanation, or hypothesis,* to account for your observations (attempting to understand *why* some letters and not others are dotted), and (5) *predicting future occurrences of the event* (dotting the appropriate letters, according to your hypothesis, in a new sentence) play a large part in scientific thinking.

Our example of sentence-deciphering is analogous to the decoding of reality that scientists attempt. (Cf. Kuhn, 1970, Ch. 4, for a picture of the scientist as solver of puzzles.) Our example, however, is an analogy and only an analogy. As such, it possesses some considerable flaws. The actual process and application of scientific method, and the formation and testing of hypotheses in the behavioral and life sciences, are significantly more complex. The increased complexity in a large number of cases derives from the techniques of observation that have been developed. The scientist often employs instruments to increase the power and efficiency of his otherwise limited and unaided human senses. As an illustration, imagine that each of the words in Lewis Carroll's sentences were microscopic cells no larger than one fifty-thousandth of an inch. Of the various types of cells represented by the differing words, some are susceptible to viral invasion. Each dot now represents a virus (considerably smaller, and therefore less visible than the already minute cell in which it is embedded). The biologist who could discover the reason or general principle underlying his observation that only certain of the cells (words) are invaded by viruses (dots) would make an important contribution to the store of biological knowledge. Perhaps more to the point, the biologist is first in need of instruments and techniques that will enable him to observe cells and viruses that lie outside the range of normal human vision. The electron microscope and tissue-staining technology are important contributions in their own right for just this reason: these tools make observation possible. With the appropriate instrumentation at his disposal, the scientist can proceed from his observations to the offering of tentative explanations and from there to the needed testing and corroboration of his explanations.

We will consider each of these concepts separately in our attempt to understand the nature of scientific thinking and how it applies to the science of psychology and to allied behavior and life sciences. An important part of our task is to come to some understanding of the functions and usefulness of theory, one of the products of scientific method. Although we are getting ahead of our story, we should mention in passing that a theory serves to organize large groups of isolated observations or data into a whole, and that the whole is used to explain, in an intelligible and *testable* way, a part of the reality that the scientist has observed. To be useful, a theory must enable the user to make predictions of the "what-would-happen-if" variety. It must enable the scientist to predict events, phenomena, or data not yet actually observed.

KEY CONCEPTS

Basic Processes of Scientific Thinking

1. Observation of Phenomenon's Occurrence: an empirical act sometimes requiring sophisticated and sensitive instruments

2. Discovering Similarities Among Observations: a logical operation requiring imagination and creativity on the part of the scientist seeking uniformity and regularity in natural events

3. Noting the Exceptions Among Observations: another empirical act usually requiring some form of measurement, the most simple kind being that of counting

4. Offering Hypothetical Explanation of Phenomenon: another logical operation akin to number 2 above, but further requiring a skeptical state of mind in the scientist that says, in effect, "This is what *could* be. Let's wait and see"

5. Predicting Future Occurrences of Phenomenon: an act of deductive logic based on steps 1 through 4 and serving as a means of testing the hypothetical explanation

Observation as the Basis of Early Man's Magic and Science

Although no one knows for sure the exact moment in the history of early man when science as a mode of thinking and a method of observation was born, it is reasonable to assume that when early man, in his struggle for survival, found it necessary to observe the conditions that led *reliably* and *consistently* to desired effects, science was born. James George Frazer, in his monumental work, *The Golden Bough,* presents an intriguing discussion of the events that led early man from magic to religion to science. Although Frazer's account has come to be regarded as somewhat speculative, there is some reason to believe that tribal magic was the mother of science, religion, and art. Frazer's thinking on this topic has served as the starting point for many modern anthropologists interested in the relationships between magic and science, and for this reason we will stay very close to Frazer's account in our discussion.*

The Thinking and Motives Underlying Magic

Confronted by strange and seemingly arbitrary events like floods, crop failures, sickness, and death, early man, unable to explain these mysteries in terms of natural and predictable causes, sought aid and understanding in ceremonies designed to control his world. Frazer points out that the underlying thought processes involved in magic are anchored in the concrete and the experiential. Early man structured his thinking about his world on the premise that events, though apart in time or geography, can influence and act on each other through secret and unknowable means. Further, he believed that imitation of the desired event produces the event: a kind of primitive cause and effect, called *sympathetic magic.* Sympathetic magic may be further divided into two subclasses: *homeopathic* (imitative) and *contagious* magic.

Homeopathic (imitative) magic is based on the principle of similarity, that is, "like produces like." Early men, in other words, assumed that they could produce any desired effect by imitating the effect in their own actions. For example, many primitive tribes believe that by destroying an image of an enemy, one can harm the enemy himself. A more practical example of imitative magic, as given by Frazer, concerns man's attempts to secure food:

> The Indians of British Columbia live largely upon the fish which abound in their seas and rivers. If the fish do not come in due

* A sound introduction to these ideas and their application to the science of biology is provided by Paul B. Weisz in his text *The Science of Biology.* Alternative points of view to Frazer's are available to the student. Bronislaw Malinowski's *Magic, Science and Religion* might prove to be a good starting place. Both books are listed in the bibliography at the end of this book.

season and the Indians are hungry, a Nootka wizard will make an image of a swimming fish and put it into the water in the direction from which the fish generally appear. This ceremony, accompanied by a prayer to the fish to come, will cause them to arrive at once.

(1963, p. 20)

We can see that the motive behind homeopathic magic is to control and predict the events that mean survival and other desirable secondary outcomes. Additionally, no matter how peculiar the reasoning seems, it must be remembered that homeopathic magic is an attempt to control by understanding. The same kinds of aspirations are involved in the second variety of sympathetic magic, contagious magic, but different means are employed in executing a contagious ritual.

Contagious magic is based on the principle of contact or contiguity, that is, things or events that have once been in contact or enjoyed a close relationship continue to act on each other at a distance. For example, early men believed that an object that had been in the possession of a person continued to affect that person even when no longer in contact with him. Removal of hair and fingernail clippings from a fellow tribesman assured the early magician of some measure of control over the fate of that tribesman. The intention of the magician might be to cause the tribesman to fall in love or to fall ill or dead. Whatever the intention, the motives underlying contagious magic revolved around man's attempt to understand his universe and to affect it in some way.

The principles of association, similarity, and contact, though certainly not formulated by early man, or even recognized as such by him, formed the basis of his approach to reality. These same principles underlie current scientific thinking in many instances. However, unlike modern scientists, early magical thinkers misapplied these principles, or, more correctly, applied them in the wrong places to the wrong events:

A ceremony intended to make the wind blow or the rain fall, or to work the death of an enemy, will always be followed, *sooner or later,* by the occurrence it is meant to bring to pass; and primitive man may be excused for regarding the occurrence as a direct result of the ceremony, and the best possible proof of its efficacy. Similarly, rites observed in the morning to help the sun to rise, and in the spring to wake the dreaming earth from her winter sleep, will invariably *appear* to be crowned with success, at least in the temperate zones; for in these regions the sun lights his golden lamp in the east every morning, and year by year the vernal earth decks herself afresh with a rich mantle of green. [Italics added.]

(Frazer, 1963, p. 68)

Because success occurred at least some of the time, only the closest scrutiny would have detected the unrelatedness of magical "cause" to observed effect. How could primitive man doubt that his ceremonies, followed by these eventual successes, were the necessary and sufficient cause of these desirable events? The rare skeptic who suggested that the rising of the sun and the magic ceremony have little or nothing to do with each other would have been dismissed as patently mad. The day of experimental testing of this hypothesis had not yet come.

KEY CONCEPTS

Homeopathic (Imitative) and Contagious Magic Compared

Sympathetic Magic (Law of Sympathy)

Homeopathic Magic (Law of Similarity)	Contagious Magic (Law of Contact)

(Adapted from Frazer, 1963, p. 14)

Sympathetic Magical Thinking: the set of beliefs that objects, persons, or events may exert influence on each other though separated by distance, time, or relevance.

1. The process of influence is irrational, alogical.

2. Frazer believed magical thinking was an error in the association-of-ideas process.

3. Frazer called this error the "Law of Sympathy."

4. Homeopathic and contagious magic are branches of sympathetic magic and are related ". . . since both assume that things act on each other at a distance through a secret sympathy, the impulse being transmitted from one to the other by means of . . . a kind of invisible ether . . . to explain how things can physically affect each other through a space which appears to be empty." (1963, p. 14)

Homeopathic Magic: (Similarity)   governed by the "law of similarity," that is, "Like produces like." **Example:** Injure an enemy by injuring an image or statue of him.

Contagious Magic: (contact)   governed by the "law of contact." "Once in physical contact, two things forever influence each other, even when now separated." **Example:** Some natives believed that an extracted tooth or a hank of hair, when in the possession of an enemy, could be used to exact revenge.

The Overpowering Flaw of Magic: Unreliability

Sometime, somewhere, those whom Frazer calls the "shrewder minds" among the members of the tribe must have realized that magical ceremonies and incantations did not produce the results that were observed. There were still events that could not be controlled by magic and, more importantly, could not be understood or explained within the assumptions on which magic is based. Weisz (1967), in discussing this issue, suggests, for example, that bacterial or viral attack, unknowable and lethal, destroyed crops and people alike. Despite the best efforts of magic, crops and people often did not survive. The fatal flaw in magic was that for some events it was not reliable:

> . . . the analogy between the magical and scientific conceptions of the world is close. *In both of them the succession of events is assumed to be perfectly regular and certain, being determined by immutable laws, the operation of which can be foreseen and calculated precisely;* the elements of caprice, of chance, and of accident are banished from the course of nature. . . .
>
> The fatal flaw of magic lies not in its general assumption of a sequence of events determined by law, but in its total *misconception of the nature of the particular laws* which govern that sequence. [Italics added.]

(Frazer, 1963, p. 57)

IMPLICATIONS

The Mystic Bottle: Dunninger's Complete Encyclopedia of Magic describes the following demonstration: A quart bottle is placed upside down (on its neck) on a table top. The magician covers the bottle momentarily by placing a cardboard cylinder over it. After recitation of the appropriate incantation, the cardboard cylinder is removed and the bottle—to everyone's surprise—is seen in an upright position.

Problem: The implication of this trick, and in fact, of all "magic" tricks, is that the magician exerts mystical control over space, time, and matter so that the impossible—within known natural laws—is accomplished.

1. Can this illusion be analyzed in terms of the five processes of scientific thinking discussed previously?

2. Offer several *possible* explanations of how this magical effect was accomplished.

3. Can each of your explanations be tested? If so, how?

4. What conditions, if they existed and could be discovered, would refute the implication of this trick as stated above?

Magic ceremonies that do bring about the desired effect must actually be applied science, based on accurate observation of what condition leads to what effect; magic that does not work is true magic because it is pursued in the absence of total success. True magic thus fails the critical test that must be passed by applied science or common sense: *Does it work?*

Animatism and Man's Feeling of Powerlessness

Whenever magic, and the underlying conception of reality on which it is based, failed primitive man, he was left mystified. His attempts at understanding his world and his endeavors to control it were stymied. He could only assume that unseeable beings were responsible for his successes or his failures. In making such an assumption, he had to relinquish the notion that *his* magic, *his* control, steered the world.

> Not that the effects which he had striven so hard to produce did not continue to manifest themselves. They were still produced, but not by him. The rain still fell on the thirsty ground; the sun still pursued his daily and the moon her nightly journey across the sky. . . .
> All things indeed went on as before, yet all seemed different to him. . . . For he could no longer cherish the pleasing illusion that it was he who guided the earth and the heavens in their courses, and that they would cease to perform their great revolutions were he to take his feeble hand from the wheel.
>
> (Frazer, 1963, p. 66)

Man was forced to realize that his magic was impotent. He suspected that there must be higher and more powerful forces than himself at work. Thus, magic had indirectly given birth to, and had been usurped by, religion. We can again see that the motive underlying both magic and religion was an attempt to understand, predict, and control the world.

Early man then began to attribute animate, even godlike being to the inanimate and uncontrollable things of his world. The anthropologist E. B. Tylor has suggested the term "animism" to designate a belief in spiritual beings. To distinguish this general belief in spiritual beings from the specific conviction that inanimate objects also embody spirit, the term "animatism" was introduced by R. R. Marett. Natural events and forces were thus construed as living personages with an almost human propensity for mischief.

James A. Michener, in his novel *The Source,* provides us with a fictionalized but dramatic illustration of primitive man's animatism. A primitive family, struggling to eke out an existence from the land, is confronted with one of nature's more spectacular events:

> Ur's son was at this moment watching the iridescent bee catcher dart among the cypresses for his prey, and he observed, "If we knew some way to make the rain and sun appreciate our problem." But the family could think of no way to accomplish this, and late that afternoon they discovered that their enemy might lie in other directions than the ones they feared, for a towering storm brewed over the Carmel and moved north accompanied by flashes of lightning and the roar of thunder. Drops of rain fell in the dust and splattered like broken bowls of broth across the flat rock. Others followed, and soon a slanting wall of water was dropping from the sky, filling the wadi and sending a yellow flood swirling among the trees.
>
> "It's reaching for the house!" Ur shouted, and he saw that if the deluge continued, his wife's fields must be swept away.
>
> "The storm fights us for having stolen the wild wheat," his wife wailed as the turbulent flood sent its fingers into her fields.
>
> Ur was no more willing to surrender to the flood than he would have been to flee a lion. Running to the house he grabbed his best spear and with it rushed to the edge of the wadi, a bandy-legged old man ready to fight the elements. "Go back!" he roared at the raging storm, not knowing exactly where to throw his spear. Always before when floods came, he had retired to the cave to sit out their subsidence, but now that his home was in the middle of the storm he was involved and there was no retreat, no refuge. "Go back!" he roared again.
>
> But his son saw that if the rain stopped falling in time, say, within the next few moments, he might by building a dike hold back the wadi and prevent it from washing away the fields. Accordingly, he began running about placing rocks and sticks and mud along the lower portions of his land, diverting the water.
>
> . . . Ur saw his wife standing in the storm, her tired face uplifted, crying, "Storm, go back! Go back and leave our fields!"
>
> When the storm was gone Ur sat bewildered on a rock marveling at how close the flood had come to destroying his home. . . . Then, out of the corner of his eye, he saw his wife doing a most perplexing thing. "Wife," he shouted, "what are you doing?" And as she threw handfuls of wheat into the swirling waters she explained in a low voice, "If the storm has left us our wheat, the least we can do is offer him some in thanks."
>
> (1967, pp. 103–4)

Ur's son, no doubt, represents the budding skeptic in this drama. He alone initiates positive steps to interfere directly with the approach of the storm. But although the storm does not destroy Ur's home and his wife's crops, and abates in time, Ur's wife makes a thanksgiving offering possibly intended to prevent future catastrophes.

KEY CONCEPTS

An Alternative to Frazer's View of Magical Thinking

Frazer's view of the origins and functions of magic among "primitive" peoples has been criticized for attributing too sophisticated a motive to people who are thought to be "uncivilized." Gustav Jahoda, in his book *The Psychology of Superstition* (1970, pp. 100–101) provides a summary of an alternative point of view; speaking of Lévy-Bruhl, a disciple of the French sociologist Durkheim, Jahoda writes:

> He reproached Tylor and Frazer for the fact that they took it for granted that the mental functioning of primitive people was identical to our own, and were thereby prevented from considering alternative hypotheses. . . . The outcome [of his own work] suggested to him a qualitative difference: *while civilized thought is rational, logical and scientific, primitive thought is affective, poetic and mythical.* . . .
> What Lévy-Bruhl was saying is that primitive and civilized men have the same biological characteristics, but owing to the divergent social influences impinging upon them, their outlook on the world is vastly different. One of Lévy-Bruhl's major contributions is the avoidance of the confusion implicit in Tylor's and Frazer's account between the *process* of thinking and its *content.* They had written as if they had a special window into the "savage's" mind, observing it at work, when in fact they were dealing with the nature of the content, and that often filtered through sources of doubtful reliability. Moreover, although he perhaps placed insufficient stress on this, Lévy-Bruhl definitely recognized that what he called pre-logical modes of thinking [akin to Frazer's magic] *persist side by side with logical ones in civilized societies.* [Italics added.]

The Disappointment of Religion

Eventually, the even brighter, shrewder minds must have come to realize that religious rites and ceremonies designed to propitiate the gods and secure their blessing on man's endeavors had equally as little to do with the order of things as did magic. Here, perhaps, the application of the laws of association leaned more heavily on direct observation of causes and their effects: Good grain leads to good crops when there is sufficient rainfall; insects cause the destruction of some grains; a dammed river can be controlled to provide needed water where one would like to have it; and so on. Observation of a limited sort began to replace man's conception of a universe ruled by mighty and capricious beings. Thus science was born.

Religion, unlike magic and science, had been based on the premise that the universe is changeable and variable, controlled by gods and spirits who intervene in the order of events. Magic and science, however, shared the assumption that the universe and the processes of nature are orderly and invariable in their operation. It was, therefore, man's task to discover this order and to understand how it could be predicted, for with prediction comes control. Magic had been one such attempt at understanding and prediction. As Frazer points out:

> Thus, in so far as religion assumes the world to be directed by conscious agents who may be turned from their purpose by persuasion, it stands in fundamental antagonism to magic as well as to science, both of which take for granted that the course of nature is determined, not by the passions or caprice of personal beings, but by the operation of immutable laws acting mechanically.
>
> (1963, p. 59)

IMPLICATIONS

1. Can each of the following situations be classified as either imitative or contagious magic (or, perhaps, as both)?
   a. People knock on wood to ensure good luck.
   b. Brides usually try to fulfill the custom on their wedding day of having something old, something new, something borrowed, and something blue.
   c. Autograph- and souvenir-hunters expend a great deal of energy and time collecting personal articles and writing samples of famous people. In Hollywood, California, there is a store that sells garments worn only a few times by celebrities.
   d. Knights in shining armor often took with them on quests a token of their fair lady's love. Usually this took the form of a personal possession or article of apparel.
   e. A man playing roulette at a casino believes that his losing streak will end when the brunette next to him stops playing and leaves the table.
   f. Bowlers and pool-players use "body-english" to direct the ball to the desired location. Often, this takes the form of a bizarre ballet punctuated by grimaces and grunts.

2. How are the motives behind the above activities comparable to the motives exhibited by early man in practicing magic? What part does failure play?

3. Do any of the situations in items a through f illustrate Frazer's assertion that magic ceremonies will be followed sooner or later by the events they are meant to bring about? Would the length of time between the ritual and the outcome be important?

In summary, we can compare the two conflicting views of magic-science and religion in their attempt to understand reality. With magic, man is self dependent, trusting in his own capabilities to meet the dangers and stresses of his world. He believes in an established order that he both

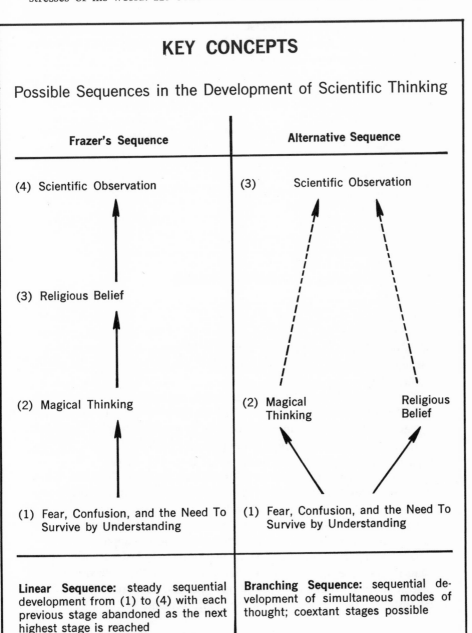

KEY CONCEPTS

Possible Sequences in the Development of Scientific Thinking

Frazer's Sequence	Alternative Sequence
(4) Scientific Observation	(3) Scientific Observation
(3) Religious Belief	
(2) Magical Thinking	(2) Magical Thinking Religious Belief
(1) Fear, Confusion, and the Need To Survive by Understanding	(1) Fear, Confusion, and the Need To Survive by Understanding
Linear Sequence: steady sequential development from (1) to (4) with each previous stage abandoned as the next highest stage is reached	**Branching Sequence:** sequential development of simultaneous modes of thought; coextant stages possible

understands and is able to control by his rites and incantations. When magic was discovered to be unreliable, and therefore man's understanding to be inaccurate, he surrendered his control and presumed understanding to unseeable and unknowable beings whom he hoped to influence. In acknowledging his inability to control, he also relinquished his belief in an orderly universe. But, with the passing of time, the readily apparent order and uniformity of his universe caused man to seek a more profound answer to his questions:

> Thus the keener minds, still pressing forward to a deeper solution of the mysteries of the universe, come to reject the religious theory of nature as inadequate, and *to revert* in a measure to the *older standpoint of magic by postulating explicitly,* what *in magic had only been implicitly* assumed, to wit, an inflexible regularity in the order of natural events, which, *if carefully observed, enables us to foresee their course with certainty* and to act accordingly. In short, religion, regarded as an explanation of nature, is displaced by science. [Italics added.]
>
> (Frazer, 1963, p. 825)

Magical Thinking: A Behavioral Analog

Whereas magic rests on the assumption of a sympathetic influence between separate events or between a replica and a real event, science depends on keen and controlled observation of the order and sequence of natural events as they occur and, later in man's development, on the capacity to imagine events that have not actually occurred but *might* occur.

The essential difference between magic and science can be seen in the old but persistent anecdote often found as a favorite among devotees of bubble-gum comics. Asked why he was parading up and down in front of his house snapping his fingers and blinking his eyes, the boy replied, "To keep wild elephants away from my house." "But," responded the amazed questioner, "there are no wild elephants for a thousand miles." Unabashed by this pedestrian wisdom and continuing to snap and blink, the boy stated with assurance, "See, it works!" Magic is based on this kind of backhanded observation, but scientific observation requires a realistic *test* of the efficacy of finger-snapping.

B. F. Skinner demonstrated an analog of this kind of adventitious, or chance, response in the pigeon. Skinner labeled the behavior of the pigeon in this situation "superstitious" because it bore no *causal* relationship to the presentation of the reinforcement.

> A pigeon is brought to a stable state of hunger by reducing it to 75% of its weight when well fed. It is put into an experimental

cage for a few minutes each day. A food hopper attached to the cage may be swung into place so that the pigeon can eat from it. A solenoid [electric switch] and a timing relay hold the hopper in place for five seconds at each reinforcement. If a clock is now arranged to present the food hopper at regular intervals *with no reference whatsoever to the bird's behavior,* operant conditioning usually takes place. . . .

One bird was conditioned to turn counterclockwise about the cage, making two or three turns between reinforcements. Another repeatedly thrust its head into one of the upper corners of the cage. [Italics added.]

(1948, p. 168)

This bizarre behavior is the result of having the reinforcement occur accidentally during a segment of ongoing behavior that bears no relationship to the presentation of the food reinforcement. Of course, the bird does not "know" this. In the usual operant-conditioning procedure, the experimenter selects an instrumental response, or operant, of the organism that occurs spontaneously and attempts to increase the chance that it will occur by reinforcing it with food or water. In this more usual case, the animal's behavior *does* bear a relationship to the presentation of food or water. The animal customarily presses a bar (the operant response) and is rewarded with a loud click that signals the release of a pellet of food into the hopper. In future responses the animal presses the bar more and more frequently until satiated with food. The pellets, in other words, reinforce, or increase the probability of, the lever-pressing response, at least when the pigeon is hungry. What makes the above-described procedure so unusual, however, it that the pigeon is adventitiously, or *randomly,* reinforced regardless of what he happens to be doing at the moment. Whatever behavior the pigeon is engaging in at the instant the clock triggers the reinforcement is reinforced, and the frequency of its occurrence increases. One pigeon apparently happened to be turning slightly when the food was delivered. From then on, the pigeon performed a kind of grotesque ballet as long as the food pellets continued to be delivered regularly. The pigeon's behavior was *not* responsible for the occurrence of the desired event (food pellet).

Much like Skinner's superstitious pigeon, early man assumed that his magic rituals were responsible for the results that he observed. In this regard, he was taking the initiative. But, unlike the pigeon, the more intelligent members of the tribe discovered their error. These "shrewder minds" sought to test their observations and explanations and to seek more causal explanations of the events that were of importance to them. Their attempts, like those of the modern scientist, were aimed at understanding their universe. With understanding, and perhaps the resultant wisdom, comes the possibility of scientific wisdom and understanding in the form of prediction and control.

TABLE 1

Magical and Scientific Thinking Contrasted

Similarities

1. Both magic and science assume that man *can* understand the world in which he lives.

2. Both magic and science require the belief that nature proceeds in orderly sequences of events that can be known.

3. Both magic and science seek to control the sequence of events as known and understood in an effort to alter outcomes.

4. The goals of magic and science are the same: *to understand the universe.*

Differences

Science	*Magic*
1. Science is based on experience, observation, and empirical procedure.	1. Magic is based on accident and tradition, often with logical but unquestioned rationale.
2. Science is guided by reason and corrected by observation and experimental tests under controlled conditions.	2. Magic flourishes in an atmosphere of mysticism, which ignores reason or observational tests of its assumptions.
3. Science is open to all; it provides public and repeatable explanations and tests.	3. Magic is restricted to some individuals who acquire secret knowledge and procedures.
4. Science is based on the conviction of naturally occurring events rooted in the material world.	4. Magic is based on the conviction of supernatural, impersonal forces, intangible and unseeable.
5. Science recognizes that only probabilistic statements are possible about nature: If such and such happens, then the probability of so and so is . . .	5. Magic relies on absolute statements or relationship between ritual and outcome: If such and such is done, then so and so will happen.

Source: Adapted and enlarged from Malinowski, 1954.

IMPLICATIONS

1. Are there any modern endeavors that resemble early man's use of magic?

2. Is it possible that modern man unconsciously or intentionally avoids facing causal explanations of certain human activities (e.g., falling in love, inheritance of intelligence, the origin of the universe)? Explain.

3. Suppose that Frazer were incorrect in postulating that man developed science in a linear (straight line) sequence that involved passing first through magic, then religion, and then observation and science.

   a. Is this sequence the only logical one in which science could have developed? Why or why not?
   b. Experiment in imagination with other possible sequences. What are the consequences of assuming alternative sequences? (For scientists, for example, what would be the consequences if religion developed from science?)

4. Biologists are investigating the possibility of artificial wombs in which a developing zygote might be implanted and mature to full prenatal development with no assistance from the mother. One criticism leveled at this project by outraged laymen points out that the birth process would become an impersonal, mechanical process. Has man gone too far in the employment of his science? Should scientists be allowed to develop an artificial womb and its associated technology (including sperm and egg banks)? What are the advantages and disadvantages?

Magical Thinking in Children

In the first few months of life, the human infant deals with reality on a vastly different basis than does the human adult. Objects, people, and sequential events do not exist for the infant. He must construct these realities for himself through a step-by-step biopsychological process. In fact, we could say that the infant is engaged in constructing his universe (Piaget, 1951).

At first, the universe and its contents are tentative: They exist only insofar as the baby has immediate sensorimotor contact with them. Later, when he is in his early teens, not only will reality have assumed permanence, but the child will even be able to construct imaginary situations that never existed in his experience—situations that will now exist only as products of his symbolic thought.

Between these phases of primitive sensorimotor intelligence and reflective adult intelligence, each child also engages in magical construction of reality, whereby cause and effect are related solely through his egocentric intervention. Thus, for example, a child may believe that all moving objects are alive, because he himself is alive and moves, or that the sun and moon follow him when he walks. The details of the development of intelligence and the sequence of fascinating changes in the child's construction of reality have been the concern of Jean Piaget and his collaborators at the Rousseau Institute in Geneva, Switzerland, for close to fifty years. Although a detailed account that would do full justice to Piaget's work is far beyond the scope of this chapter, we will consider Piaget's findings in reference to the first stage of development, sensorimotor intelligence. (Consult Hunt, 1961; Flavell, 1963; Piaget, 1952 and 1954; and especially Piaget and Inhelder, 1969, for more detailed accounts of the full theory and research methods.) Our primary interest in considering this aspect of the Genevan research is to broaden the picture of magical thinking we have been considering, its origins and its contrast to scientific, causal thought.

SENSORIMOTOR INTELLIGENCE

From birth to approximately eighteen months of age, the child confronts his world without the capability that language affords for symbolic representation of what he experiences. Nonetheless, the infant is capable of intelligent and directed behavior. He is able to construct a complex system of action schemes based on his immediate perceptions of stimuli and on his movements in response to such perceptions. Coordination of these sensorimotor (perception and movement) schemes takes place without the intervention of symbolic representation or thought (Piaget, 1952 and 1969).

Piaget divides the sensorimotor phase into six substages of intellectual development, which, unfortunately, we have not the space to consider here. (However, we shall consider the six changes of causal thought.) The essential point for our purposes is that the child in the sensorimotor phase of development responds to his world, and interprets his perceptions of it, solely in terms of his own activity and his own responses to currently available stimuli. When a stimulus is withdrawn so that it cannot be perceived, it ceases to exist. Objects that are not *now* in perception have no permanency. For example, if one dangles a pocket watch on a chain in front of the infant of five to seven months he will reach up and grab for it, coordinating his perception of the watch with his motor response of reaching and grasping. But if you drop the watch below his view, its disappearance elicits no search behavior by the infant. He does not seek it out at this stage, because for him it simply no longer exists.

Toward the end of the sensorimotor period, the infant achieves object permanency. Now if you show him the watch and then hide it behind an upturned book acting as a screen, he will seek out the watch behind the screen. He realizes that it still exists behind the book and has merely changed location. In Piaget's terms, he understands that the watch is "permanent": It has only changed its geography.

Magical Causality

Our discussion to this point has been a lengthy but necessary background to the topic of our main interest. The infant's conception of causality during sensorimotor development is centered in his own actions. Because his world consists of objects *he* can perceive and to which *he* can respond, the only cause he knows is himself. He does not yet grasp that temporal and spatial sequences of physical contact operate between events any more than he grasps the existence of the hidden watch. Thus, in playing with dangling crib toys, the infant does not comprehend that the toy he is pulling on is connected to the others by physical connection, a string, and that it is this connection which allows his "pulling scheme" to successfully shake them all. To prove this inference, walk up close to the crib and make some sound; the infant is likely to employ his same "pulling scheme" response to make the *sound* happen again. In effect, he thinks that since he caused one event, he can cause another (another sound) by the same means. He fails to grasp the necessity of operating appropriately on external, physical means.

Piaget provides an amusing example of such magical thinking in one of his own children:

> At 0;8 [months] Jacqueline is lying down looking at a saucer which I swing about 50 centimeters in front of her eyes. She reveals a lively interest and expresses her pleasure by the well-known behavior of arching herself upward, with her weight on her feet and shoulder blades, and then letting herself fall in a heap. I pass the saucer before her again. She watches it, smiling, then stares at it seriously and attentively and arches upward a second time. When Jacqueline has fallen back again I pass the object before her once more; the same play three more times. After this I hold the object motionless before her; she arches herself again two or three times, then proceeds to something else. I resume twice; as soon as the saucer is motionless Jacqueline arches upward again. I definitely pause in my game; Jacqueline nevertheless draws herself up five or six times more, while looking at the object, then tires of it. Every time the child's gesture has been followed by the saucer's movement, Jacqueline has manifested great satisfaction; otherwise, an expression of disappointment and expectation.
>
> (1954, p. 269)

Jacqueline has magically tried to cause the saucer movement through the arching response. Piaget is at pains to point out that, although the child's actions seem to evidence a magical belief in causality without material connection, her use of familiar behaviors to bring about new end goals indicates that she is on the threshold of intelligence (Piaget, 1969, p. 10). Thus the essence of sensorimotor development is its practicality—"aimed at getting results rather than at stating truths"—and its most important result lies in the structuring of reality that is accomplished for later *symbolic* manipulation of the world. Sensorimotor intelligence "organizes reality by constructing the broad categories of action which are the schemes of the permanent object, space, time and causality, [physical] substructures of the notions [abstract ideas] that will later correspond to them." (1969, p. 13)

An important point to keep in mind is that not one of these categories of space, time, or causality is available to the child at birth. His universe is centered on his own body and on his own actions in a total egocentrism. This egocentrism is equally unconscious since the infant lacks even awareness of self as independent of everything else he experiences. Magical thinking, therefore, is essentially an egocentric orientation toward reality that claims to control the universe in terms of self-initiated actions that may or may not be appropriate to the effect intended. The concept of *external* causation, spatial contact, requires symbolic representation of a permanent and independently existing external world. The child must be able to internalize his motor responses and schemes and convert them to cognitive or mental schemes.

The Origins of Causal Thought

The child's concept of causality, to repeat an essential point, is originally egocentric, focusing on the relations between the self and the world in a global and fused fashion. "Self" and all that is "not-self" are fused into a single mass of ongoing experience. It is only when the self is dissociated from the "everythingness" of the universe as an independent object among equally independently existing objects "out there" that the more abstract concept of causes and their effects can be realized.

> Hence causality presupposes at all levels an interaction between the self and things, but if the radical egocentrism of the beginnings first leads the subject to attribute all external events to personal activity, the formation of a permanent universe subsequently enables the self to be located among things and to understand the totality of the sequences which it sees or in which it is engaged as cause or effect.
>
> (Piaget, 1954, p. 357)

Thus *the apprehension of the universe and its contents as having permanent and independent existence is the necessary condition for the development of the notion of causality as contrasted with magical thinking.* For Piaget, then, causality must be definable in terms of the structure the developing intelligence imposes on reality. As intelligence develops its structuring of reality, the child's conception of cause and effect matures to adult status.

An essential question now poses itself: What is the sequence of development in the child's maturing conception of causality?

The Developmental Sequence

The infant is ignorant of his own existence. He perceives reality only through his own activity. Consequently, the picture Piaget draws of the child's developing sense of his universe begins at ground zero: no causality beyond self. The developmental sequence ends for the child in a cognitive revolution by which the universe becomes populated with independent, permanently existing objects and externally caused events. It sounds very much like Frazer's account of early man's development. From start to finish the process involves six phases.

STAGES ONE AND TWO: GLOBAL CAUSALITY AND FEELINGS OF EFFICACY
The infant makes contact with his world through his inborn reflexes. He learns to suck, grasp, look at what he grasps. But in all of these activities he shows no evidence that he retains stimuli. That is to say, he behaves as if once a stimulus is out of sight, it no longer exists and has no continued permanence. Recall the example of the pocket watch. The absence of a sense of object permanence marks stage one. However, through his reflexes the infant eventually develops certain habits by which he learns to associate the presence of one stimulus with another. This is stage two, habit formation. Thus, for example, he learns that a given face accompanies feeding (food), along with characteristic sounds, smells, and touches. But he cannot yet anticipate one stimulus from the presence of another. They must both be present *simultaneously* for them to exist.

Causality, at this stage, therefore, is a primitive feeling that: "Something is happening, but I don't know why." Cause cannot be assigned to stimuli in the external world since he does not yet conceive of a permanent or solid universe. Neither can he assign cause to the internal world of self since this is as yet undistinguished from the global state of experience. In short, for the infant the universe and self are one and the same—a diffuse, global aggregate. He is all that is. At best, causality can be a primitive feeling of efficacy or success when effort is accidentally perceived to bring about some desired state. But the feeling of efficacy can be experienced only in terms of stimuli immediately present, since foresight of stimuli yet to come, or its opposite, memory of past stimuli, requires a sense of a permanent universe. The global causality of the first two stages is therefore best summarized by saying that the infant dimly perceives that he is at the center of what is happening without being able to distinguish what happens *to* him from what happens *because* of him.

STAGE THREE: MAGICO-PHENOMENALISTIC CAUSALITY

From this third stage on the child's behavior reveals a genuine concern for causal relations, stemming initially from the activity of his own hands and feet. He observes his limbs shaking the crib, bassinet, or the dangling objects over his crib. From such exploration and experimentation a conception of his relation to the world emerges. His feelings of efficacy (power), developed in the first two stages, are expanded when he discovers that one may *intend* to bring about some state of affairs: one may intend to slap a dangling rattle with this object called a hand and presto! the rattle moves! But what he does not yet grasp is that it is the *physical contact* between his hand and the rattle that is responsible for the result. He may try just the gesture of swinging the hand without the necessary ingredient of *contact* with the target and be greatly confused and disappointed when the expected outcome does not materialize. His behavior signifies his belief that, to bring about the repetition of an originally accidental outcome, it is necessary only to repeat the exact original gesture. The gesture alone, he surmises, is sufficiently charged with the necessary efficacy. Recall Jacqueline's arching upward to make the saucer move as it had done once before as she arched. Or, for that matter, recall Skinner's superstitious pigeon repeating his accidental movement to procure a reinforcement. Piaget provides a further example in an observation of his son, Laurent, at three months, fourteen days of age:

> . . . having fortuitously shaken a chain and heard the sound of the [connected] rattles thus shaken, Laurent waves his *empty* hand as if this movement were the sole cause of the effect (sound) perceived. Then, little by little, he discovers that the chain is necessary. [Italics added.]
>
> (1954, pp. 266–67)

The infant behaves in this stage as if the true cause of the effects he observes is the power of his desires, his efforts, and the movement of his body alone, without regard to intermediate physical links. He feels omnipotent because he has yet to distinguish self from external-world causes.

Piaget calls this type of causality *magico-phenomenalistic:* "magico" because it is based on the actions of the subject (infant) without regard for external physical connection between cause and desired effect, and "phenomenalistic" because phenomenally (subjectively) observed coincidence in time of two events is sufficient to make them appear causally related (Piaget and Inhelder, 1969, p. 18). Of course, this is precisely the same variety of semicognitive operation that Frazer termed sympathetic magic. Power or efficacy lies in your ritual, not in the external environment. And so, the magician believes, does causality.

STAGE FOUR: ELEMENTARY EXTERNALIZATION AND OBJECTIFICATION OF CAUSALITY

In the previous stage, when he acts, or believes that he acts on the external world, the infant still has no real awareness that his body is an object in a world of objects. He does not link his body movements directly to the effects perceived. But in this fourth stage, roughly extending from nine to eleven months of age, objects begin to acquire causality in themselves, at least to the extent that they directly involve activity on the part of the infant. For instance, the child has learned to coordinate hand and eye to grasp objects, though he still does not comprehend that physical contact between object and hand is necessary to possess the object. But he will comprehend this notion now when he realizes that *another* person's hand is grasping some desired object, and that to possess this object in his own hand, he must brush aside the *external* obstacle. A concrete example will make this clear:

At 0;8 [months] (8) [days] she pushes away my hand which grasps her duck at the same time she . . . [grasps it], and at 0;8 (17) she pushes away the hand which offers her unpleasant medicine. Hence she endows the hand or the person of another with a spatialized causality distinct from her own.

Furthermore, simple acts have given way quite soon to more complex series during which the child incontestably attributes causality to someone else's hand. I hold with my hand Jacqueline's feet which are hidden under a coverlet. She sees neither her feet nor my hand. First she tries to disengage herself, but not succeeding she leans over and pushes back the part of my arm that is visible. . . . we may definitely conclude that my arm is conceived by Jacqueline as the cause of the retention of her foot.

(1954, p. 293)

Observations such as the above are taken as evidence that the child now perceives images external to the self as independent centers of action or causality for the first time. To prevent another's hand from achieving its effect, it must be grasped or brushed aside. Thus, in the fourth stage the child ceases to regard his own body as the sole origin of causality. Other bodies are sources of other causes.

STAGE FIVE: REAL OBJECTIFICATION AND SPATIALIZATION OF CAUSALITY

The chief characteristic of the fifth stage is a consolidation of the advancements of the previous stage into an informal and subjectively realized truism: "I am only one cause among many in the universe." Still limited to immediately present perceptions, the child is yet unable to achieve the degree of abstraction that would allow him to deduce the cause of an event from observation of the event alone. In short, he perceives the causes of events correctly, but he does not know how to evoke them at will. To illustrate the point, consider the following observation:

> At 1;1 [one year and one month] Jacqueline touches with her stick a plush cat placed on the floor, but does not know how to pull it to her. The spatial and optical [visual] contact between the stick and the cat seem to her sufficient to displace the object. Causality is therefore spatialized but without yet making allowance for the mechanical and physical laws that experience will reveal (need for pressure of the stick in certain directions, etc., resistance of the object, etc.).
>
> (1954, p. 321)

Causality has been externalized (spatialized); it is no longer solely egocentric and global. But it is not yet precise enough to divest itself of attempts at magical efficacy.

STAGE SIX: REPRESENTATIVE CAUSALITY

In the final stage of the development of causal thinking, the child is capable of adopting a truly "scientific" attitude. He is able to reconstruct a cause from the presence of its effects. In short, he is capable of inference or logical deduction. Furthermore, once shown a *potential* source of action, he can foresee its effects. He is thus able to make predictions of a limited sort, and to test their outcome by observation.

Causes now are located externally and are interpreted in the light of experience. Language has begun to develop and the child may now use it as a tool for abstracting and reconstructing reality. For example, the child perceives effect B and, to interpret it, he evokes an absent cause A:

> At 1 year 4 months, Laurent tries to open a garden gate but cannot push it forward because it is held back by a piece of furniture. He cannot account either visually or by any sound for the cause that prevents the gate from opening, but after having tried to force it he suddenly seems to understand; he goes around the wall, arrives at the other side of the gate, moves the armchair which holds it firm, and opens it with a triumphant expression.
>
> (1954, p. 335)

KEY CONCEPTS

Piaget's Developmental Scheme for the Origins of Causality

Stage One: Global Causality From the first few weeks of life to around four months of age, the infant interprets his world egocentrically. He makes no distinction between self and not-self, and he does not recognize that objects have permanent existence once out of sight.

Stage Two: Feelings of Efficacy From about five to seven months, the child has developed simple reflex habits in which he associates images and sounds together, as in feeding. But he does not yet anticipate one stimulus from the presence of another. He functions totally in terms of immediately present stimulation. None other exists. His sense of causality is one of diffuse feelings of efficacy when some effort on his part accidentally is perceived to bring about some desired effect.

Stage Three: Magico-Phenomenalistic Causality At around eight or nine months of life, the child has begun to externalize and spatialize causality, but always in terms of his own action only. He discovers that one may intend to bring about an effect, but fails to grasp that physical or spatial contact between the cause and the effect are necessary. Thus he operates magically on his surroundings to bring about phenomenal or naively perceived effects that happen to be contiguously connected to his efforts.

Stage Four: Elementary Externalization and Objectification of Causality Roughly extending in time from nine to eleven months of age, the fourth period sees the child distinguishing between self and non-self obstacles to perception. He brushes aside the hand of another which holds a desired object, thus evidencing his comprehension of external causality. His egocentrism is diminished.

Stage Five: Real Objectification and Spatialization of Causes He perceives that he is only one object in a world of objects, and that causes directly operate on objects to bring about effects. In this fifth stage, extending from approximately twelve to fifteen months of age, the child perceives the external causation of effects correctly, but does not know how to evoke them at will.

Stage Six: Representative Causality At approximately eighteen months to two years, the child is able to abstract reality. He can reconstruct a cause from the presence of only its effect. Language has developed and allows him to take into account stimuli that are not immediately present. Past experiences are now meaningful.

The unseen and the unheard are now taken into account. Symbolic imagery, the capacity to apply previous experience—experience which is not now physically present—to the problem at hand is the chief characteristic of representative causality of the sixth stage. It is this capacity

to transcend the immediate and the tangible, to search beyond the present to what *might be,* that characterizes the efforts of scientists and
children.

Magic, Science, and Children: Some Parallels

It is possible to draw parallels between the intellectual development of
the child as described by Piaget and the hypothesized intellectual
development of the human race as pictured by Frazer. For one thing,
early man was rooted in the practicality of existence. His magic rituals
and explanations were designed to achieve survival. Insofar as he was
interested in abstract truths at all, they were truths that would increase
his control of his immediate existence, much as a child attempts to
control *his* world. Although the cognitive basis of Piaget's sensorimotor
description and Frazer's account of sympathetic magic are startlingly
similar, we must not be led to believe in a one-to-one correspondence.

It would be incorrect to assert that early man never escaped the
sensorimotor phase of intellectual development just as it would be incorrect to conclude that sensorimotor intelligence is an isolated phase of
a child's intellectual development. Sensorimotor intelligence overlaps
with, and blends into, later stages of cognitive functioning, including
symbolic functioning, imitative play, reflective thought, and representative causality. The important point is that the cognitive basis of both
sensorimotor intelligence and magical thinking is the inability or the
unwillingness to process reality on its own terms, in the abstract, without
reference to one's self.

True reflective, cognitive, operational intelligence requires the capacity to imagine what is not immediately present, what has not yet come
to pass, what has not yet been observed. And then the frame of mind is
required that allows one to view such abstract mental productions
skeptically enough to create situations in which their validity may be
tested against observation. In this regard, Piaget's account of the
origins of causal thinking goes beyond Frazer's *descriptive* account by
demonstrating the *developmental* relationship between magical and
causal thought. Piaget himself compared his work to that of Frazer in
one of his early books, *The Child's Conception of the World* (1929),
and hastened to point out the difference between Frazer's *descriptive*
account and his own *explanatory* and genetic history of causality.

In any event, it is clear that the significance of Piaget's observations
lies in their capacity to extend our understanding of intellectual functioning beyond, but in the same direction as, Frazer's theorizing. By
his stark contrast of magical and causal thinking in children, Piaget
demonstrates that in essence the two forms of thought are not radically
different, nor are they diametrically opposed. Magical structuring of

reality is simply developmentally (and necessarily) prior to the type of causal thought so characteristic of the contemporary scientific enterprise. Because Piaget's formulations are conceived in terms of stages, we must not lose sight of the fact that one stage hinges on, and depends for its own successful outcome, on the previous stage. Questions about the nature, origin, and ultimate obsolescence of magical thought can thus be answered by the observational methods Piaget has made available to psychology for studying the sequential nature of cognitive development.

It would be unwise to devalue Frazer's account of the intellectual tribulations of early man, for it is this account, so closely complementary to Piaget's, that allows us to discern the differences between a scientific and a nonscientific attempt to explain reality. In short, Piaget's children serve to aid our understanding of human development, while Frazer's early man demonstrates the development of human understanding.

IMPLICATIONS

Jerome Bruner proposed four criteria against which to test the usefulness of any theory of cognitive development (1966, in Bruner, 1973, pp. 313–15):

1. "Any theory of intellectual growth . . . must characterize the operations of mind in some formal and precise fashion. . . . The description of what a child has done when he is thinking through or thinking about a problem must include as close an analytic account of his operations from a logical point of view as possible.

2. "A theory of intellectual growth must take account of the natural ways of thought, the ones that seem ordinary or intuitively obvious . . . and give these some special status.

3. ". . . any account of cognitive growth (or any form of human growth, perhaps) should take into account the nature of the culture in which a human being grows. For . . . a culture is, among other things, a system of techniques for giving shape and power to human capacities.

4. "A theory must take into account man's primate ancestry and consider the manner in which the evolution of primates and of man imposes a pattern on his growth."

Problem:

1. Considering Piaget's theory of the growth of causal thought presented in the text, why must each of these criteria be met in order to have an adequate theory?

2. Does Piaget's theory meet each of these criteria? If not, which does it fail to meet?

Magical Thinking as an Alternative to Causality

Consider once more Skinner's superstitious pigeon. The bird makes a response, accidentally, in the presence of a reinforcement. He behaves as

---

IMPLICATIONS

Sigmund Freud, inventor of the theory of psychoanalysis as an explanation of personality and as a form of psychotherapy, had some comments on a form of magical thinking found in one variety of personality disorder. Obsessive-compulsive neurosis is a disordered behavior pattern in which intense anxiety from a variety of dimly perceived causes induces the neurotic to defend against the anxiety-provoking thoughts by engaging in distracting behaviors. These behaviors often take a bizarre form and resemble ritualistic actions. For example, compulsive repetitive hand-washing, repeating a certain phrase over and over, counting your heartbeats, or making a certain gesture before going to sleep can all be counted as attempts to distract the conscious mind from pondering unpleasant, frightening, and intolerable thoughts. It is as if the neurotic were afraid of the power of his own thoughts. Freud described the situation as follows:

> The existence of omnipotence of thought is most clearly seen in compulsion neurosis, where the results of this primitive mode of thought are most often found or met in consciousness. . . . In every one of the neuroses it is not the reality of the experience but the reality of the thought which forms the basis for the symptom formation. Neurotics live in a special world in which . . . only the "neurotic standard of currency" counts, that is to say, only things intensively thought of or affectively [emotionally] conceived are effective with them, regardless of whether these things are in harmony with outer reality. . . .
>
> A compulsion neurotic may be oppressed by a sense of guilt which is appropriate to a wholesale murderer, while at the same time he acts toward his fellow beings in a most considerate and scrupulous manner. . . . And yet his sense of guilt is justified: it is based upon intensive and frequent death wishes which unconsciously manifest themselves towards his fellow beings.*
>
> (Freud, 1938c, p. 874)

Problem: In the foregoing passage, the neurotic is depicted as having to defend himself against his own thoughts. He regards his thoughts as all-powerful (omnipotent).

1. Compare Freud's use of the term *omnipotent* with Piaget's use of the term *egocentric*. Are they similar? In what ways are they different?

2. Is the motivation for creation of compulsive symptoms by a neurotic similar to the motivation in (a) a magico-phenomenalistic child, (b) early man's magic rituals? Explain.

---

if his response were the cause of the reinforcement. In fact, the automatic food dispenser regularly delivers a reinforcement at uniform intervals regardless of the bird's behavior at the moment. The pigeon has the advantage over primitive man since his desired outcome (food) appears on a temporally consistent basis. If the food were to stop appearing, the pigeon's response would eventually terminate or extinguish. Primitive man's schedule of reinforcement for his magical rituals was far less regular and consistent. Yet he continued in his pursuit. The difference between man and pigeon probably lies in man's unlimited capacity to generate rationalizations or *ad hoc* explanations for his failures. However, without the capacity for rationalization, even the pigeon can be placed on an irregular schedule of reinforcements, if this is done gradually enough to accustom him to receiving only partial reward. But in both cases a simple truth remains: both the pigeon's and early man's behavior are not the causes of their perceived effect. The responses of man and bird are related *acausally* (literally, "without cause") to the outcome. Response and outcome simply occur together in time. They are only temporally contiguous, but both man and pigeon perceive a causal *meaning* connecting the two events. Causality, then, exists not in the relationship of one event to another, but in the perceiving organism.

We can interpret magical thinking as a psychological event that has meaning for the organism beyond its perceived efficacy in obtaining desired outcomes (e.g., survival for man, food for pigeon). We might hypothesize that *some* events of the universe are *causally* related. But there are other events that are related in an *acausal* way that, by its one-sided interest, science has excluded from its explanation of reality. Carl Gustav Jung, personality theorist and psychotherapist, proposed just such a hypothesis.

Two events of the universe, A and B, Jung reasoned, can be related through *meaning* that emerges from the unconscious in response to those very events, which are governed not by causality, but by simultaneity. To such a relationship Jung gave the name "synchronicity" (Jung, 1969, *Collected Works*, Vol. 8).

The Principle of Synchronicity

To Jung it seemed that there are events so startlingly coincidental that to dismiss them as mere accident would be to ignore their essence. We have all had the experience of some uncanny coincidence: dreaming of a relative shortly before his death; a run of similar numbers from our theater ticket to our laundry bill and library card; thinking of someone we have not seen in a long time and then immediately receiving a phone call or visit from him. In none of these cases would we attribute a cause-and-effect relationship to the events: dreaming of a relative does not cause his death. In fact, Jung points out that a causal relationship between these events is not even within our intellectual capability to propose. It is not even thinkable because we could not understand how such relationships could come about. And yet, on the other hand, we are confronted with an equally inexplicable fact: the two events are related so closely and so *meaningfully* as to be uncanny. They compel us to believe that there is more operating here than a mere chance connection. Jung saw this situation as evidencing the need for postulating a principle in addition to causality to explain the operation of the universe. The new principle was not to be conceived as merely opposite to causality but as complementary to it in creating a unified and whole picture of reality. Synchronicity thus assumes status as a scientific principle of equal rank to causality; it also provides an explanation of those phenomena that causality cannot account for: "Synchronicity . . . means the simultaneous occurrence of a certain psychic state with one or more external events which appear as *meaningful* parallels to the momentary subjective state—and in certain cases, vice versa."* (Jung, 1969, p. 441; italics added).

Thus, simultaneity and meaningfulness are the essence of this acausal explanation of phenomena. An internal psychic state corresponds with an external event by sharing a similar meaning with the external event. The internal state does not cause the external event any more than the external state—which is not yet known—can cause the internal state. To assume that, for instance, the internal state (e.g., a dream about a relative) causes the external event (his death) would be tantamount to magical thinking. Jung is careful to avoid this logical fallacy, but runs up against a logical impasse instead. Both internal and external states exist in time together, correspond in meaning, and bear no cause-and-effect relationship to each other. How, then, did they both come about? Jung has no ready answer for this problem. He simply postulates that the existence of the simultaneity problem forces one to conclude that there is a force or principle operating in the universe which runs counter to our traditional expectations. He calls the principle *synchronicity*:

> Synchronicity is no more baffling or mysterious than the discontinuities of physics. It is only the ingrained belief in the sovereign power of causality that creates intellectual difficulties and makes it appear unthinkable that causeless events exist or could ever occur. But if they do, then we must regard them as *creative acts,* as the continuous creation of a pattern that exists from all eternity, repeats itself sporadically, and is not derivable from any known antecedents. We must of course guard against thinking of every event whose cause is unknown as "causeless." This . . . is admissible only when a cause is not even thinkable. . . .
> Meaningful coincidences are thinkable as pure chance. But *the*

* See footnote on page 33.

more they multiply and the greater and more exact the correspondence is, the more their probability sinks and their unthinkability increases, until they can no longer be regarded as pure chance, but, for lack of a causal explanation, have to be thought of as meaningful arrangements.* [Italics added.]

(1969, pp. 518–19)

Thus Jung was able to tolerate the ambiguity that the inevitability of his reasoning left for him. He was to provide a partial psychological explanation for causeless events in terms of the archetypes of the collective unconscious, but before we consider his formulation let us examine an example of synchronicity.

An Illustrative Case of Synchronicity

Jung's most famous example of synchronicity involved a dream of one of his patients:

A young woman I was treating had, at a critical moment, a dream in which she was given a golden scarab [an ornament in the shape of a beetle]. While she was telling me this dream I sat with my back to the closed window. Suddenly I heard a noise behind me, like a gentle tapping. I turned round and saw a flying insect knocking against the window-pane from outside. I opened the window and caught the creature in the air as it flew in. It was the nearest analogy to a golden scarab that one finds in our latitudes, a scarabareid beetle, the common rose-chafer (*Cetonia aurata*), which contrary to its usual habits had evidently felt an urge to get into a dark room at this particular moment. I must admit that nothing like it ever happened to me before or since, and that the dream of the patient has remained unique in my experience.*

(1969, p. 438)

Jung is suggesting in this recounting of his experience that there is an objective, meaningful parallel between events external to the individual and his internal psychic states that is perceived during the moment of simultaneity of the two events with the help of unconscious processes. The two events (i.e., the dream of the scarab and the arrival of the beetle) are *not* causally connected. In fact, a causal connection between the two is not even thinkable. But their occurrence together is so meaningful and so unlikely by chance that Jung was convinced that the perception of the similarity of their meaning (dream scarab and flying scarab) by the unconscious was the only possible explanation. He went so far as to propose that synchronicity demonstrates a form of psychological relativity equal and complementary to the space-time relativity of physics. For Jung, therefore, the physical world has its opposite poles: "Space-Time versus Indestructible Energy," while the psychological world is structured around the opposite poles of: Constant Cause-and-Effect Connections versus Inconstant Coincident Meaning Connection of Synchronicity.

The Psychological Basis of Synchronicity

As part of his theory of personality, Jung proposed the existence of a "collective unconscious" in addition to the personal unconscious composed of each individual's life experiences. The collective unconscious is not the product of the *individual's* experience, but rather the amalgam within an individual of the experiences of the human race as a whole. Thus, the collective unconscious is the inherited reservoir of a number of emotionally tinged images called *archetypes* that are common to all men. Archetypes are universal emotional *dispositions* to action symbolized by certain images, such as *Death, Power, God, Demon, Wise Old Man, Mother,* or the *Hero.* Archetypes are not inherited in the sense of full-blown memories or pictures, but in the sense of predispositions to respond to reality arising from the past experiences of the human race in dealing with its world. Because certain experiences have been repeated so often by our ancestors, the race has evolved in a way that makes possible certain constant modes of response. It is these modes we inherit.

Unfortunately, this explanation borders closely on the discredited Lamarckian view of evolution that acquired characteristics (experiences) can be passed on to offspring. (Cf. Darwin's theory in Chapter 2.) By this reasoning, if carried to its logical conclusion, any *experience* of a parent can be inherited by the offspring, including black eyes resulting from angry punches, sunburn resulting from overexposure on the beach, and strong or weak muscles, depending on the occupation of the parent. Nonetheless, Jung insists that the archetypes are not inherited as fully developed images, but as potential determinants to action. Thus, for example, the archetype of "Mother" does not mean that the child has a photographically accurate representation of his mother stored in his brain from birth. It means, instead, that he will respond to his mother and mother-related stimuli in certain ways that are similar to the ways our ancestors in the remote history of our race responded to this emotional image. (Cf. Hall and Nordby, 1973, pp. 41–43, for a sympathetic account of Jung's theory.)

Relying on the concept of archetypes, Jung explained the *perception* of meaning (but not its existence) between causelessly related events as a function of the operation of an individual's archetypes. "Meaning" refers to the apparent, sometimes symbolic, *equivalence* of the simultaneous events (Jung, 1969, p. 482). Archetypes, therefore, represent a special form of psychological relativity, a psychic probability that

KEY CONCEPTS

Jung's Principle of Synchronicity: Acausal Relations

Carl G. Jung was struck by the meaningfulness of so-called "chance" events like dreams which predict disaster or death. To dismiss such uncanny coincidences as merely accidental is to deny, in Jung's belief, the real essence of such events.

The universe is structured along two principal dimensions, according to Jung, the dimension of cause and effect versus the dimension of *synchronicity*. Synchronicity refers to events that are coincident in time and meaning, as opposed to events related in a causal way. Jung pictured the relationship between these two dimensions as complementary. That is, to obtain a full picture of reality, we must be able to explain the coincidental equivalence that causality cannot. He pictured the principles of cause and effect and synchronicity as follows:

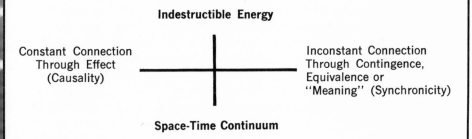

Indestructible Energy

Constant Connection Through Effect (Causality) — Inconstant Connection Through Contingence, Equivalence or "Meaning" (Synchronicity)

Space-Time Continuum

(Jung, 1969, p. 514)

Thus, for Jung, the universe is structured around the *physical* dimensions of physics' principle of indestructible energy versus space-time, while the *psychological* dimension is structured in that same universe around the opposite poles of causality and synchronicity.

Criticism: The chief criticism leveled against Jung is that the events he interprets as meaningfully connected are in fact chance events with perfectly material, accidental causes that are perceived as meaningful by the persons involved.

directs the perception of reality "out there" in terms of what is happening "in here," and provides an interpretation of the two. It is from the archetypes that the individual's *interpretation* of the meaning or equivalence he perceives between simultaneous events emerges. The meaning itself exists independently of his perception of it. Thus, the accidental similarity that we perceive in coincidences like dreams and subsequent deaths is not accidental at all. It is governed by the control of the collective unconscious over the probability of perceived equivalences between internal and external events. In short, archetypes increase the probability that causeless events which have meaning (equivalence) will be perceived as meaningful by the individual. Because, for Jung, the unconscious often knows more than the conscious mind, our unconscious archetypes focus our conscious attention on the similarity of our "superior" inner knowledge to external events. One does not cause the other: *perceived* meaningful coexistence is the essence of synchronicity.

Evaluation of the Principle of Synchronicity

Jung's theorizing bears strong resemblance to magical thinking, yet he insisted that he was not proposing a magical explanation for observed phenomena. He was, rather, trying to account in *psychological* terms for *psychological* phenomena. However, his formulations leave a great deal to be desired. Acceptance of the principle of synchronicity would mean the abandonment of causal thinking since it is the scientist's firm belief that all observable effects have observable causes. Jung did not believe, however, that one principle had to be abandoned in favor of the other. Synchronicity and causality are opposite, but complementary, explanations of the universe. Where causality fails, synchronicity succeeds in providing a unified, holistic account of nature. But, for the contemporary scientist, admission of a noncausal principle operating in nature is equivalent to being denied the right to ask "why" questions of the phenomena he observes. The principle of synchronicity demands an acceptance of a logical contradiction that in effect says, "This is so *because* there is no other explanation available." Unfortunately, the contemporary scientist has less tolerance for such ambiguous faith than Jung supposed.

Acceptance of the logically contradictory belief that at least a part of nature is subject to causeless regularity, which therefore lies beyond human power to understand, signals an abandonment of a basic attitudinal orientation of the scientist. He believes, as Frazer points out, that man can and will understand his world and that prediction and control of its phenomena are feasible. Just as early man abdicated this self-reliant stance in accepting a universe populated with capricious and unknowable gods, acceptance of the principle of synchronicity signals a return to this ignorant and helpless state.

Confronted with the unreliability of his magical control, early man was forced to relinquish his cherished trust in the power of his understanding to control his own fate. He hesitatingly faced the unpalatable alternative that mysteriously more powerful gods intervened inexplicably in his world. The contemporary scientist prefers to pursue his professional activities in the belief that all phenomena are potentially under-

IMPLICATIONS

The following excerpt from Freud's *Totem and Taboo* (1938c, p. 881) is a case history of an obsessive-compulsive neurotic. For details of obsessive-compulsive neurosis, refer to the previous Implications section in this chapter.

The neurosis of this woman was directed against her husband and culminated in the defence against the unconscious wish for his death. But her manifest systematic phobia concerned the mention of death in general, in which her husband was altogether eliminated and never became the object of conscious solicitude. One day she heard her husband give an order to have his dull razors taken to a certain shop to have them sharpened. Impelled by a peculiar unrest she went to the shop herself, and on her return from this reconnoiter she asked her husband to lay the razors aside for good because she had discovered that there was a warehouse of coffins and funeral accessories next to the shop he mentioned. She claimed that he had intentionally brought the razors into permanent relation with the idea of death. This was then the systematic motivation of the prohibition (relating to the razors), but we may be sure that the patient would have brought home the prohibition relating to the razors even if she had not discovered this warehouse in the neighborhood. For it would have been sufficient if on her way to the shop she had met a hearse, a person in mourning, or somebody carrying a wreath. The net of the determinants was spread out far enough to catch the prey in any case, it was simply a question whether she should pull it in or not.

Problem:

1. Judging from the above passage, would this woman be engaging in magical thinking as defined by Frazer and Piaget?

2. Basing your answer on Freud's last three sentences, would he have accepted Jung's notion of synchronicity? If not, what would his objections be?

3. How would Jung answer Freud?

4. Would Jung consider the occurrence of the woman's premonition of the death of her husband and her discovery of the funeral warehouse a case of synchronicity? Support your answer.

standable through the same principles and the same methods of investigation he has so far employed with atoms and cells, dinosaurs and rats, disease-producing bacteria, and children-producing parents.

Consequently, the modern scientist would look at Jung's dilemma with an eye open to possible alternative, causal explanations.

A Reinterpretation of Synchronicity

Jahoda (1970) has criticized Jung's formulation on the grounds that coincidences can be explained causally, or at least in alternative terms to synchronicity. Consider Jahoda's reinterpretation of Jung's example of the patient's scarab dream:

> The story is presented in such a manner as to maximize its appearance of improbability, but it *can* be viewed somewhat differently. The patient, it will be recalled, had a dream in which she was given a golden scarab, and while she was telling this dream to Jung a similar insect flew against the window pane. Now perhaps it is not unfair to presume that it was the season of the year when rose-chafers were about; this fact might well have been *causally connected* with the patient's dream, *the golden scarab being an elaboration of the actual sight of a rose-chafer;* since many of them were about, it is perhaps not really very surprising that one of them bumped against the window, even though it was darker inside the room. [Italics added.]
>
> (1970, p. 118)

In Jahoda's view the significance of the two events lies not in their synchronicity or acausal relationship, but in the patient's *imposition* of meaning (with Jung's help) on two causally related events that are not then recognized as such. Because the season guaranteed the presence of rose-chafers, the patient's dream was probably in response to a previous daytime perception of their presence. Thus the presence of rose-chafers *caused* the dream in the first place. In the second place, the report of the dream to Jung happens to coincide with the presence of a rose-chafer and Jung capitalizes on its presence to confirm his theory. It is not, as Jung would have it, that the unconscious detects meaning between meaningfully related events, but that ". . . a coincidence is meaningful when it is experienced as such by the people affected; moreover, one can go a step further by saying that *the meaning is imposed upon the pattern of events by the people involved"* (Jahoda, 1970, p. 119; italics added).

Jung's version of the story seems to be a case of the cart before the horse. Meaning for paranormal "psychic" events exists only after the involved individuals create it.

The importance of Jung's theorizing lies not in its usefulness for explaining phenomena but in the lesson it conveys about scientific method. When the scientist abandons his belief that observed events have explainable causes, he simultaneously abandons science. Science progresses by shedding light on those areas that were once seen as mysterious or "spontaneous" events. Explanation of such phenomena usually proceeds by elucidating the intricately concealed causes underlying them. Because some phenomena are currently unexplained by causal thinking is no reason to assume that they are inherently unexplainable by its application. Jung's difficulty did not lie in the application of his imagination to the creation of new ideas—which were prodigious. His weakness lay in his abandonment of a fundamental belief in the more mundane view that effects have their causes.

Overview and Implications of the Chapter

Science is the name we give to one of the many approaches that man uses in his attempt to understand the universe. The method of science requires that observations be made and hypotheses subjected to test.

For primitive man, sympathetic magic rituals and ceremonies served to aid him in his attempts to understand and to survive his world. In imitative rituals designed to make crops flourish or fish plentiful, and in contagious magic rituals designed to control enemies, sickness, and death, early man laid the foundation for science and religion. Belief in unseeable and mighty beings developed in response to man's inability to reliably control his world through his magic. But the substantial orderliness and consistency of the sequence of natural events prompted the more intelligent members of the human community to return to the outlook implicit in magic, and to abandon total dependence on the divine.

Man can control his universe through his understanding if he devotes his attention to the observables of cause-and-effect sequences in nature. With this kernel of wisdom—that observation lies at the foundation of scientific thinking—wishful or superstitious thinking becomes less prevalent. However, as we will see in the next chapter, this hard-won knowledge was lost to man for a while with some of the ancient Greeks. When man regards the products of his own mind as above the understanding of that which exists in the universe, reality is no longer to be explained, but to be explained away.

Several varieties of magical thinking comparable to Frazer's descriptive account of the intellectual growth of the human race were considered as a contrast to causal, scientific thinking. Piaget's observations and research into the nature of the development of intelligence and causal thinking revealed that magico-phenomenalistic thought is a kind of midpoint in the maturation of the child's construction of reality. From an essentially egocentric, global conception of a self fused with the world, the child sequentially achieves more and more internalization and abstraction of thought.

At first, the notion of permanent objects located in space is a major goal to be sought for. Having achieved object permanence of things like disappearing watches, the child possesses a primitive sense of causality, a kind of magical feeling of efficacy or power in controlling his world. Finally, with the emergence of the concept of self as an object in a world of permanent objects, the child is able to grasp abstractly the spatial and physical contact between cause and effect. He is able to infer one from the other and to go beyond the raw data of immediate phenomenal experience to imagine and to create thoughts that are freed of their dependence on available and present stimuli. This form of thought, near the end of the sensorimotor period, most nearly resembles the thinking of scientists as they investigate nature.

With Carl Jung's formulation of the principle of synchronicity we can observe a sophisticated attempt to account for a part of reality on a noncausal basis. Believing that certain events that are coincident in time and that share a similarity of meaning are not explainable through traditional causal understanding, Jung set out to propose a complementary principle to causality operating in nature. Internal and external events correspond in time and share parallel meaning through equivalence of content in the perception of the individual. Premonitions of death in dreams, or lucky runs of similar numbers, or waking events that bear similarity to dream events were offered by Jung as examples of synchronicity. When a causal relationship between any two of these events is not thinkable, one must resort to causeless explanation.

Jung's formulation has been criticized on two grounds: (1) Causeless regularity is a contradiction in terms; its acceptance denies the scientist the possibility of asking "why" questions of nature, and signals a return to the ignorant and helpless attitude of early man's abandonment of his magical, though unreliable, control. (2) Alternative explanations of synchronistic events are possible and more feasible. It may be that meaning does not exist between events in a *causeless* way, to be detected by unconscious operation of the inherited archetypes, but rather that individuals *impose* meaning on events that, unknown to them, bear a cause-and-effect relationship.

The important point is that man is motivated by a fortuitous combination of necessity and curiosity to explore his universe and to understand its workings. When he discovers that one mode of thought is unreliable, necessity and curiosity impel him to seek other modes. Science, therefore, is not only a collection of facts, findings, and concepts, but it is also a way of thinking, a method of coping with necessity and of focusing curiosity. Science is, furthermore, a collection (albeit, an *organized* collection) of fears overcome, falsehoods debunked, and frustrations surmounted. Scientists, philosophers, theologians, alchemists, and psychologists are alike in at least one respect: they think. There are enormous differences among them in the ways that they employ thought; but the goal of their thoughts is strongly similar: to understand man and the universe in which he evolved.

Recommended Further Reading

Gustav Jahoda provides a broad survey of magical thinking and superstitious behavior considered as psychological processes in his *The Psychology of Superstition* (Baltimore: Penguin Book, 1970).

Sir James George Frazer's *The Golden Bough* (New York: Macmillan, 1963; also available in paperback) is still the best prime source for a consideration of the varieties of sympathetic magic among early men. Frazer's account is colorful and worthwhile reading.

Alternatives to Frazer's viewpoint, as pointed out in the text, can be had in Bronislaw Malinowski's *Magic, Science and Religion* (New York: Doubleday-Anchor, 1954), and in Claude Lévi-Strauss' classic, *The Savage Mind* (Chicago: University of Chicago Press, 1966). While more difficult reading than Frazer or Malinowski, Lévi-Strauss provides tantalizing, almost poetic insight into the customs, taboos, and thoughts of "savages."

Sigmund Freud, the founder of psychoanalysis, about whom more will be said in Chapter 3 of this book, dealt with magical thinking, neurosis, and the Oedipal complex against the background of Frazer's thoughts in *Totem and Taboo* (London: Hogarth Press; Vol. 13 of *The Standard Edition of the Complete Psychological Works of Sigmund Freud*. 1953). More readily obtained editions of *Totem and Taboo* are also available: in paperback by W. W. Norton, and in *The Basic Writings of Sigmund Freud* (New York: Random House, 1938). Freud dealt with magical thinking from the perspective of psychoanalytic theory and its emphasis on unconscious conflict.

An ingenious experimental analysis of magical thinking as revealed in perception is provided by A. Michotte in *The Perception of Causality* (New York: Basic Books, 1954).

Michotte designed some cleverly original experiments to determine how people attribute causality to moving objects despite the lack of true cause-and-effect relations between them. Piaget's more direct approach to the same problem, with children as subjects, is chronicled in a large number of his books spanning fifty years: perhaps his easiest and yet most comprehensive treatment is given in *The Child's Conception of The World* (London: Routledge & Keegan Paul, 1929). For readers interested in a concise and authoritative overview of Piaget's entire approach to cognitive development there is a brief, but somewhat difficult, treatment by Piaget and Inhelder in *The Psychology of the Child* (New York: Basic Books, 1969; available in paperback).

Any description of causal thinking would be incomplete without mention of David Hume's classic account in *An Inquiry Concerning Human Understanding* (Indianapolis: Bobbs-Merrill, 1955; paperback). Sections VI and VII of Hume's essay deserve special attention.

Jung's own presentation of his principle of synchronicity may be found in "Synchronicity: An Acausal Connecting Principle" (Vol. 8, *The Collected Works of C. G. Jung,* Bollingen Series XX, Princeton, N.J.: Princeton University Press). Because Jung's writing is often difficult, an introductory-level overview of Jung's thinking may be found in Frieda Fordham's *An Introduction to Jung's Psychology* (Baltimore: Penguin Books, Pelican Edition, 1953), or in the more recent *A Primer of Jungian Psychology* by Calvin S. Hall and Vernon J. Nordby (New York: New American Library, Mentor Edition, 1973). Either of these paperbacks will provide the diligent reader with a detailed but understandable account of Jung's theory. The closest thing to an introduction to his theory composed by Jung himself is *Analytical Psychology, Its Theory and Practice* (The Tavistock Lectures, New York: Random House, 1968; also available in paperback).

2

Observation, Hypothesis, and Experiment: The Formal Scientific Method

Science is first of all a set of attitudes. It is a disposition
to deal with the facts rather than with what someone has
said about them. Rejection of authority was the theme
of the revival of learning, when men dedicated themselves
to the study of "nature, not books." Science rejects even
its own authorities when they interfere with the observation
of nature.

Science is willingness to accept facts even when
they are opposed to wishes. Thoughtful men have perhaps
always known that we are likely to see things as we want
to see them instead of as they are, but thanks to Sigmund
Freud we are today much more clearly aware of "wishful
thinking."

B. F. SKINNER
Science and Human Behavior

Prospectus

"Seeing is believing!" a phrase which fit snugly into every old-time
magician's stage patter, was designed to draw attention to the obvious
impossibility of the feat just performed. As audiences became more
sophisticated, rabbits out of hats, swords through beautiful girls, and
disappearing ladies became less the objects of "seeing-it-is-believing-it"
awe, than occasions to prompt the inevitable, "It's a trick, all done with
mirrors. Pretty good, though." Now we view sleight-of-hand magicians
with a different kind of awe. We recognize that the principle "seeing is
believing" is true only to the extent that the magician allows us to see

43

some things and not others. The delight that magic shows still hold for children is probably due to the fact that they have had relatively few experiences requiring them to distrust their own senses.

In much the same way, man had to transcend his own intuitive view of the world, leaving behind his magic in favor of direct observation. Plato suggested, as we will see in this chapter, that contemplation of the ideal, not observation of the real, is the path to true knowledge of the universe. Aristotle, abandoning Platonic idealism, struck out for more direct empirical investigation of the world, but like our magician friend, for Aristotle, seeing *was* believing. Not until the time of Galileo was the intuitive acceptance of observation replaced with a more imaginative, questioning world view, a world view requiring the observer to devise situations in which questions could be asked of nature and the answers tested.

Psychology, the almost-science, has begun to travel this road, attempting to apply scientific method and experimentation to the problems of behavior. Scientific method, then, may be thought of as a technique of asking questions, developing possible answers, and questioning the answers.

The Forever Changing, Unreal World

Consider the possibility of a race of people who from birth are not allowed to see or to touch anything. These unusual individuals live out the whole of their lives within the confines of an underground cave. Further suppose that you are one of these imprisoned people, and the conditions of your imprisonment are as follows. Your legs and neck are chained, as are those of all your comrades, in such a way that you cannot turn your head or your body, nor can you reach out and touch the individual next to you. The cave is very dark so that you cannot even make visual contact with the person next to you. Above and behind you, at some distance, a fire blazes, but it affords no direct illumination. Between the fire and you there is a raised way or incline on which is built a low wall similar to the screen used in puppet shows. This wall or screen, the fire, and the entry to the cave are all behind you in increasing order of distance from you, the screen or wall being the closest. You sit with your fellow prisoners facing the rear wall of the cave, with your back to the screen, fire, and cave entrance. Along the wall, to the rear, pass all varieties of men carrying all sorts of vessels, and statues and figures of animals made of wood and stone. These objects are held just above the level of the screen. Shadows cast by the held objects are cast along the cave's rear wall, which you face. You do not see the objects themselves, only their shadows. From birth this has been your environment. The echoing voices of the men who carry the objects are heard all over the cave. To repeat: You and your companions have no direct knowledge of these things and events that lie just behind you; all the experience you have acquired from birth consists of shadows and voices. The question that is immediately prompted by this surrealistic nightmare of a theater is: *what conception of reality would you have if questioned on the subject? Further, how closely would your concepts of your world correspond to what in fact exists in your world?*

Distrust of Empirical Observation

By now, the reader has probably realized that this bizarre fantasy resembling a primitive sensory-deprivation study is really a paraphrase of Plato's famous cave allegory, from Book VII of *The Republic*. Plato, in the context of a dialogue, drew a number of inferences from the cave story. We can paraphrase some of the "questions" Plato asked:

> *If the prisoners were able to converse with one another about the shadows they dimly saw, would they not believe they were discussing the* real *world?*
>
> *Would not these prisoners also believe that the echoing voices they heard were the voices of the shadowy objects and persons?*
>
> *What would happen if we liberate one of the prisoners and force him to walk out of the den into daylight?*

The first two questions are obviously rhetorical, containing their own answer, but the third question Plato answered in some detail.

> At first, when any of them is liberated and compelled suddenly to stand up and turn his neck round and walk and look towards the light, he will suffer sharp pains; the glare will distress him, and he will be unable to see the realities of which in his former state he had seen the shadows; and then conceive someone saying to him, that what he saw before was an illusion, but that now, when he is approaching nearer to being and his eye is turned toward more real existence, he has a clearer vision—what will be his reply? . . .
>
> Will he not fancy that the shadows which he formerly saw are truer than the objects which are now shown to him?
>
> (Plato, Jowett translation, Book VII)

Our liberated prisoner has now been made aware that reality has at least two levels: his familiar reality of the cave, and this new, untrustworthy experience of the world outside the den. If we allow him to become accustomed to the world outside his den until his eyes are able to tolerate a direct gaze at the sun, would he not come to believe that *this* world is reality and his former existence was a mere representation of true reality? Plato goes on to suggest that, in remembering his fellows still imprisoned in the den, he would congratulate himself on his changed condition, and pity them. Our liberated prisoner would reject his former existence and choose his new-found "reality." Plato concludes the cave allegory with an early version of social-psychological prediction. If our liberated prisoner were to be returned to the cave, his former companions would assume that he was mad, judging by his wild stories of the outside, lighted world. No doubt they would try to prevent him from freeing any of the prisoners. Why ascend to the world outside the cave if madness is the result?

The essential point in Plato's allegory for our study of scientific method in psychology is the attention it draws to the early Greek distrust of empirical observation. For Plato, all men are like the prisoners of the cave. All we can gather from our senses are mere shadows of reality; observation of the world is a poor substitute for the higher faculty of reflection. Knowledge of the true state of reality is not available through empiricism—that is, through use of the senses. The "true" state of reality is present to all men before birth. The real essence of the universe, Plato believed, is acquired by the soul *pre*natally, and the goal of education and science is to recapture this forgotten knowledge by reflection and thought. As we have seen, reflection and thought, in the absence of careful observation, can lead to magical, or at least inaccurate, explanations.

The Rejection of Observation

The important kernel of knowledge that primitive man had acquired —that *observation* of what conditions lead to what effects must be undertaken to understand and to control his world—was lost to mankind for a time with the Greeks some 300 years before the birth of Christ.

To illustrate Plato's doctrine of Ideal Forms, as it has been called, consider how Plato might have gone about understanding what a tree is. The essence of a tree, he would reason, lies not in observing, measuring, or examining many trees in all possible circumstances, and then in drawing conclusions to be tested by experiment or further observation. Rather, the real understanding of a tree can be had by reflecting on the nature of "tree." What makes a tree a tree? What is the thing without which a tree would not be a tree? The answer to these questions— "treeness"—is the remembrance of the *ideal* tree known by the soul before birth. Observation and experience were dismissed as inferior methods of knowing reality in favor of philosophical reminiscence of

KEY CONCEPTS

Plato's Idealism and Contemporary Empiricism: Comparison Summary

Plato's Idealism	Contemporary Empiricism
1. Accurate concepts of "things" are present to the mind before birth.	1. Individuals begin life without prior knowledge.
2. These prenatal ideas or Forms are universal, perfect essences and are real and objective.	2. Knowledge is attained only through sensory experience.
3. Knowledge of the world that is accurate or infallible can be had only by "recollecting" the prenatal ideas.	3. Sensory experience (empirical observation) must be repeated and checked to determine its reliability.
4. Reminiscence, *not* sensory experience, is the road to knowledge.	4. Extreme empiricists hold that only that which can be observed exists, and, to paraphrase E. L. Thorndike, if a thing exists, it exists in some quantity and can be measured.
5. Empirical acts (sensory experience) provide unsound information about particular, transient things.	5. Prime interest is in the tangible, material and potentially predictable things and events around us.

Forms. Sensory experience allows one to know only the unreal, shadowy, forever changing world. The Ideal Forms of the soul are not just memory images, but are the real stuff of the universe of which sensory knowledge is but a representation.

Modern Science as an Escape From Greek Thought

George Gaylord Simpson, a renowned biologist, has summarized the rise of modern scientific method as an escape from Greek thought:

> The element of confusion is well illustrated by a recent statement that science is "thinking about the world in the Greek way." This is in fact an important thing that science is not. It has often been argued that the Greek sense of order was a necessary condition for the rise of science. *Necessary, perhaps; sufficient, definitely no.*

IMPLICATIONS

1. Carl G. Jung, originally an adherent of Freud's psychoanalysis, broke with Freud and developed his own school of analytic psychology. One of the chief differences between Jung and Freud consisted of Jung's reanalysis of the unconscious into a personal unconscious, as Freud held, *and a collective unconscious* (cf. Chapter 1). Read the following passage from Jung's *Archetypes and the Collective Unconscious,* and try to determine whether Jung is suggesting a modern psychological interpretation of Platonic Ideal Forms:

   > A more or less superficial layer of the unconscious is undoubtedly personal. I call it the *personal unconscious.* But this personal unconscious rests upon a deeper layer, which does not derive from personal experience and is not a personal acquisition, but is inborn. This deeper layer I call the collective unconscious. I have chosen the term "collective" because this part of the unconscious is not individual but universal; in contrast to the personal psyche, it has contents and modes of behavior that are more or less the same everywhere and in all individuals. It is, in other words, identical in all men and thus constitutes a common psychic substrate of a suprapersonal nature which is present in every one of us.*
   >
   > (1959)

2. The collective unconscious harbors images common to all men called *archetypes.* Archetypes always carry great emotion with them, and we see evidence of archetypes in myths and fairytales which employ almost universal symbols, like the Great Mother. Here is what Jung had to say on the subject:

   > In former times, despite some dissenting opinion and the influence of Aristotle, it was not too difficult to understand Plato's conception of the Idea as supraordinate and pre-existent to all phenomena. "Archetype," far from being a modern term, was already in use before the time of St. Augustine, and was synonymous with "Idea" in the Platonic usage. . . . Were I a philosopher, I should continue in this Platonic strain and say: Somewhere, in a "supracelestial place," there is a prototype or primordial image of the mother that is pre-existent and supraordinate to all phenomena in which the "maternal," in the broadest sense of the term, is manifest. But I am an empiricist, not a philosopher; I cannot let myself presuppose that my peculiar temperament, my own attitude to intellectual problems, is universally valid.*
   >
   > (1959, p. 328)

   Yet, Jung concludes that there are behaviors manifest in man that are not explainable on a truly empirical basis.

   Can the theory of archetypes and collective unconscious be reconciled with empirical scientific technique? If not, why not?

---

* Reprinted by permission of Princeton University Press and Routledge & Kegan Paul, Ltd., from *The Collected Works of C. G. Jung,* ed. by G. Adler, M. Fordham, H. Read, and W. McGuire; translated by R. F. C. Hull, Bollingen Series XX, vol. 9i, *The Archetypes and the Collective Unconscious,* copyright © 1959 and 1969 by Bollingen Foundation.

The actual origin of science in the modern sense involved a revolt against thinking in the Greek way. . . .

[For some Greek thinkers] . . . the essence of things was believed to reside in a philosophical ideal, and observation of real phenomena was considered not only unnecessary, but also positively wrong. . . .

Facts were not to be explained, but to be explained away. [Italics added.]

(1963)

Modern science, in Simpson's view, rests firmly on empirical, observational foundations. Such a view should not be taken to mean that reason, imagination, and logic are abandoned in pursuing a scientific explanation for the material universe. It would be more correct to say that the modern scientist reasons, deduces, and constructs logical and plausible explanations of natural phenomena that have been observed. Then his explanations must be tested by further observations of the events (under *controlled* conditions whenever possible) to determine their *degree* of accuracy. In the end, the scientist, like primitive man before him, must demonstrate the accuracy of his explanation either by correctly predicting occurrences of the event, or by bringing the event under control. Prediction and control—these are the hallmarks of the scientist's attempt to understand his universe.

The Induction-Deduction, Universal-Particular Merry-Go-Round

The difficulty of escaping the influence of early Greek effort at scientific explanation and replacing it with a more empirical approach can be capsulized as the problem of the "universal versus the particular." Plato's Ideal Forms are assumed to be universal representations of a given reality that can be known only by reflection. There is one universal essence that is common to all trees. The same is true of elephant essence, banana essence, human essence, chair essence, or anything you care to think of. Plato was not interested in the particular elephant, the particular banana—*this* brown and yellow, roughly upholstered, swivel desk chair with the nick in the lower left arm rest. "For Plato, the world of individual things was not worth the philosopher's attention— 'This book is red'—the particular book and its redness were of little consequence to the philosopher. Only the universals or concepts 'book' and 'red' were significant, since only about these and their relations could we have clear knowledge" (Theobald, 1968, p. 47).

For the contemporary scientific psychologist, an analogous problem over the relationship between the universal and the particular exists and in psychology is nowhere more easily seen than in the area of personality. Allport was among the first psychologists to point out the difficulty inherent in attempting to understand an individual, particular personality in all of its *uniqueness* while simultaneously grasping *universal* variables common to all human personality. The *idiographic* (particular, unique) approach to personality investigation attempts to reveal the individual pattern of a single personality. *Nomothetic* (universal, or at least, general) techniques of personality study seek to establish regularities and uniformities of a whole class of individuals. This second approach is concerned more with measurement and statistical relationships, whereas the idiographic or individual method may actually combine both statistical and clinical technique in studying an individual personality (Allport, 1960, and 1961; Falk, 1956).

At first it may seem as though there is no conflict between the two approaches, but closer scrutiny reveals that the psychologist is faced with a choice at the outset of his research. He can either be concerned with in-depth clinical study of individual personality themes in terms of a single person's *personal* history, *idiosyncratic* responses to ink blots and ambiguous pictures, *unique* answers to open-ended statements (When I am alone, I usually . . .) and *singular* perceptions of stimuli; or he can concern himself with analysis of *groups,* collections of data from many individuals. Some scientists feel that science must build on individual cases to abstract what is common to them all in order that universal laws be established. Science as such deals only with the universal, general, not with the particular case. Allport has argued that the idiographic and nomothetic approaches must be blended:

Psychology, it seems to me, must be equipped to deal with the *whole* of personality. . . . What is "distinctive," what is "characteristic" must be included. . . . Our difficulty here lies in the cultish conception of science, which bedevils most of us simply because of the incalculable prestige of those disciplines that have dealt so successfully with *inanimate* nature. If we no longer rivet our attention to their methods . . . and if we ask what the *aims* of science are, the dilemma can be resolved. *Science aims to achieve powers of understanding, prediction and control above the level of unaided common sense.* . . . Knowledge of general laws . . . quantitative assessments and correlational procedures are all helpful; but with this conceptual, [nomothetic] knowledge must be blended a shrewd diagnosis of trends within an individual, an ability to transcend the isolated common variables obtained from current measurement devices and to estimate the ego-structure of the individual. Unless such idiographic [particular] knowledge is fused with nomothetic [universal] knowledge, we shall not achieve the *aims* of science. . . . [Italics added.]

(1960, pp. 146–47)

The question immediately arises of how, beyond the context of personality investigation, universal and particular methods can be blended. In a somewhat oversimplified way, we can describe the blend as the induction-deduction merry-go-round.* Science begins with observations of individual events. The similarities, if any, among the separate events lead the scientist to draw a general conclusion about the entire class of such events. This is the *inductive* phase of scientific investigation. For example, if a psychologist observes that individuals who report they are anxious about something, say an upcoming exam, always evidence sweaty palms, frequent trips to the bathroom, and rapid heart beats, he may in *future* cases of individuals reporting anxiety assume that sweating, bathroom urgency, and rapid heartbeat are present. After observing several cases, he *generalizes* his conclusions to all similar cases of the phenomena. Induction, then, may be described as proceeding from the particular to the general. But the merry-go-round must come full circle. The scientist now proceeds from his general conclusions to new particular observations. He reasons that if his analysis of the original separate observations was correct, and therefore his general principle is correct, then he can now predict the occurrence of observations not yet actually made. This phase of scientific investigation is called *deduction*.

For example, our psychologist studying anxiety might deduce that the bodily signs of anxiety (sweating, bathroom urge, rapid heartbeat) always occur when someone reports he is experiencing the emotion of anxiety *because* these bodily signs *are* the emotion. In effect, the psychologist would be speculating on the possibility that felt emotion and physical arousal are one and the same thing. This hypothesis is in fact very close to William James' theory of emotion. Now our psychologist is in a position to predict a new particular observation: If bodily arousal could be induced in a subject (say, by the injection of an arousing drug) who is otherwise free of any intense emotional state, that subject will report a feeling of anxiety when experiencing the arousal, even though he has no logical reason for so doing. This deduction predicting a new observation provides the scientist with the means of testing his conclusion. As it turns out, his conclusion would be only partly correct. Schacter and Singer (1962) conducted an experiment similar to our hypothetical situation, but employing several different drug conditions, and several different information patterns to which subjects were ex-

* The difficulty of inductive and deductive methods, their logical relationships and priorities have been a source of controversy in the philosophy of science for a long period. Students seeking information on the nuances of this material are directed to Kant's (1950) *Prolegomena to Any Future Metaphysics,* and to Hume's (1955) *An Inquiry Concerning Human Understanding* as starting points for further reading. The present discussion will deal only superficially with the topic.

KEY CONCEPTS

The Induction-Deduction Merry-Go-Round and Idiographic Versus Nomothetic Description

Induction (from individual particular observations to a general inclusive statement)

Deduction (from the general statement to new particular observations)

Nomothetic (the generalities, regularities of a class or group of individuals)

Idiographic (the unique qualities of the individual)

Problem: Psychiatrist knows that certain tranquilizers are beneficial in treating anxiety neurotics who evidence high emotional arousal. The tranquilizer calms them and makes them more amenable to verbal interchange such as psychotherapy. On the basis of his past experience with such patients, the psychiatrist *inducts* a *general rule* of treatment and *deducts* a *particular* patient's prognosis (prediction).

Psychiatrist's Induction

John, an anxiety neurotic, was calmed by tranquilizer.
Bill, an anxiety neurotic, was calmed by tranquilizer.
Phil, an anxiety neurotic, was calmed by tranquilizer.
Mary, an anxiety neurotic, was calmed by tranquilizer.
All profited from tranquilizer enough to make therapy worthwhile.

Generalization: Anxiety Neurotics Profit from Tranquilizers.

Nomothetic Description

Psychiatrist's Deduction

New patient, Sam, is an anxiety neurotic. He will profit from tranquilizers.

Outcome: Sam does not profit from tranquilizers.

Conclusion: Sam was not an anxiety neurotic; or, general rule does not always hold; or, Sam is anxiety neurotic and general rule does not hold for *him*, but does hold for all other anxiety neurotics.

Idiographic Description

posed. Emotion, it seems, is dependent on bodily arousal, but the specific label a subject is willing to attach to the arousal varies with the situation in which he finds himself.

The importance of the induction-deduction merry-go-round for the development of science should not be lost in our discussion of emotion. Induction and deduction form an intimate pair of thinking techniques that structures the efforts of the scientist and allows a systematic analysis of his efforts. It is unlikely, however, that any scientist proceeds with the induction-deduction paradigm foremost in mind before starting an investigation. Few, if any, scientists awake in the morning to greet the new day with the thought "Today, I'll be inductive, and complete a great many observations, so that tomorrow I can deduce a few predictions and test a few hypotheses."

We can summarize the universal-particular/induction-deduction merry-go-round by keeping in mind that the inductive phase is essentially an empirical act that requires astute observation through the senses (an act Plato would have frowned upon). The general abstraction formed by induction from several specific cases allows the scientist to deduce new observations. In short, *induction requires that we proceed from the particular instance to the general, while deduction requires we proceed from the general principle to the particular.* Then, of course, our new deductive particulars require a return to the inductive mode. Induction-deduction is summarized on page 52.

Science Becomes Empirical: Naive Observation

Although it is true that scientists, and psychologists among them, are interested in establishing general, even universal, "laws" of explanation for events, it is equally true to say that Plato's nonempirical contemplation of universals would find little favor with contemporary scientists. As we have seen, Simpson observes that modern science is an escape from the Greek way of thinking. Modern scientists insist, by contrast, that science proceed from observation, and that all observations be tested. Greek thought developed a path away from the nonempirical contemplation of the universe and, with Aristotle (384–323 B.C.), evolved toward a brand of empiricism, a forerunner of contemporary empiricism.

Aristotle began his philosophic career with Platonist precepts. However, probably because of his early medical training and interest in biology, Aristotle saw the importance of making observations, but the conclusions that he drew from his observations were not subject to further test. The modern scientist recognizes that unaided observation and common-sense explanation allow only a limited and naive investigation of the universe. As Theobald has said of Aristotle, ". . . for him what there was to the world *was* what met the eye." He goes on to say:

Aristotelian explanation, then, is not explanation as we understand it in terms of comparisons of actual states of affairs, with theoreti-

---

IMPLICATIONS

The acquisition, development, and use of language have been studied by psychologists in an attempt to understand the principles governing this complex form of behavior. One school of thought, behaviorism, interprets language as simply a more complex form of behavior than lever-pressing, but a form of behavior that nonetheless obeys the same laws of reinforcement. Language is acquired by the child, according to this view, through the reinforcement he receives for correctly imitating the verbal responses of those around him. The reinforcement consists of either obtaining the thing asked for, or of the social approval and contact that results when baby speaks a correct word or phrase. In short, language is *learned* behavior, acquired through imitation and reinforcement.

Another school of thought, represented by Noam Chomsky, the noted linguist at Massachusetts Institute of Technology, has severely criticized the behaviorist position on language. Chomsky suggests that humans are *born* with a language facility, a group of universal principles of language construction, that allow the child to produce sentences and phrases which he has never heard, but which are grammatically and syntactically correct. This creative ability, the capacity to generate sentences that have never been heard, is possible because humans inherit a set of conceptual tools that structures reality as it is experienced. For the Chomskians, language is not *simply* learned, but is learned because of inherited knowledge, concepts, or grammatical rules.

1. Which of these two positions on language can be characterized as empirical, and which as rational or Platonic? Explain your answer.

2. Is Chomsky's criticism of the behaviorist school a valid one? Can originality of language use be accounted for in learning theory by resort to stimulus generalization principles?

3. How would you test Chomsky's assertion that rules-of-grammar are inherited?

4. John B. Watson, a behaviorist, once suggested that thinking and mental activities were just covert, subvocal speech behavior. Does Chomsky's position, if true, contradict this possibility? If so, how?

5. Investigate the philosophy of René Descartes. Are there any similarities among Descartes, Plato, and Chomsky? If so, what are they?

6. The Sapir-Whorf hypothesis states that the way we use language structures the way we perceive our world (*not* the other way around: i.e., that language is structured by the way we see our world). In other words, the innate categories of labeling objects set up by our language forces us to perceive events *only as we can label them*. For example, if we had no label for the color "orange," but did have a label for "red," the hypothesis predicts that we would conceptually lump reds and oranges in the same group and fail to perceive any real differences. Could this type of innate structuring of reality be similar to Plato's concept and to Chomsky's? Explain.

cal ideas about those states of affairs, but explanation by the precise description of what could be ordinarily seen by the man in the street.

(1968, pp. 50–51)

Theobald further observes that Aristotle's world view was not yet ready to accommodate the idea that the universe was not created in a special act of providence, and that the universe is not ordered, but is possibly random—with man not at the center but at the periphery.

. . . thus to describe in detail what there was to be seen with the eyes, *was* to explain it significantly, as part of the whole. This was the way Aristotle understood the world. . . .
    Aristotle's world was made once and for all—there were no guesses to be made.

(1968, p. 51)

Aristotle's kind of empiricism might be described as naive, in the sense that interference with or manipulation of the phenomena to be observed was not considered. Things are as they appear to be. The role of the scientist, in Aristotle's view, is to observe and record the frequency of occurrences, the directly apparent characteristics, and the readily visible wholeness of phenomena, allowing similarities to emerge wherever possible. The merry-go-round comes half circle. Individual events, particular observations, are intelligible only to the extent that they occur regularly, without exception. One-time events are not lawful, and they are to be dismissed as chance. Here again, we see the conflict between the idiographic and nomothetic approaches to scientific thinking.

Kurt Lewin and Galilean Psychology

Beginning in the 1920's, Kurt Lewin focused his attention on the contrast between Aristotelian and Galilean scientific method and the implications for psychology. Lewin, attempting to develop a dynamic theory of motivated behavior, urged scientists to abandon the Aristotelian, intuitive world view in favor of the creative outlook exemplified by Galileo.

Where Aristotle's view of the world depended upon the assumption that things are what they are because of their intrinsic quality, Galileo focused not only on the objects of observation themselves, but on their surroundings, their contexts, their environment. For example, Aristotle believed that man's world consisted of four elements: earth, water, fire, and air. Each of these elements has a characteristic motion: earth and water fall; air and fire rise. The motion of bodies could be explained to the extent that they exhibited the properties of one of these elements. Observation of bodies in motion requires the observer, in Aristotle's view, to record many different occasions of bodies in motion and to abstract the lawful principle that most frequently characterizes the behavior of an object. (See Atkinson, 1964, Chapter 4, for more complete examples.) Such observation leads to intuitive conclusions that are reasonable and logically valid, but which may not be empirically accurate. For instance, intuitively, heavy objects seem to fall faster than light objects. In other words, for Aristotle, the speed of a falling object depends only on how much earthly substance an object contains, not on external conditions like the distance of the fall. But Galileo and his contemporaries demonstrated that the longer an object falls in time, the faster it does so. An object falling for x amount of time is falling less than half as fast as an object falling for $2x$ amount of time. Not only the inherent nature of the object, but also environmental conditions determine rate of fall. To have discovered such a principle meant that Galileo had to remove himself from purely intuitive, naive, direct observation and substitute imagination. He had to devise "what if?" questions; he had to imagine events he had not actually observed; and further, he had to intervene in nature and construct possible explanations that could be tested by observation. This special form of creativity, this unwillingness to accept observations at their face value, and this capacity to devise situations that do not naturally occur are the characteristics of truly contemporary science.

Lewin was convinced that a truly dynamic Galilean psychology must take account not only of the characteristics of persons, but of their total psychological environment. No longer should psychology adhere to the Aristotelian tradition of dichotomizing events into separate classes, distinct and separate like fire and water. Rather, psychology should begin a process of synthesis, a searching for general laws that summarize diverse instances of behavior. Instead of establishing generalizations based on the most *frequently* observed behavior, and ignoring the exception as unlawful, psychology should develop precise laws of individual behavior. Persons are not motivated solely by innate factors, but by a combination of those innate variables *and* current situational variables. Only when *both* person and environment are understood can behavior be meaningfully and lawfully described. It is worth quoting Lewin's famous statement of this principle:

. . . to understand or predict the psychological behavior (B) one has to determine for every kind of psychological event [actions, emotions, expressions, etc.] the momentary whole situation, that is, the momentary structure and state of the person (P) and of the psychological environment (E).

$$B = f(P, E)$$

[Behavior is a function of the person and his immediate environment.]

(1935, p. 79)

We can summarize the distinction between Aristotelian and Galilean modes of thought as follows:

1. *Aristotle*'s method of observation is naive, accepting at face value what can be seen unaided and unquestioned.
2. *Galileo* actively intervenes in the phenomena observed to propose imaginative questions and to structure for observation situations that do not occur naturally.
3. *Aristotle* assumes that events can be explained by resort to their

---

KEY CONCEPTS

Aristotelian and Galilean Psychology

ARISTOTELIAN ASKS	GALILEAN ASKS
1. What are the *inherent* qualities or characteristics of this thing?	1. What are the qualities of this thing *in its situation* as I now observe it?
2. What *has been* the most common or most frequent behavior of this thing?	2. What would happen *if* I changed the conditions under which I have observed this thing to such and such conditions?
3. What common property or cause governs most occurrences of this thing (on the average)?	3. How can I measure the difference between the most common type and those that deviate from this type? Is there regularity to the occurrence of exceptions?

In effect, the Aristotelian asks:
"What have I most often observed about this thing?"
while the Galileian asks:
"What would happen if . . . ?"

Plato, Galileo, Aristotle, and early man share a common motive: *to understand and to control the known universe.*

innate properties, by description of the class of element to which they belong. Class descriptions are constant and unchanging.

4. *Galilean* thought takes account not only of the property of the observed object, but also of the surrounding circumstances, situational factors.

5. *Aristotelian* thinking depends upon frequency of occurrence for its definition of lawfulness. The most frequently occurring event is lawful; exceptions are random and unlawful.

6. *Galilean* thought demands a concrete description of the event and its surroundings, seeking explanation for the usual *and* the exceptional. Mathematical analysis is often employed.

We can conclude our discussion of the development of the contemporary scientific way of thinking by noting that the Aristotelian mode of thought is limited to events *as they occur,* whereas the Galilean mode of thought is more active in creating situations that do not yet exist. Clearly the *motivation* behind Plato's, Aristotle's and Galileo's modes of thought is strikingly similar to early man's: *an attempt to understand and control, in a reliable way, the known universe.*

Overview of Prescientific and Postscientific Thinking: The Darwinian Revolution

Perhaps at this point an example of a modern scientific theory that partakes of both the pre- and postscientific modes of thought might serve to illustrate the essential difference between a scientific and a nonscientific approach to explanation.

In 1859 Charles Darwin published his classic, *Origin of Species.* Darwin proposed that the differences among various species of animals arose not through a divine special creation (in which elephants were made elephants, pigs were made pigs, amoeba were made amoeba, etc.), but through a natural process of interaction between an organism's environment and the physical capacity of the organism to utilize the environment's resources. Organisms not possessing the physical capability to survive in a given environment have less chance of mating and of reproducing offspring similar to themselves. Thus a population of organisms changes over time as conditions of the environment change to "naturally select" different adaptive characteristics in the members of the population. About the same time, another naturalist, Alfred Russel Wallace, independently of Darwin, reached almost identical conclusions about the nature and course of evolution.

Before Darwin and Wallace's time, it was generally assumed that the Biblical story of Genesis was literally true. Man and animals had been created by God along with the rest of the known universe. There are two important implications in such belief. First, it is implied that there can be no change in species without another act of divine intervention (a notion which is somewhat Aristotelian in flavor). Whatever species were created in the beginning have survived unchanged. Thus, the total number of types of creatures that came into existence at the creation of the world has not changed. A fundamentalist religious belief in the creation story recognizes neither the possibility of decreases in biological variety (e.g., extinction), nor the possibility of increases in biological variety (e.g., sexual recombination or mutation). Obviously, such belief is difficult to reconcile with direct observation of changes in species that have occurred. Moreover, the demise of dinosaurs and the existence of viruses would prove to be embarrassing facts. Any cattle breeder is able to demonstrate that changes in physical appearance and characteristics, through interbreeding and selection, are possible and desirable.

The second implication of a belief in special creation is a bit more complex. According to the Bible story (Genesis 2:27) man was created in God's image. Taken literally, it was assumed that man was therefore distinctly different from animals. Men and animals are different in *kind* or *quality* of being. Further, it was assumed, almost matter-of-factly, that all living things other than humans were intended for man's pleasure. The purpose of the animal kingdom is to accommodate man, the highest earthly creature. Darwin's observations and theory, based on a five-year, worldwide voyage aboard H.M.S. *Beagle,* were destined to abrasively disengage man from his cherished Aristotelian conviction that he was the center of the living creation.

There is a somewhat amusing and double-edged irony in the fact that the captain of the *Beagle,* Robert Fitz Roy, had, as one of his intentions in inviting a naturalist aboard for the five-year voyage, the goal of obtaining geological evidence to refute some early theories of evolution that were beginning to gain attention throughout Europe (Engel, 1961, p. xv). Captain Fitz Roy was a fundamentalist believer in the Genesis account of divine creation. He would no doubt have been appalled had he been able to foresee that the young Charles Darwin would develop a comprehensive and eminently successful theory of organic evolution from observations he would make during the voyage of the *Beagle.*

The second edge of this irony is that Charles Darwin himself began the voyage as a believer in the Biblical account of creation. It was only after his reading of Sir Charles Lyell's *Principles of Geology,* a book he took along on the voyage, that Darwin's religious convictions succumbed to doubt. Lyell's book advanced the radical premise that the earth's physical features were a product of geological forces acting over immense periods of time—periods incomparably greater than the few thousand years since the Creation in the Genesis account. (Engel, 1961,

p. xv.) By the third year of the voyage, Lyell's book and his own observations of the fossil record had reduced Darwin's belief in divine creation to nil. "But he refrained from voicing much of what he thought in order to avoid giving offense [to Fitz Roy]" (Engel, 1961, p. xv).

In a separate book, *The Descent of Man* (1871), Darwin concluded that the species to which man belongs arose from a long chain of development *within the animal kingdom,* the same kind of development through which apes, finches, and anteaters had evolved. Darwin did not, as popular misconception would have it, suggest that man descended *from* the great apes, but rather *with* them, from common, remote primate ancestors. With Darwin and Wallace, man was no longer different *in kind* from the animals, but different only in *degree.*

The Scientific Basis of Natural Selection

Natural selection, as Darwin termed the mechanism of evolution, involved three essential components:

1. The reproductive capacity of a species of organisms to generate more offspring than are able to survive
2. The existence of naturally occurring differences or variations in physical structure among members of a given population (e.g. long tails, short tails, medium tails, etc.)
3. The advantage of some variations of given members of the population in coping with and adapting to their environment in their "struggle for existence"

Darwin had observed that, owing to changing conditions and pressures of the environment, not all members of a species survive. He had also observed, as had others before him, that offspring tend to resemble their parents; they inherit slight differences or variations possessed by their parents. Although he had no clear notion of the genetic basis of this inheritance, one fact stood out clearly: some of these variations are "favored" by the environment. Perhaps, for example, a long, pointed beak, as opposed to a rounded short beak, in an environment sparsely populated by insects is advantageous in penetrating the crevices and cracks of tree limbs and bark where insects nest. Birds with rounded, stubby beaks might be less successful in obtaining food, and, in the long run, stubby-beaked birds survive less often in this environment, having fewer offspring like themselves. The trait of "stubby-beakedness" tends to decrease in this population, in this environment. Eventually, this population of finches is characterized by all more or less long, pointed-beaked birds; the population has evolved. Darwin gave another example of his thinking on natural selection:

Let us take the case of a wolf, which preys on various animals, securing some by craft, some by strength, and some by fleetness; and let us suppose that the fleetest prey, a deer for instance, had from any change in the country increased in numbers [becoming a source of food that was desirable though difficult to secure] . . . during that season of the year when the wolf was hardest pressed for food. Under such circumstances the swiftest and slimmest wolves would have the best chance of surviving and so be preserved or selected. . . .

(1958, p. 94)

Earlier in the book, Darwin wrote poetically about the subtlety of natural selection:

It may metaphorically be said that natural selection is daily and hourly scrutinizing, throughout the world, the slightest variations; rejecting those that are bad, preserving and adding up all that are good; silently and insensibly working *wherever and whenever* opportunity offers, at the improvement of each organic being in relation to its organic and inorganic conditions of life. *We see nothing of these slow changes in progress until the hand of time has marked the lapse of ages,* and then so imperfect is our view into long past geological ages, that we see only that the forms of life are now different from what they formerly were. [Second italics added.]

(1958, p. 91)

Darwin was pointing out that evolution by natural selection is a dramatically slow process involving eons of time, and therefore a process not susceptible of direct observation. But from the evidence available, in the Galilean tradition, Darwin constructed his theory in imagination to be tested in reality.

Observational Basis of the Theory of Natural Selection

The theory as presented here had been derived by Darwin from three sets of observations (de Beer, 1958, in Fried, 1968). On his visit to the Galapagos Islands on the *Beagle* Darwin noticed that species of finches differed from island to island but showed resemblances to each other as well (Darwin, 1845, in 1962). If Darwin had been a true Aristotelian, he would have simply recorded the similarities and differences, noted the most frequent type, and dismissed all others as random exceptions. But Darwin, in a truly Galilean spirit, saw his observations as a problem to be solved. If the Bible story were true, how could finches, on *separate islands,* of *apparently different species,* resemble each other?

Secondly, in his travels over South America Darwin had noticed the same kind of phenomena. Species in one geographical region, though slightly different in some respects, resembled other species in neighboring regions. Lastly, Darwin also noticed that certain fossil remains of extinct animals resembled living species. Why should extinct animals be constructed like presently living animals in some respects and differently in others?

One way to account for these observations is to assume that species change gradually over time; they evolve. Here is an explanation proposed in imagination, requiring confirmation in further observation. Darwin had taken his observations and supplied an underlying network of logically connected conclusions. This is an impressive display of the induction-deduction merry-go-round in action. Some of Darwin's assertions have been tested observationally by employing fossil remains, conducting blood-serum- and protein-typing tests on distantly related species, and by direct experimental manipulation of breeding populations under controlled conditions. To a large extent, Darwin's theory is confirmed and accepted, though with modification, by all modern biologists. The modifications have come mostly in the area of genetic explanation for the observed variations, a topic about which Darwin knew little!

Darwin's Impact on Scientific Psychology

Darwin's theory became the impetus for studying individual differences in humans, the forerunner of the mental-testing movement. The theory also served to provide a rationale for the objective study of human behavior by the methods used in studying animal behavior. If man belongs in the animal kingdom, so does his behavior. The theory also served, in somewhat less desirable fashion, as a springboard for the comparison of animal behavior and human behavior in the attempt to explicate complex human traits by resort to less complex, analogous animal traits. The most we can say here is that sometimes analogizing works, and sometimes it fails miserably.

We need now turn to a more formal study of contemporary scientific method in psychology before we end our selective survey of pre- and postscientific thinking.

The Formal Statement of Scientific Method

Comparison of Platonic, Aristotelian, and Galilean thought emphasizes three significant concepts:

1. Without empirical observation of natural events (including behavior), reason alone is a meager tool for understanding and controlling reality.

KEY CONCEPTS

The Structure of Darwin's Theory of Natural Selection

Darwin's (and Wallace's) theory of natural selection is based on three *observations* and on two *conclusions* drawn from these observations:

Observation One

Without environmental pressures, every species tends to multiply in geometric progression. In other words, a population doubling its number in a first year possesses a sufficient number of individuals to quadruple its number in a second year, to increase eight-fold in a third year, and so on.

Observation Two

Under real environmental conditions, the size of the population remains remarkably constant over long periods of time. The geometric increase does not occur.

Conclusion One

Evidently, not all mating leads to viable offspring, and not all viable adults survive to reproduce. There must be a "struggle for existence," which some members of the population do not win.

Observation Three

Not all members of a species are alike; considerable differences (variations) can be observed.

Conclusion Two

In the struggle for existence, therefore, individuals exhibiting favorable variation will enjoy a competitive advantage over others. They will survive in proportionately greater numbers and will produce offspring in proportionately greater numbers exhibiting the favorable variation.

(Back to **Observation**)

(modified slightly from Weisz, 1967, pp. 768–69)

2. Direct, intuitive observation, unaccompanied by questioning, imagination, or creative intervention, is a limited and misleading prescientific technique.

3. Galileo's most significant contribution lay in the precedent he set for future scientists actively to intervene in natural events and actively to construct an imaginative picture of reality (what we now call theory), which was to be tested by further observation.

What, then, is that systematic mode of thought that characterizes the modern scientist's approach to understanding and control of reality? It has traditionally been called "The Scientific Method," often with a tone of such reverence in the voice, and with such emphasis on "*the*," that beginning science students feel that they are about to be admitted to some profound and sacrosanct cult. Nothing could be further from the truth. Actually, it is incorrect to speak of *the* scientific method, as if there were one and only one right way to "do" science. Scientific method is simply a form of thought, a collection of techniques, and a set of principles by which controlled environments are constructed in which hypotheses can be tested.

Classical scientific method involves experimentation, the active intervention in ongoing events, under controlled conditions. However, there are several other approaches to investigating nature that do not employ experimentation. Natural observation of animals or human groups in their environments without intervention by the observer is a scientific technique. Clinical observation of patients in psychotherapy is another scientific technique that does not employ experimentation. Surveying a selected sample of voters' attitudes and analyzing the results in statistical form is yet another scientific method that makes no use of experimentation. Yet each of these techniques lays claim to scientific status, and finds a ready place within the body of established science, because each technique provides information that is not available in any other way. We will briefly examine several of these "scientific methods" after we have first given consideration to the traditional statement of experimental scientific method.

The Steps of Scientific Method: The Traditional View

It is worth emphasizing that scientific method is introduced in textbooks as five interlocking, succinct steps, conveying the impression that all scientists proceed from *step one through step five* like cooks following a recipe. The steps are not distinct and separate, and the scientist does not proceed rigidly in hierarchical succession. A better way of characterizing the formal methodology is to recognize that this is a statement of the way scientists *generally* behave in attacking problems. However, scientists do not memorize the five steps and recall them each time they attempt to solve a problem. It is often said that the closest a working scientist ever gets to "The Scientific Method" is in his reading of introductory textbooks on the subject. Karl Popper has suggested, in addition, that scientists actually proceed in a somewhat different way than the method implies. We will examine Popper's views in the next chapter.

The prime purpose of scientific method is to provide (*1*) *an organized, systematic approach to observation, (2) a method of controlling all factors that might influence the observation, and (3) a technique for testing proposed solutions to problems defined by observation.*

As you already know, the starting point for scientific investigation is observation. The scientist, on the basis of his observations and the observations reported by others, has noticed the existence of certain phenomena. *Step one, therefore, is observation,* observing instances or occurrences of an event, pretty much as you did in Chapter 1 when you observed that the letter *b* was dotted wherever it appeared. Observation also involves one of the *processes* of scientific method, induction. When we observe particular instances of an event, we try to generalize from each separate instance to the class of instances as a whole. In other words, we try to go from the particular to the general, from the individual observation to the universal. For example, when we saw that the first *b* was dotted, and the third *b* also, we were ready to make the generalization that all *b*'s would be dotted.

However, we also noticed that twice in those lines of nonsense poetry the letter *u* appeared with dots. This observation does not seem to fit our generalization that *b*'s are dotted. In fact, when we notice that only *some u*'s are dotted (as in "frumious"), but that others are not (as in "Jubjub"), we begin to suspect that the placement of dots is not lawful or orderly, as we first thought. In other words, our observations have led to the discovery of a problem. *This discovery is step two of the method, defining a problem.* It means that we must ask *relevant* questions of the phenomena we have observed. "How does it come about?" "What causes it to happen?" Or, very specifically, "How do dots come to appear on certain of the letters?" (Or, if dots were viruses, and words were cells: "How do certain cells succumb to the attack of viruses?") Defining the problem is often very difficult. In fact, sometimes only the most creative or imaginative scientist can even see where a problem exists. For example, before Darwin took up the issue, variations in species were not considered a problem. It was ignored, explained by religious dogma, or dismissed as random and accidental.

Once the problem is recognized and stated, however, the scientist begins again to use his faculties of reason, logic, and imagination, and oftentimes, just plain old hunches, to offer a *tentative* (subject to change) explanation of the problem. He proposes a *possible* answer, recognizing that his speculation, however soundly based, is subject to modification or outright rejection. This tentative solution to the problem is called a hypothesis. *Statement of the hypothesis is the third step of the method.* Usually, an hypothesis is stated in the form of an "if . . . then . . ." statement: "*If* dots are assigned only to words with *b*'s in them, *then* all future words with *b*'s will have dots," or "*If* high metabolic rate provides a good medium for viruses, *then* all cells with high metabolic rate will be attacked by viruses."

The "if . . . then" form of the hypothesis is useful in pointing up the tentativeness of the stated solution, and puts the solution in a form that can be tested by proper arrangement of the stated conditions. If we discover cells with *low* metabolic rates that are invaded by viruses, then we must revise our hypothesis and search for other possible explanations.

In all cases the important point is that the hypothesis must be tested in some way. It is not sufficient simply to propose a possible explanation and then accept it as final. A situation must be devised in which all factors that *could* affect our observation are *controlled,* and only one factor, that which is suggested by our hypothesis, is allowed to operate. We observe the results, and wait for our prediction (hypothesis) to be confirmed or rejected. This testing of the hypothesis in a controlled situation constitutes the *fourth step of the method, experimentation.* We will discuss the requirements of experimentation more fully in a later section. First we must consider the last step of the method.

Having performed a series of suitable experiments, the scientist may generalize from the resulting experimental data (results) to formulate an explanation of the phenomena that is both comprehensive and inclusive. The important point to bear in mind, however, is that no single experimental result is taken as final. Many replications and modifications of the experiment by both the original investigator and other independent investigators are required before we can obtain any level of confidence in the results. Even if these requirements are met, the results of experiments are still subject to interpretation, a point to which we will return later. But for now, we can simply say that the results of many experiments often lead to the formulation of a theory. *Theory formulation is the fifth step of the method.*

A theory is a general statement, couched in precisely defined language or in mathematics, that attempts to explain and to account for the phenomena observed. A good example of theory is Darwin's formulation of the principle of natural selection to account for his diverse observations. Theories also serve a number of other important conceptual functions for the scientist. We shall spend much more time in the next chapter detailing the functions and uses of theory in psychology, but we can make some general statements in the present context.

First, theory serves as a kind of scientific shorthand. Theories summarize a myriad of facts, observations, and relationships derived from experimentation or other research methods. Thus, in Darwin's statement of natural selection, we see summarized several of his observations and conclusions. Secondly, a theory is said to have predictive power when deductions about new phenomena not originally included in the theory can be made. To return to Darwin's theory: As more became known about the functioning of genetic mechanisms and the inheritance of traits, scientists were able to predict (i.e., deduce) that seemingly widely divergent species were actually related in past evolutionary history. To check the prediction (deduction), cell samples and blood-protein analyses were made for several species to ascertain whether any similarity in chromosome number or type existed. This method, requiring enormous technical skill, not only confirms the theory in many respects, but serves as means of testing the theory.

Finally, theory may serve to identify new problem areas requiring research. Sometimes, when a theory is successful in explaining a series of observations, it not only points the way to new observations that can be made, but often leads scientists to explore new areas of research that did not *seem* related before the theory pointed the way. A good example can again be drawn from Darwin's theory. Exobiologists are interested in the possibility that organic evolution has taken place on other planets in the universe. From what is known about the development of life and the conditions that foster this development, systematic guesses can be made to the effect that life in other solar systems is not only possible but probable. Fascinating questions can now be posed that were once only a part of the science-fiction literature.

Bearing in mind that it is only a textbook technique of studying scientific activity, we can now summarize the classical statement of scientific method.

1. *Observation*: The empirical act of gathering information about the material world
2. *Defining the Problem*: Asking relevant questions of our observations
3. *Proposing a Hypothesis*: Stating a *possible* solution to the questions asked
4. *Experimentation*: Testing the accuracy of the hypothesis under controlled conditions of observation
5. *Theory Formulation*: Generalizing from many experimental and non-experimental results to propose a conceptually whole explanation that summarizes the data, predicts new observations, and guides further research

IMPLICATIONS

In the late 1950's Professor H. B. D. Kettlewell of Oxford University set out to test the principle of natural selection. For over 100 years in England two varieties of moth have been known to exist. One type of moth, which we will call the C type, is light in color; the other type, B, is darker. Observation through the collection of samples showed that the light colored form was more common, existing in greater numbers. The reason was that light colored moths are protectively colored when they rest against light colored, lichen-covered trees, and thus are less often prey to hungry birds. The darker form, B, stands out against the light tree and is hunted avidly by birds. The environment thus selected *against* the trait of darkness. However, in certain areas of England, the dark form began to increase in number, almost displacing the light form. Highly industrialized cities like Birmingham, with their soot and air pollution, tended to have trees with darkly covered bark on which the darker B moths were protectively colored, but not the light C moths. Kettlewell raised both dark and light moths in the laboratory in equal numbers, then released them in both industrial areas and in nonindustrial areas. Each moth was marked with a spot of white paint to identify it as a laboratory-raised moth. Baker and Allen (1967, p. 505) arranged the hypothesis of the experiment as follows:

Hypothesis: If . . . natural selection favors darker moths in industrial regions and lighter moths in nonindustrial regions . . .

Prediction: then . . . releasing equal numbers of light and dark forms in both regions, and recapturing the survivors after a period of time, should show definite changes. In the industrial region, far more dark forms should be recovered than light forms; in the nonindustrial areas the reverse should be true.

After a period of time using large lanterns in the woods at night, Kettlewell set about collecting the moths in both regions.

Results confirmed the hypothesis: Kettlewell collected more dark surviving moths in the industrial areas than in the nonindustrial areas.

1. Is Kettlewell's experiment adequate experimental proof of Darwin's theory of natural selection? If not, why not?

2. Is predation by birds the only explanation that can account for the results? Support your answer.

3. What variables connected to the recollection of the released moths need to be controlled for the results to be accurate?

4. Can you design a similar experiment to test Darwin's notion of natural selection?

The Art and Science of Experimentation

In an experiment, the scientist attempts to change or vary *one* of the conditions stated in the hypothesis. Simultaneously, he must hold constant *all* other conditions which could affect the phenomenon under study. This mediation between change and constancy is the ideal experimental situation. It is rarely, if ever, achieved. As a general rule of thumb, the more control the investigator exerts over the variables of the experiment, the more satisfactory, reliable, and valid are the results. The essence of experimentation is control.

Once again, we can resort to an analogy to make the concept of experimental control clear. Picture the following fantastic situation: During a time of emergency, you are placed in charge of the control panel of switches that regulates all the electric power in your city. A further emergency arises in which it becomes necessary for you to cut power to all parts of the city, *except* the nearby hospital, which can be seen from a window near your control panel. Let us assume that your control panel contains only five switches, each capable of turning off power to a different part of the city. Because you are unfamiliar with the panel, and because the switches are labeled only in code numbers, the probability of your turning off the correct switches and leaving on only the hospital switch is not very encouraging to the heart patients dependent on their electrically powered stimulators, the paralysis patients being kept alive by their artificial lungs, and the surgery patients on the table in a potentially dark operating theater. There is one final difficulty. You cannot simply turn on and off each switch, watching the lights in the hospital from your window until you locate the hospital switch by trial and error. After each switch is thrown, it must remain in that position for fifteen minutes to prevent a power surge, which would permanently burn out the circuits.

PROBLEM
One switch must be kept on. All others must be turned off.

In the language of experimental method, the switches over which you decide to exert control by choosing to turn them off are the *independent variables*: they can be changed in a known way at will. The lights and electrical power of the hospital, *which depend* on one of the switch circuits, are the *dependent variables:* their "behavior" depends on the action you take with the independent variables (switches).

Two outcomes are possible: (1) You choose correctly to turn off switches 1, 3, 4, and 5 (leaving switch number 2 unchanged) and the hospital lights remain on. In this case, the *dependent variable's* lack of change (hospital lights remain on) confirms your hypothesis that independent-variable-switch 2 controls power to the hospital. (2) The alternative outcome, in which you choose incorrectly to shut down switches 1, 2, 4 and 5 (leaving switch 3 unchanged), results in the hospital's power going off. In this case, the *dependent variable's* change demonstrates that your guess (hypothesis) about switch 3 controlling the hospital's power is wrong. In either case, the independent variables are always those conditions of an experiment that the scientist himself manipulates, changes, or controls.

Dependent variables are all those conditions of the experiment in which the scientist looks for some change or outcome as *he* changes the independent variables. Generally, although not always, the *dependent* variables in a psychological experiment are the *responses* of the organism the psychologist is working with. Dependent variables, therefore, tend to be *behavioral outcomes:* What did John's eye do when I puffed the blast of air against his eyelid? John's response, the eyeblink, is the *dependent* variable, while the puff of air that I administer in a known intensity and at a known frequency rate is the *independent* variable.

Using the electric-power-emergency analogy, if we do not attempt to stretch the comparison too far, we can see how not all experimentation is as precise as it might seem. Often, a scientist's guesses, or hypotheses, about the outcome of an experiment are based on intuitive, hunchlike

KEY CONCEPTS

Experimental Terms: Summary

Independent Variable(s) (stimulus)	All of those conditions of the experimental situation which the experimenter controls or changes at will. Typically, but not always, independent variables are all those stimuli that affect the subjects of the experiment.
Dependent Variable(s) (response)	Are usually some form of behavioral outcomes that depend on the effects of the independent variable(s). Dependent variables tend to be the experimental-group subject's responses.
Experimental Group	A population of subjects (human or animal) that is exposed to some special treatment under the control of the experimenter.
Control Group	A population of subjects (human or animal) that is either denied the special treatment of the experimental group, or given a differing treatment, so that a comparison with the experimental group's performance is possible. In all other respects, the control-group subjects are identical to the experimental-group subjects.

reasoning. At some level of his awareness, and because he is immersed in the knowledge of his field, the scientist can often develop hypotheses about which he has no conscious assurance of accuracy. For example, you might have noticed that the code number for switch 2 was H-7511; no other switch code number had an H in it. Of course, the patients in the hospital might not like to be told that you made your decision on the basis of one letter in a code number. Scientific experimentation is both an art and a science. It is often frustratingly difficult to separate the two. While the science of hypothesis *testing* can be learned, the art of hypothesis *development* requires a creative imagination.

A Model Experiment: Can a Memory Be Biologically Changed?

On the basis of past experimentation and research in genetics and biochemistry, a biological psychologist suspects that the same substance that stores genetic information in all cells may also function to store memory (see Gurowitz, 1969). Deoxyribonucleic acid (DNA) is the chemical substance that stores in its molecular structure the genetic constitution of all organisms and is the means by which offspring inherit parental traits. In other words, DNA is a biological information-storage system contained in the nucleus, and perhaps the cytoplasm, of every living cell. DNA, in short, contains the molecular plans for the development and functioning of the organism. Our psychologist has the hunch that the mechanism for storing genetic information might also serve to store incoming sensory information. He hypothesizes that DNA, or allied genetic compounds like RNA, are the physical basis of memory. The scientist might set up his general hypothesis as follows: If *DNA or RNA code information and store it as memory,* then *anything that interferes with DNA or RNA production in the nervous system will also interfere with memory.* This is a very general hypothesis that would have to be made more specific in terms of the actual experiment designed to test its validity.

The psychologist now tries to construct a situation in which he can control and manipulate the variables involved and determine changes in the dependent variable, memory. The experimenter trains a group of twenty white mice to jump over a small hurdle at the sound of a buzzer. The hurdle is placed in the center doorway of a two-compartment shuttle box. On the floor of compartment 1 is an electric grid that can deliver a painful but harmless shock to the feet of a mouse. A given mouse is placed in compartment 1 and allowed to roam freely about the compartment. Figure 1 illustrates the experimental arrangement.

After three or four minutes in compartment 1, a buzzer is sounded. If the mouse does not jump over the hurdle into compartment 2 within

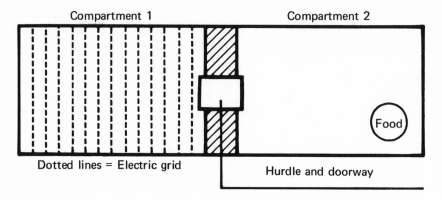

Figure 1. Shuttle-box (viewed from above)

25 seconds after the buzzer has sounded, electric shock is administered through the floor-grid of compartment 1, and the shock is continued until the mouse jumps the hurdle. In about ten such sequences of buzzer and shock for each mouse, the group learns to jump from compartment 1 to compartment 2 at the first sound of the buzzer. To prevent anticipation jumps, the interconnecting doorway is kept locked until just before the buzzer signal is sounded.

The entire group of mice, up to this point, has been treated as a single population. Each mouse is trained, fed, shocked, caged, and handled in the same way. This consistency of procedure is one form of control to insure that any results ultimately obtained are not due to different pre-experimental handling or training. Holding pre-experimental training constant for all subjects is the first *independent* variable. Now the group is divided *randomly* into two smaller groups, an *experimental group* and a *control group*. Each of these subgroups is composed of ten mice. The division is accomplished as randomly as possible to again insure that there are no significant *pre*-experimental differences between the experimental and the control groups. Almost always, experiments involve control groups. As we have seen, a control group is a population of organisms identical to the experimental group in all respects *prior* to the experiment. During the experiment, the control group will be treated differently in *one* significant way. That difference is usually the absence of *one* independent variable: *the* independent variable that is expected to produce the sought for change in behavior. In other words, the essence of a control group is comparison. Control groups serve as multiple replications of the experiment to provide a frame of reference for what transpires with the experimental group. In brief, the only way to determine whether the *independent* variable is the cause of changes in the *dependent* variable (behavior) is to deny some of the subjects access to the independent variable.

In our memory experiment, the psychologist decides to administer to the experimental group an injection of Actinomycin D, a drug which inhibits or prevents the normal functioning of DNA. The injection is given directly into the brain. Hopefully, if the psychologist's hypothesis is correct, mice injected with Actinomycin D will forget the correct response to the sound of the buzzer. But suppose that it is not the Actinomycin DNA inhibitor which causes the forgetting? Suppose that poking a hypodermic needle into brain tissue itself is the cause. In other words, there is the possibility that the independent variable, the drug, is not the cause of the dependent variable, the forgetting. Brain damage, not chemical inhibition, is the cause. Here is where the control group comes in. Each of the control mice is also given an injection, but instead of Actinomycin D, a placebo or fake injection compound is used. Usually it is saline solution, a salt-water mixture having no significant physiological effects. Therefore, the control group undergoes the same hazardous injection, but is denied the independent variable. Its performance on the shuttle-box problem can now be compared to the experimental group's performance.

Experimental Results

If all the variables have truly been controlled, the experimenter's hypothesis that the mice given the drug will forget the correct response, while those given the placebo will not forget, will be given a fair test and, hopefully, supported as valid. Of course, things are never quite this simple. It may be that some mice in both groups forget the response. Then the experimenter would have to employ statistical techniques to determine if there is a significantly greater number of forgetters in the experimental group. It may be that all mice in both groups remember the correct response, thus rejecting the hypothesis. The reason may be that the hypothesis is invalid, or that Actinomycin injection is not the best method to test the hypothesis. It is difficult to be certain that a given method is the best of all possible methods. This is the reason that a single experimental result is never taken as final.

Let us consider the happy event of 100 per cent of the experimental group's forgetting the response and 100 per cent of the control group's remembering it. In this unlikely event, there are still problems to bedevil the wary psychologist. A critic might argue that since Actinomycin D is a DNA-inhibitor, and normal DNA functioning is necessary for general good health, the mice given the drug did not *forget* the response, they were simply so sick and disoriented that they were *unable* to make the response. The experiment does not prove that DNA or anything else is the basis of memory. What is the psychologist's solution to this dilemma? Better-designed experiments, with control groups of various dosage levels of the drug to determine the threshold of sickness and the degree of forgetting, if any. It is probably not out of place to suggest that even well-controlled experiments are often subject to the best-laid-plans-of-mice-and-men syndrome.

IMPLICATIONS

You are an educational psychologist, and you are wondering about the effectiveness of teachers' classroom tests in measuring not only a student's learning progress but the test's actual effectiveness in producing learning. On the staff of your school, there are two teachers of equal competence giving biology courses. Teacher A, Sam Scarem, likes to give only multiple-choice, objective exams and to impress the students with the importance of knowing the correct answers. As one student in Mr. Scarem's class put it: "He likes to yell a lot, gives enormous homework assignments and tests which can only be described as horrendous." Teacher B, Miss Bertha Sunshineinthemorning, prefers to give only essay type exams, in which students must recall the studied information (not just recognize the right answer as in multiple-choice questions), because she believes part of learning is being able to organize and express information learned. Your task is to design an experiment to determine which type of testing produces the most efficient learning of biology.

Step One: Your hypothesis or guess about which type *is* most effective is:

Step Two: You begin to list the variables that will have to be controlled. Some of these are:
a. Effects of the personalities of the teachers on their classes.
b. Intellectual abilities of each teacher's students.
c. Motivational factors of each teacher's students.
d. Amount of material covered by tests to be compared.
e. Conditions and time of administration of tests (e.g. after a weekend, or holiday, on a Monday, during mid-term week, etc.)
f. Amount of previous learning of each class before test is given.
g. Grading criteria for the essay type exam: what is an A for one teacher may be a B or C for another.
h. Other factors:

Step Three: Your Experimental Design (Hint: You might be able to divide each teacher's class into halves and cross-combine them for each type of test and teacher.)

1. List your independent variables and dependent variables.

2. Describe what kind of results would give a significant amount of support to your hypothesis.

3. Can your design include the possibility that a mixed test (half multiple choice, half essay) is the superior format? Explain your answer.

Guiding New Research

Having performed a series of suitable experiments on the biochemical basis of memory, the scientist may generalize from his data to formulate a theory of explanation. For example, if it were established beyond reasonable doubt that DNA is the basis of memory in nervous tissue, the psychologist might go on to speculate on the basis of his general theory about ways to improve memory. He might predict that *increasing* the DNA content of certain locations in the brain might expand or improve memory functioning in humans. Large doses of DNA might be administered to humans, and experiments might then be designed to test the effects on memorized material. Thus experimentation and theory formation may guide further research and allow predictions of new observations yet to be made.

Nonexperimental Methods

In addition to testing hypotheses by experiment, several methods have been devised that do not employ experimental method. Nonetheless, these techniques yield valuable results that compare favorably in accuracy to experimental method. We shall consider briefly two nonexperimental methods in order to gain some understanding of this approach.

The Method of Natural Observation

There are phenomena in the natural world that require scientific study but cannot be experimentally manipulated without destroying the phenomena. The scientist does the next best thing. He isolates variables for study, records his observations, and attempts to reach sound conclusions in the absence of absolute control (which is rarely achieved anyway) of the variables. A fine example of a situation in which experimental, laboratory investigation would "control away" the very event to be studied is Jane van Lawick-Goodall's research with chimpanzees in the Tanzanian jungle (1971). Without detailing the personal events and trials of Jane van Lawick-Goodall, which are recorded admirably in her book, *In the Shadow of Man,* we can quote a passage of the book that reveals both the natural observation method and the excitement of scientific discovery:

> Hauling myself up the steep slope of Mlinda Valley I headed for the Peak, not only weary but soaking wet from crawling through dense undergrowth. Suddenly I stopped, for I saw a slight movement in the long grass about sixty yards away. Quickly focusing my binoculars, I saw that it was a single chimpanzee, and just then

he turned in my direction. I recognized David Graybeard [a name that she assigned to this chimp from previous observation].

Cautiously I moved around so that I could see what he was doing. He was squatting beside the red earth mound of a termite nest, and as I watched I saw him carefully push a long grass stem down into a hole in the mound. After a moment he withdrew it and picked something from the end with his mouth. I was too far away to make out what he was eating, but it was obvious that he was actually using a grass stem as a tool. . . .

For an hour David feasted at the termite mound and then he wandered slowly away. When I was sure he had gone I went over to examine the mound. I found a few crushed insects strewn about, and a swarm of worker termites sealing the entrances of the nest passages into which David had obviously been poking his stems. I picked up one of his discarded tools and carefully pushed it into a hole myself. Immediately I felt the pull of several termites as they seized the grass, and when I pulled it out there were a number of worker termites and a few soldiers, with big red heads, clinging on with their mandibles. There they remained, sticking out at right angles to the stem with their legs waving in the air.

(1971, pp. 50–51)

There are several significant points in this passage. First, note how careful the observer is to avoid disturbing the chimpanzee during the ongoing behavior sequence. Human contact at this point, if it would not frighten him off, might very well interfere with the natural, "spontaneous" pattern of his behavior. Second, although tool-using behavior had been studied in the laboratory years before by Wolfgang Köhler (1917, in 1959), it was not known in any definite way whether chimps could devise and employ tools in their natural surroundings. The discovery that chimpanzees not only can be prodded by experimental food deprivation into using sticks to grab out-of-reach bananas, but that they naturally construct and use tools without human intervention, was an exciting one. As Jane van Lawick-Goodall pointed out:

Previously man had been regarded as the only tool-making animal. Indeed, one of the clauses commonly accepted in the definition of man was that he was a creature who "made tools to a regular and set pattern." The chimpanzees, obviously, had not made tools to any set pattern. Nevertheless, my early observations of their primitive tool-making abilities convinced a number of scientists that it was necessary to redefine man in a more complex manner than before. Or else, as Louis Leakey put it, we should by definition have to accept the chimpanzee as Man.

(1971, p. 52)

The method of natural observation is not free of difficulty when it comes to assessing the accuracy of its results. One danger lies in interpreting implications of the results. Unless a particular observation fits into an entire pattern of observations, it is difficult to understand its meaning in human terms. The danger of anthropomorphizing animal

---

IMPLICATIONS

Wolfgang Köhler, a Gestalt psychologist, devised situations for chimpanzees to display insight learning. Briefly, insight learning involves the sudden solution of a problem by restructuring the elements of the problem to accommodate the situation. Here is one of Köhler's observations in his own words:

1   Sultan was a *clever* chimpanzee. He was *quite familiar* with the solution
2   of the following problem. *A banana is attached to the ceiling* of the labo-
3   ratory, *far too high to be reached by a chimpanzee even when he jumps.*
4   Several yards away from this place, however, is a box of considerable
5   size. *In this situation, Sultan never hesitated; he dragged the box until it*
6   *was just underneath the banana,* climbed to its top, and *from here*
7   *jumped up to reach the fruit without the slightest trouble.* One would
8   think that when another chimpanzee is present, and sees what is hap-
9   pening, he must afterwards be capable of repeating this simple per-
10   formance when a new banana is attached to the ceiling. . . . Now this, I
11   soon had to realize, is a bit of a myth (imitation of one chimp by an-
12   other). It does happen that a chimpanzee repeats what others have been
13   doing in his presence—always supposing *that he is sufficiently in-*
14   *terested in that particular action,* and that he is *sufficiently intelligent*
15   to *understand* [original italics] what he has seen. But a chimpanzee
16   of particularly restricted intellectual gifts may be quite incapable of
17   repeating what another chimpanzee has just done—*simply because he*
18   *has failed to grasp certain relations which are essential* to the other's
19   performance. [All italics except as noted, were added.]

(Köhler, 1969, pp. 156–57)

1. Is this account an example of natural observation, or of experimental investigation? Give reasons for your answer.

2. Assuming that the foregoing *is* natural observation, can you distinguish between statements of *pure description* of events and statements of *interpretation?* Classify each italicized word or phrase in the above passage as description or as interpretation.

3. In lines 7 through 15, is Köhler reaching a justified conclusion on the basis of his observations, or is the conclusion exaggerated?

4. Do lines 15 to 19 show any evidence of anthropomorphism (the attribution of human traits or thoughts to the chimps)?

5. In what specific ways do you think that Köhler's account could be improved in the scientific sense?

behavior is well known. Aside from this difficulty, even when the method is used with human subjects, results must always build solidly on previous knowledge in the field. In the first place, only through previous knowledge can the investigator select the variables or behaviors that he considers significant enough to warrant study. In the second place, this reliance on previous knowledge can paradoxically serve as a hindrance to the natural observer. Previous knowledge may compartmentalize and categorize his perception of the ongoing event to such a degree that significant variables controlling the behavior go unnoticed. Despite these limitations, systematic natural observation is an essential, though limited, tool for the scientist seeking to understand uncontaminated, unmanipulated events in naturally occurring environments (cf. Chapter 4, How Theories Change: The Quiet Revolution.)

The Correlational Method

In most respects, the correlational method is not significantly different from the method of natural observation. Again, the investigator is interested in naturally occurring events and wishes to select variables for study. Again, he is unable or unwilling to create an artificial, controlled situation in which to manipulate certain variables. And again, the investigator is interested in discovering significant relationships among variables. However, the correlational method has one refinement of technique not usually empoyed (although it may be) in natural observation and description. This technique is statistical correlation, a mathematical analysis that quantifies the degree to which one variable is associated with ("goes with") another variable. A correlation coefficient does not, however, demonstrate that because two variables are related, one variable is the cause of changes in the other. All that is demonstrated by this form of mathematical manipulation is that two variables are often associated, often occur together. (Any other interpretation is magical thinking.) It may be that one causes the other; or, that both are caused by some third, unknown factor. Hilgard, Atkinson, and Atkinson cite the following example:

> Another example which is frequently used as an illustration is the high positive correlation obtained for the number of storks seen nesting in English villages and the number of child births recorded in the same communities. We shall leave it to the reader's ingenuity to figure out all possible reasons for such a correlation, without postulating a cause and effect relationship between babies and storks.

> (1971, p. 18)

Turning to a more serious example, suppose an investigator wished to discover whether a relationship exists between neurotic breakdown and preneurosis personality pattern? He could not select a sample of normal individuals, administer personality tests to each, and then undertake a systematic program of harassment to discover which personality type becomes neurotic. Aside from the ethical considerations, technical feasibility limits the amount of emotional damage even psychologists can inflict. Instead, the psychologist can turn to nature, where this experiment has already been conducted, so to speak. There are neurotic individuals of various types and degrees, and there are personality assessment instruments to categorize personality type. For example, Eysenck (1967) has conducted research for many years into the relationship between introversion-extroversion personality types, and neuroticism-normality emotional patterns. Generally, using a complex statistical technique called factor analysis, he finds that the shy, withdrawn, intellectually oriented introvert succumbs to anxiety neurosis, when and if he becomes neurotic. Extroverts, on the other hand, outgoing, socially minded, less arousable, succumb to hysterical and psychopathic breakdowns. This does not mean that introversion is the cause of anxiety neurosis any more than extroversion is the cause of psychopathic behavior. Rather, whatever central nervous system process is responsible for introversion may also be responsible for the type of symptom picture that results *when and if* neurotic breakdown occurs.

IMPLICATIONS

In his charming book on animal behavior, *King Solomon's Ring*, the eminent ethologist, Konrad Z. Lorenz gave this defense of his somewhat poetic descriptions:

> You think I humanize the animal? Perhaps you do not know that what we are wont to call "human weakness" is, in reality, nearly always a prehuman weakness and one which we have in common with the higher animals? Believe me, I am not mistakenly assigning human properties to animals; on the contrary, I am showing you what an enormous animal inheritance remains in man, to this day.
>
> (1952, p. 152)

1. Is Lorenz's statement above a sound defense of natural observation reported in human terms? Why or why not?

2. If we follow the logic of Lorenz's reasoning, can we demonstrate that what we see in an animal's behavior is humanized in description because of our own animal inheritance? Is this an example of cart-before-the-horse reasoning? If not, why not?

Notice that the scientist does not manipulate the variables under study. He attempts to observe their relationship as accurately as possible, and to quantify it mathematically if possible. But again, difficulties of interpretation may prevail when he begins searching for causal relationships.

A Final Word on Scientific Method and an Almost-Science

Textbooks in psychology customarily define this discipline as the science of human and animal behavior, or use some equivalent formulation containing the word "science." It probably would be preferable to define psychology as "the almost-science of human and animal behavior." Not intended to demean or belittle the achievements of contemporary psychology, the modified definition simply is meant to call attention to those unique characteristics of psychology as it deals with *living* elements of the natural world.

There are two components to this uniqueness that make psychology an almost-science. First, the degree of control exerted by the physical and natural sciences over their subject matter is rarely achieved in psychology, except, perhaps, in the psychobiological investigations of nervous system functioning. But in the more characteristic investigations, in areas like attitude formation and racial prejudice, personality development, psychotherapy, and the treatment of mental disorders, in cognitive functioning and the development of intelligence, psychology is a long way from establishing a predictive and explanatory theory of the magnitude, say, of evolutionary theory. This is not to imply that a priori it is not possible for psychological science to do so. One hopes that because as a discipline, psychology is young, the difficulty is more a matter of elapsed time than deficient methodology (Cf. Chapter 4).

Second, psychology, like medicine, is both an art and a method of scientific investigation. Large segments of psychology are devoted to the application of psychological principles: testing, psychotherapy, teaching, city-planning, human engineering, to name a few. Psychologists who work in these areas are not only working scientists, but practitioners interested in applying knowledge to human situations. Careful investigation makes possible careful application. The real art is to muster the skill to test the science.

Overview of the Chapter

Plato's cave allegory points up the essential difference between modern science and early Greek science, and the contrast is instructive. Where Plato denied the importance of direct observation of reality in favor of contemplation of prenatally acquired Ideal Forms, modern science rests

KEY CONCEPTS

Scientific Methods of Investigation: A Comparison Summary

Experimental Method	Natural Observation	Correlation
1. Selects, manipulates, and controls variables under study.	1. Selects variables for study.	1. Selects and partially controls variables for study.
2. Custom-designs situation or setting in which to study variables.	2. Restricted to naturally occurring settings since interest is in "spontaneous" behavior.	2. Custom-designs method of collecting data from already-existing settings or populations. "Nature has already conducted the experiment."
3. May ask "what if?" questions before, during, and after manipulation of variables, continually refining the control of variables. (Galilean method)	3. Not usually possible to ask "what if?" More likely to ask: "Have we observed all that can be observed without interfering with the phenomenon?" (Similar to Aristotelian method.)	3. May ask "what if?" questions, but answers cannot be stated in terms of cause and effect, only in terms of possible relationship among variables.
4. Employs crude to sophisticated measurement techniques to test hypotheses.	4. Does not typically employ sophisticated measurement techniques nor the construction and testing of hypotheses.	4. Typically uses sophisticated to ultrasophisticated measurement techniques. Hypotheses may be tested.
5. Because experimenter controls the conditions of the experiment, he can specify his procedure so that the experiment may be repeated by others.	5. Naturally occurring conditions cannot be repeated in identical ways on successive occasions.	5. Multiple repetitions of data selections are possible, but conditions vary.

soundly on an empirical basis. Modern science *is* observational. However, Artistotle's version of observation as a direct, intuitive, even naive, trust that what there is to the world is what there appears to be had to be replaced by a more dynamic, questioning approach. Galileo's scientific method more nearly resembles contemporary scientific method in the creative intervention in natural affairs that is attempted in experimentation. Kurt Lewin has focused attention on the distinction between Aristotelian and Galilean outlooks in psychology by pointing out that the typical Aristotelian method is to look for lawfulness in the most frequently occurring event, ignoring the exceptions as random. Galilean method, on the other hand, seeks to encompass even the exceptions within lawful relationships, and proceeds to a more concrete analysis of the event and its surrounding conditions. Lewin's famous programmatic formula, $B = f(P,E)$ (Behavior is a function of the person and *his* immediate environment), summarizes this position well for psychology.

Modern scientific method may be formally stated in five steps:

1. Observation
2. Defining a problem
3. Proposing a hypothesis
4. Experimentation
5. Theory formulation

In addition to testing observations by experiment, several nonexperimental techniques exhibiting lesser control of the variables have been developed to provide information when experimentation is not feasible. Experimental method itself is characterized by the attempted control of all variables. Those variables held constant or changed in a known way by the experimenter are called *independent variables*. Those variables which undergo change as a direct result of manipulation of the independent variables are called *dependent variables*.

Dependent variables, in psychology, tend to be identified with behavioral outcomes. As a means of comparison, an experiment is usually designed with one or more control groups. The control group is denied access to one or more of the independent variables to determine their effect on the dependent variable. The experimental group is treated with the independent variables, and their results can now be contrasted with those of the control group in testing the hypothesis.

The method of natural observation and the method of correlation both attempt to select and study naturally occurring variables and to seek out significant relationships. Van Lawick-Goodall's study of the spontaneous behavior of chimpanzees in their natural habitat provides a good example of natural observational technique.

Eysenck's research into the relationship between mental disorder and introversion-extroversion personality types provides a useful example of correlational research. In both cases, Eysenck's and van Lawick-Goodall's, the degree of control exerted over the studied phenomena is less than in an experiment, but experimental manipulation is not feasible in either case.

Psychology, the almost-science, makes use of scientific method, but is not yet in the position of physics or biology, and does not possess predictive or explanatory theories of wide scope. Further, psychologists, in areas such as testing, teaching, psychotherapy, and human engineering, attempt to apply what little is known to human situations. Application is more art than science, but is dependent wholly on science.

Recommended Further Reading

An undertaking that will well repay the effort involved would be a reading of Book VII of Plato's *Republic*, where the cave analogy is proposed. (A variety of paperback editions are available. The Jowett translation can be had from Random House, Modern Library edition, New York; undated.) Robert I. Watson's *The Great Psychologists*, Chapters 1, 2, and 3 (Philadelphia: Lippincott, 1968) is very readable and authoritative in describing the early Greek philosophers and their impact on the history of psychology.

For anyone who wishes to pursue the early history of experimental method in psychology, the standard reference work, and by far the most detailed account, is E. G. Boring's classic, *The History of Experimental Psychology* (New York: Appleton-Century-Crofts, 1957). Less detailed, but no less authoritative or useful, is the recently revised volume by Gardner Murphy and Joseph Kovach, *Historical Introduction to Modern Psychology* (third Edition: New York: Harcourt Brace Jovanovich, 1972). Chapter 9 of the Murphy and Kovach book details the contribution of Darwin's evolutionary writings to psychology's development and the impact of Darwin's theory in fostering animal experimentation in psychology. Excellent for both its editorial commentary and selection of readings is E. G. Boring's and Richard Herrnstein's *A Source Book in the History of Psychology* (Cambridge: Harvard University Press, 1966). The original writings of key figures in the history of psychology are anthologized, edited, and annotated by Herrnstein and Boring in an attempt to expose students to ordinarily hard-to-obtain sources.

The distinction between Aristotelian and Galilean thinking in psychology is discussed by Kurt Lewin in Chapter 1 of *A Dynamic Theory of Personality* (New York: McGraw-Hill, 1935; paperback). Of Darwin's works, perhaps the most readable is *The Expression of the Emotions in Man and Animals.* (Chicago: University of Chicago Press,

1965), which provides some of the flavor of this great biologist's thinking. His classic works, *The Origin of Species* and *The Descent of Man,* while more tedious and painstaking in style, deal directly with the issues raised in this chapter. (Both books are available in a one-volume, unabridged edition from Random House in New York; separate paperbacks of both books are also obtainable.) Darwin's own account of his five-year voyage with Captain Fitz Roy is to be found in *The Voyage of the Beagle* in a beautifully edited and annotated edition by Leonard Engel (New York: Doubleday–Museum of Natural History, 1962).

A thorough, but very readable, introduction to the philosophy of science, including an account of induction, deduction, and scientific laws, will be found in D. W. Theobald's brief book *An Introduction to the Philosophy of Science,* Chapters 3, 4, and 6 (New York: Barnes and Noble, 1968; originally published in England by Methuen & Co.). Stephen Toulmin's *The Philosophy of Science: An Introduction* (New York: Harper & Row, 1953) covers much the same ground as Theobald, and it is considered to be an authoritative reference. Extremely difficult reading without a thorough background in philosophy, logic, and psychology, yet the most substantial presentation of the scientific status, rationale, and logical underpinnings of psychology is Egon Brunswik's *The Conceptual Framework of Psychology* (Chicago: University of Chicago, 1950; Vol. 1, No. 10 of the *International Encyclopedia of Unified Science*). Brunswik's monograph is a work to be taken in small doses, to be savored, discussed, and then reread.

Gordon Allport's distinction between idiographic and nomothetic method may be found in his *Pattern and Growth in Personality,* Chapter 1 (New York: Holt, Rinehart & Winston, 1963).

An exciting and unusual perspective on scientific method is provided by B. F. Skinner in his narrative of the beginnings, pitfalls, lucky discoveries, and generally pragmatic nature of his early career in psychology in the paper "A Case History of Scientific Method" (*American Psychologist,* 1956, *11,* 221–233); this paper has been widely anthologized in introductory-psychology reading books.). For an equally readable and adventuresome account of natural observation, Jane van Lawick-Goodall's *In the Shadow of Man* (New York: Dell, 1971; paperback), describing her work with free-living chimpanzees in the Tanzanian jungle, is unbeatable.

Wolfgang Köhler's historically important work with apes on problem-solving tasks makes a nice contrast to van Lawick-Goodall's investigations. Köhler's clever experimentation with these creatures is to be found in *The Mentality of Apes* (New York: Random House, Vintage Books, 1959).

3

Theory and Its Limitations as a Tool for Scientific Understanding

Stentor is a relatively complex, stalked, tube-building protist (semi-microscopic animal). If it is continuously irritated by a stream of India ink particles, it goes through a series of changing responses in spite of the fact that the stimulus remains constant. First it bends to and fro in different directions; if the stream of particles continues it *then* reverses its cilia so as to "blow" the particles away; when this fails, it pulls itself inside its tube. Whenever it ventures out, only to find the stimulus still present, it goes straight back into the tube. It does not make the responses (bending, "blowing") it earlier made to the same stimulus. Finally (Morgan and Loeb forbid us to say "in exasperation"), it breaks away, moving off to build a new tube elsewhere. Such is genius among the protists.

GEORGE GAYLORD SIMPSON and
WILLIAM BECK, *Life*

Prospectus

In the history of science, some colossal goofs, some unbelievably lucky accidents, and some unrelenting hard work have combined to produce exciting discoveries. Contrary to the implication of the formal statement of scientific method explored in the preceding chapter, the working scientist may not "do" science in such an orderly sequence of interlocking steps from observation to theory. Problems arise that simply should not arise in terms of what is known. These problems lead to new explanations, new experiments, and new or revised theories.

Unfortunately, not all theories are useful theories. Only when a theory is stated in terms that make clear what possible observations can prove it wrong, if such observations can be made, can that theory be accorded scientific stature. When and if a theory survives the assault of experimental tests, it must also prove its usefulness in summarizing available data and observations as well as its capacity to predict new observations. In these ways, a theory becomes a scientist's understanding of a part of reality. However, a theory may also be a hindrance to understanding. Houdini's phone call, Bacon's Four Idols, and the partial failure of the drive-reduction hypothesis make clear, as we shall see, the reason for this paradox.

Behavior of the Contemporary Scientist

Most of what has been said in Chapter 2 about the nature of scientific method is simply untrue. It is untrue in the particular sense that scientists, the practitioners of the method, may not actually behave the way our formal statement of the method says they should. We pointed out in the last chapter that a statement of "the five steps of scientific method" is simply a textbook way of thinking about this important activity. The point remains that the method of acquiring knowledge about the world in science differs from the plan of attack in most other disciplines. Scientists do observe, ask questions, propose tentative explanations, test these explanations, and formulate theories, but not always in that order, nor are they bound to fulfill each of the phases as if they were steps in some recipe.

It is highly probable that some scientific endeavors, particularly in psychology, do not even begin with direct observation. Since the modern scientist, by virtue of his training, has at his disposal an already formulated and highly organized body of knowledge, he does not have to begin at the beginning, so to speak.

Problems: The Failure to Confirm Expectations

Just because the scientist is immersed in the available knowledge of his discipline, he is led to harbor certain expectations of what holds "true," given certain conditions. Therefore, instead of beginning with direct observation, the scientist sometimes initiates his scientific thinking with a full-blown problem that results when one of his expectations is violated and events do not turn out the way current scientific thinking says they should. In Chapter 4 we shall examine this situation more closely in the light of T. S. Kuhn's views on scientific revolutions. In the meantime, however, let us devote our attention to an example of the failure to confirm existing thinking as it occurred in psychology.

THE DRIVE-REDUCTION HYPOTHESIS

For many years it was widely held, on the basis of experimental evidence and theoretical prediction, that stimuli that reduce a biological drive are capable of reinforcing the behavior that leads to such stimuli. Further, it was also held that the capacity of a stimulus to reduce hunger, or thirst, or sexual desire was the *necessary and sufficient* condition to qualify that stimulus as a reinforcer. Taken literally, this means that not only *can* a stimulus that satisfies a drive be a reinforcer, but, in addition, *only* a stimulus that is a drive reducer (or one which has previously been paired with it) and no other, will be *able* to reinforce behavior. In this view, it is not merely a *possibility* that a reinforcer be drive-reducing; it is an absolute and exclusive necessity. In Clark L. Hull's masterful and influential hypothetico-deductive theory of learning, this notion was stated formally:

Whenever an effector activity (R) [response produced by a muscle or gland] is closely associated with a stimulus afferent impulse or trace (S) [incoming sensory information or stored memory information] and the conjunction is closely associated with the rapid diminution in the motivational stimulus (S_D or S_G) [e.g. hunger contractions of stomach or salivation] there will result an increment ($\triangle$) to a tendency for that stimulus to evoke that response.

(Hull, 1952, pp. 5–6)

What this rather awesome and formalized statement means is that a response that is associated with a decrease in drive will tend to be repeated (learned) because it is reinforcing in its ability to satisfy the drive. If an organism learns that pressing a lever will deliver a food pellet that reduces his hunger, he is likely to press the lever until he is sated and to return to the response of lever-pressing the next time he is hungry. So, Hull was postulating that a stimulus that reduces a biological drive is a primary reinforcer.

Hull was basing the notion of drive reduction on the reasonable assumption that organisms having the capacity to satisfy their drives for food, water, sex, and so on, will be those organisms that most adequately survive and reproduce in the course of their species' evolution. For Hull, in the wake of the Darwinian evolutionary theory, it seemed logical that natural selection would have favored organisms that possessed the innate physiological equipment to accomplish the important task of tending to their biological needs efficiently. If the organism did not have, for example, the capacity to store information about the way in which it had satisfied its needs in the past, it would have to relearn all the required behaviors involved in food-seeking and consummatory activity each time it reexperienced the drive of hunger. This inefficiency would be a most unadaptive state of affairs. In the context of this reasoning and Darwin's theory of natural selection, it seemed utterly reasonable that drive reduction was the *necessary* and *sufficient* condition of reinforcement.

The psychological literature is replete with the experimental work of Hull and many other investigators that shows this effect to be true. But suppose that drive reduction is not the whole story about the nature of reinforcement. Suppose further that drive reduction is the *sufficient* condition of reinforcement but *not* the absolutely *necessary* quality of a reinforcing stimulus. We might, in the course of routine investigation of learning variables, stumble over stimuli that are reinforcing, but which are *not* drive reducing, and which have never been paired with a drive-reducer. Yet these stimuli are capable of motivating an organism to respond, and they are also capable of maintaining that response by reinforcing it. It is obvious that we have stumbled over a problem in this discrepancy between our theory and our discovery. Our expectation that *only* primary drive-reducers and associated stimuli are capable of reinforcing a response has been violated. In actuality, many such "violations" of the drive-reduction hypothesis were observed.

From Failure to Confirm Expectations to New Data, New Explanations

One such violation of expectation was the now classic observation that nonthirsty rats would learn a response rewarded or reinforced merely by a solution of water sweetened by saccharine. Saccharine is non-nutritive, and though it is pleasant to rats and men, it cannot reduce the hunger drive (Sheffield, 1954 and 1960, in Haber, 1966). This experimental finding by itself is not a disproof of the drive-reduction hypothesis. Sheffield's finding might, however, cause us to widen our definition of a reinforcer.

Another, more dramatic problem emerged that caused greater difficulty for the drive-reduction hypothesis Olds and Milner (1954; see also in this context Olds, 1956; and Olds and Olds, 1965) published research demonstrating that electrical stimulation delivered to the septal area of a rat's brain was capable of reinforcing a lever-pressing response.

Minute electrodes had been implanted by Olds and Milner in specified areas of the rat's brain and connected, in turn, to a power supply that could be turned on and off by the rat's own response to the lever of a Skinner box. In other words, the apparatus was so constructed that each of the rat's lever presses delivered a small amount of electrical current to the electrode in his brain. The rat's behavior indicates that he will acquire and maintain a lever-pressing response for the "reinforcement" of electrical stimulation to that area of his brain at a rate equal to, or exceeding, the rate of such responding with food reinforcement. The point, of course, is that electrical stimulation does not reduce any drive, and in fact, it may actually increase the level of excitement or arousal in the rat.

Since Olds and Milner's original investigation, many such studies of electrical stimulation of the brain (ESB) have been performed. The results of these explorations have provided neuropsychologists with a rudimentary map of the "pleasure" and "pain" centers of the rat's brain. (Actually, the phenomenon is much more complicated than the simple notion of "pleasure" and "pain" centers would indicate.) More sophisticated ESB research with human subjects has been undertaken by Delgado and his co-workers (1969, for example), and a variety of criticisms and new interpretations of the effect have been proposed.

Returning to the central idea of this discussion, we can see that the failure to confirm the drive-reduction hypothesis in all of its particulars has led to new thinking and new research about reinforcement. Thus the violation of an established expectation is sometimes a direct antecedent of fresh insight into old problems and the emergence of new problems.

One of the proposed alternatives for the now semidefunct drive-reduction hypothesis takes account of the exciting effect of some stimuli that had been excluded from the drive-reduction formulation. As Judson Brown has succinctly stated the matter: "It is the problem of why, if the drive-reduction view is correct, men and animals ever behave so as to obtain more stimulation rather than less." (1954, in Haber, 1966).

Fred Sheffield has tried to take this difficulty into account in proposing the "drive-*in*duction" theory of reinforcement. The main thesis of this theory is that rewards or reinforcements can be viewed as incentives rather than satisfiers, implying that reinforcement depends on arousal rather than on reduction of drive (Sheffield, 1954). Sheffield's proposal assumes a gradient of excitement working backward from the final response (say, eating) to various neutral cues that lead up to this response. If such is the case, the rat would be motivated and reinforced for *increases* in excitement caused by his expectation of the next cue stimulus in a chain of cues leading ultimately to food.

The detailed specifics of the drive-induction theory lie beyond the scope of our discussion, but it is well to note that the difficulty experienced with original drive-reduction hypothesis has led psychologists to new formulations and new experimental work. Sheffield's suggested mechanism of reinforcement is only one of several contenders in the quest for an adequate explanation of reinforcement. The business of science is never complete, never final. Scientific explanation leads to tentative knowledge and provides the means for testing the clarity and accuracy of its proposals and predictions. Of course, this does not mean that the theory of drive-reduction will be abandoned. The theory does explain some behavioral situations, and in other situations is more useful than any proposed alternative. Theories, like the drive-reduction hypothesis, are replaced only when something more useful or more successful in meeting demands of experimental tests comes along. Another essential point to remember in all of this is that direct observation is not the only means of scientific discovery. Problems may lead to discovery.

KEY CONCEPTS

Violating Expectations: Drive Reduction Versus Induction

Classical Drive-Reduction View of Reinforcement

1. A stimulus that is associated with the reduction in the intensity of a biological drive *can be* a primary reinforcer. Drive reduction is a *sufficient* condition.

2. Association with the reduction of a biological drive is the *only* characteristic a stimulus need possess to qualify as a primary reinforcer. Drive reduction is the *necessary* condition.
   For example, food is the necessary and sufficient condition for hunger reduction. Food is a primary reinforcer.

Violation of Expectation

1. Vitamins are *necessary* to satisfy a basic biological need, but are not perceived as reinforcers.

2. Saccharine is *sufficient* to serve as a reinforcer for rats but it is *not* capable of reducing any drive.

Alternate Explanation of Reinforcement: Drive Induction

1. Stimuli which arouse or initiate drive can serve as reinforcers.

2. Reinforcers are factors that increase drive excitement.

3. A chain of responses that leads to making a final response that directly satisfies a drive increases an organism's excitement and frustration up to the moment of consummation (e.g., eating). Thus the organism is compelled to follow a course of action that actually increases his drive of excitement to obtain the final reward.

(Sheffield, 1954, in Haber, 1966)

A Revised Notion of Scientific Method

Karl Popper, an eminent philosopher of science, has suggested that scientific method actually consists of three phases: *Problems—Theories—Criticisms* (Popper, 1963, in Foley *et al,* 1970, p. 11). He has suggested in his criticism of strictly observational, inductive method that "we do not start from observations but always from problems—from practical problems or from a theory which has run into difficulties; that is to say, which has raised, and disappointed, some *expectations*" (p. 11).

The scientist must take into account both the vastness of our knowledge and the boundless, overwhelming ignorance we display. It is in the clash between these characteristics that growth in our knowledge occurs. We learn by our mistakes: ". . . a problem arises, grows, and becomes significant, through our failures to solve it" (Popper, 1963). Scientific method, then, really begins when we face a problem:

IMPLICATIONS

1. Describe some situations in which a stimulus is drive-reducing but is *not* reinforcing.

2. List situations in which a stimulus is reinforcing but does not reduce a drive.

3. How can the drive-reduction hypothesis be modified so that it takes account of exceptions, but does not become so general as to become valueless? Explain.

4. It is sometimes said that serendipity or "lucky chance" is the mother of some great discoveries in science. What might be some conditions that are necessary in order that a scientist may take advantage of accident or chance when it occurs?

5. David Premack (1962) has suggested that a common property of all reinforcers is that they are higher in probability of occurrence than are the actions which they reinforce. For example, if a child is placed in a room with a pool table and a candy machine as the only contents, either one or the other of these devices will occupy him first. If it is the candy machine, then it has the higher probability of occurrence compared to the pool table. But if we fix the candy machine so that it works only if the child has played pool for five minutes, then the candy machine is said to reinforce the behavior of pool playing. Conversely, when the child wants to play pool, we may arrange the contingencies so that the pool table is available only when and if he eats, say, five candies first. In this case, the pool game is reinforcing the behavior of candy eating. The response with the lower probability of occurrence is reinforced by the one with the higher probability.

a. How could probability be used as the basis of a theory of reinforcement? Be specific.

b. What would happen in the case of several equally probable behaviors?

c. Would Premack's model serve as an answer to Question 1 above? Explain your answer.

Once we are faced with a problem, we proceed by two kinds of attempt; we attempt to guess, or to conjecture, a solution to our problem; and we attempt to criticize our usually somewhat feeble solutions. Sometimes a guess or conjecture may withstand our criticism and our experimental tests for quite a time. But, as a rule, we find that our conjectures can be refuted, or that they do not solve our problems, or that they solve it only in part; and we find that even the best solutions—those able to resist the most severe criticism of the most brilliant and ingenious minds—soon give rise to new difficulties, new problems. Thus we may say that our knowledge grows as we proceed from old problems to new problems by means of *conjectures* and *refutations;* by the refutation of our theories, or, more generally, of our *expectations.*

(Popper, 1963, p. 11)

PROBLEMS—THEORIES—CRITICISM

This is the way scientists really behave in "doing" science. By conjecture—tentative proposal of solutions to problems (hypothesis), and by criticism—actively seeking to refute a theory, scientific knowledge progresses. The friendly "hostility" of one scientist for the theory of another provides an atmosphere conducive to rigorous thinking. Moreover, only theoretical proposals that are *susceptible* of test are admissible to scientific thinking.

The Criterion of Refutability and the Testing of Theories

A theory to explain the behavior of a rat in a maze, or the behavior of a molecule in a living cell, that is not *susceptible* of test and that is not stated in concrete, observable terms, is not a *scientific* theory.

Whenever a scientist claims that his theory is supported by experiment or observation, we should ask him the following question. Can you describe any *possible* observations which, if they are actually made, would refute your theory? If you cannot, then your theory has clearly not the character of an empirical theory; for if *all conceivable observations agree with your theory,* then you are not entitled to claim of any *particular observation* that it gives empirical support to your theory. [Italics added.]

(Popper, 1963)

If any observation that you can think of is possible under your theory, then your theory is so broad as to include everything and explain nothing. The ultimate test of scientific method is the production of theories that allow the scientist to specify what observations, if they were to be made, would refute his theory. Then, if his confidence in his theory is justified, such contradictory observations will not in fact be made; the theory is correct in asserting that such and such events are not possible, while such and so events are. However, if the scientist *cannot* specify the requirements to refute his theory, the theory is, for the time being, relatively useless. This requirement of refutability guarantees two things. First, it insures that the theory will be constructed along observable, specific, and concrete lines of evidence. Only the observable can be refuted.

Second, the criterion of refutability restricts the amount of guesswork or speculation that enters the final, formal structure of the theory. Theories cannot be stated tentatively ("It could be that . . ."), but rather must be stated in terms that allow positive confirmation and disconfirmation, that is, definitively. Hypotheses, not theories, are couched in "iffy" language. The requirements of refutability should not be interpreted to mean, however, that theories are created solely *to be* refuted; theories that pass critical tests of their accuracy and generality without succumbing to refutation increase our confidence in their ability to explain some part of nature. But a theory that is not stated in terms that allow for *potential* refutation deprives scientists of the opportunity to measure its accuracy. Such a theory is not scientific. (Cf. Popper, 1959, 1963.)

Difference Between Scientific and Nonscientific Strategies

It is evident, then, that scientific method, by its very nature, is a self-testing, self-correcting enterprise. Scientific method relies not only on empirical observations, but on reason and logic as well. But, in the end, the final arbiter of truth for a scientist is not what reason says ought to be, but what observationally is (Marx and Hillix, 1963, p. 23). A scientific theory, furthermore, must specify not only what is and what can happen, but it must clearly assert what *cannot* be, what cannot happen, according to its logic, as well. (Cf. Toulmin, 1960, Chs. III and V; and Toulmin, 1961, especially Chs. 1, 3 and 4.)

It seems that we have arrived at a definition, if only a partial one to be used as a rule-of-thumb, of "science," a term we have been using since the beginning of this book. George G. Simpson provides us with the beginnings of such definition:

> One way to approach definition is to consider science as a process of questioning and answering. The questions are, by definition, scientific if they are about relationships among *observed* phenomena. The proposed answer must, again by definition, be in *natural* terms and *testable* in some *material* way. On that basis, a definition of science as a whole would be:
> *Science is an exploration of the material universe* that *seeks natural, orderly relationships among observed phenomena and that is self-testing.* [Italics added.]
>
> (Simpson, 1963)

Notice the similarities between Simpson's definition of modern science and the motives that we presumed to exist in early man's attempts to understand his world.

The scientist's quest for knowledge and understanding is distinguished from that of other disciplines (e.g., philosophy, art) neither by its content nor by its usefulness. It is distinguished from them by its *method of search* and by its striving to reach *relatively certain* and *testable* knowledge. The criterion of refutability is the essence of this difference. It prevents, to a large extent though by no means completely, the contest of opinions that occurs when facts are in dispute. Instead of resorting to the differing opinions of authority, scientific disputes are settled ultimately by careful and exacting laboratory work. Of course, experimental results are subject to interpretation, but there is a kind of upper limit where interpretation must leave off and undisputed evidence takes over. Evidence that has met the criterion of refutability, and that has been tested, ceases to be the subject of dispute.

The Houdini Phone Call Syndrome

Perhaps an anecdote will make the importance of the notion of refutability clear. Once, in a discussion with some friends, the topic of great professional magicians and sleight-of-hand tricks came up. The discussion led to the great magician who used the stage name Houdini, and to the apocryphal tales that surrounded this master showman. It was said that at his behest a phone was to be buried in his tomb upon his death. Mysteriously, in keeping with the character he tried to convey in his professional life, Houdini had suggested that, if life after death were possible, he would place a phone call from his tomb and inform the world.

At this point in the conversation, someone commented dryly, "There goes another theory down the drain." But then, a more thoughtful member of the group contributed: "If Houdini had really been clever he would have said, 'If there is a life after death, I *won't* call!' "

Obviously, if Houdini had set up the circumstances in that second way—the condition of no call, it would be impossible to refute his claim no matter what happens after death. He would have created a situation in which any results and all results confirm his claim: "Heads I win, tails you lose." In the language of scientific testability, if he had done what was jokingly suggested, Houdini could have established an untestable, irrefutable proposition. To be sure, the belief that life after death is possible is a legitimate *belief,* but it is not subject to refutability in the scientific sense.

KEY CONCEPTS

The Criterion of Refutability

1. Theories must be stated in terms that would allow them to be refuted if you can discover the required observations to do so.

2. Theories that do not specify what it would take to prove them wrong, if this could be discovered, cannot be tested. They are non-refutable.

Since it is impossible to sample every possible observation that will have some bearing on a theory's accuracy, it is more efficient to try to discover a few observations that do not confirm the theory. The logical structure of a scientific theory has this form:

If theory X is true, then observations A, B, C should be feasible.

Observations A, B, and C are made.

Therefore theory X is confirmed.

The obvious problem with such an argument is the unasked question: What about other possible observations—observations other than A, B, and C? These other observations are potentially either confirmatory or disconfirmatory. Picture the situation as an Euler diagram:

Theory X asserts A, B, C to be true

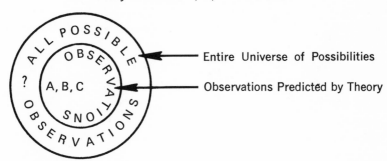

If the observations predicted by theory X are made, they demonstrate only that the theory is one of the possible true explanations. Hence, attempts to discover observations which disconfirm the theory from all those possible can lead to conclusive rejection of theory X.

(Adapted from Campbell, 1969, pp. 352–55)

The Refutable Status of Psychoanalysis: An Example

More to the point, perhaps, than the foregoing anecdote is the application of the criterion of refutability to a complex psychological theory. Sigmund Freud's psychoanalytic theory of personality and psychotherapy, without doubt, has had a wider and more lasting influence on psychologists' views of personality than any other theory. However, psychoanalysis as proposed by Freud involves a good deal of creative insight supported by clinical rather than experimental observation. Many essential aspects of the Freudian theory lack the quality of refutability or the capacity to generate testable hypotheses. Some aspects of the theory have served as the springboard for fruitful research, but in many cases this research has redefined Freudian terms so completely that even Freud would be hard put to recognize them as his own creation. Freud's creative genius lay in his ability to intuitively detect the complex motivational factors, conscious and unconscious, that lie at the base of human behavior. He was the first to acknowledge that with increases in biological and psychological knowledge, changes in the structure and content of his theory would have to be made.

The criticism that psychoanalysis does not meet the standards of scientific-theory construction has been made widely and often (cf. Hook, *et al,* 1959; Eysenck, 1953; Skinner, 1956 and 1963; Colby, 1960; Salter, 1963). Although many of these criticisms often hit their mark, it would be well to keep in mind that it is possible that psychoanalysis as a system of personality theory *for application to psychotherapy* may not purport to be a *scientific* theory (Hartmann, 1964, Ch. 15). In this frame of reference, therapeutic endeavors involve a slightly different set of standards than those of scientific-theory construction. In fact, some psychoanalysts seem to feel that, as a form of therapy (that is, a technique of clinical intervention), the theory is exempt from standard scientific evaluation procedures; they propose, instead, that success or failure with the disordered behavior of patients be substituted for the more abstract criterion of refutability in making tests of the theory (cf. Kubie, in Hook, 1959). However, as Sidney Hook points out:

> Unless psychoanalysis has better clinical or experimental successes than alternative theories, it can hardly aspire to scientific status. The difficulty is that even if it has these successes, this is not sufficient evidence for its validity. *It must find ways of eliminating other hypotheses compatible with the same results.* If as a priest of some Mithraic cult, I give an ailing penitent mouldy bread and say a prayer over him, he may recover. If recovery takes place several times when penitents are treated in this fashion, I am justified in continuing to use this technique. *But the success of the treatment is not decisive with respect to the validity of the theory*

that prayer is efficacious unless I can deduce from my theoretical assumptions something specific not otherwise known, and not explainable by any other supposition. [Italics added.]

(Hook, 1959, p. 220)

If psychoanalysis is to be of any use in predicting behavior and in determining how much more successful its therapeutic measures are than any other therapy's attempts, it must be subjected to the same standards of test that would be applied to any rigorous scientific theory.

IMPLICATIONS

1. Classify each of the following statements as refutable or as nonrefutable.

   a. Bald-headed men have no hair.
   b. New "Foamo" detergent is better.
   c. The more intelligent a person is the less likely he is to be neurotic.
   d. Racial prejudice is caused by severe and rigid authoritarian child-rearing.
   e. The first organism to evolve on this planet did not require oxygen.
   f. Strict toilet training in childhood, accompanied by threats and spankings, leads to compulsive cleanliness in later life.
   g. "Relaxo" headache tablets, with new powerful ingredients, are more powerful and relieve your headache faster.
   h. "Dento" chewing gum, without sugar, is recommended by more dentists for their patients who chew gum.

2. How can those of the above statements that are *not* refutable be revised so that they are, in principle, testable?

The Mechanism of Repression: Does It Meet the Criterion of Refutability?

Let us consider a concrete example of the application of the criterion of refutability to an aspect of Freudian psychoanalysis. Freud proposed an unconscious and automatic mechanism of motivated forgetting called "repression." In his clinical practice with neurotic patients, Freud often found that exploring memories of early childhood incidents that were connected to the patient's neurosis produced a strong resistance in the neurotic to the task of recalling the incident. Freud found, further, that without the use of hypnosis, patients often could not recall important, and sometimes traumatic, events. These events from the patient's past, Freud hypothesized, had been pushed into the unconscious to protect and to defend the conscious ego from awareness of unacceptable impulses, wishes, and desires connected to the event. Under hypnosis, the defense mechanism was held in abeyance so that the threatening memory can be recalled. Unfortunately, Freud soon found that hypnosis was not a reliable tool with all patients (Breuer and Freud [1895], 1964). This process of submergence into the unconscious, thrusting threatening material out of awareness, Freud called repression proper. For obvious reasons it is classed as a defense mechanism. In his early writings, Freud considered the discovery of the mechanism of repression to be the foundation stone of psychoanalysis. But he changed his views on the matter in later discourses, where he included repression as simply one of many unconscious and automatic defense mechanisms (cf. Anna Freud, 1946; and S. Freud [1926], 1963 appendix):

> The theory of repression is the pillar upon which the edifice of psychoanalysis rests. It is really the most essential part of it, and yet it is nothing but the theoretical expression of an experience which can be repeatedly observed whenever one analyses a neurotic without the aid of hypnosis. One is then confronted with a resistance which opposes and blocks the analytic work by causing failures of memory.*
>
> (Freud, 1938b, p. 939)

The Case of Little Hans and His Phobia for Horses

Repressed material can find expression in displaced form so that the resulting alternate symbolic or *disguised* expression can prevent the reexperience of anxiety by the conscious mind, or ego.

An illustration of the mechanism of repression in action can be found in the case of "Little Hans" as reported in Freud's famous "Analysis of a Phobia in a Five-Year-Old Boy" (1909, in 1963) and in a shortened form published after the original detailed case study (1926). Little Hans was phobic about horses. He refused to go out into the street for fear of being bitten by a horse or of seeing a horse fall down. Horses, by the way, were a common sight on the streets at this time in history. The unexplained fear of horses and the inhibition against going into the street represent the major symptoms of Hans' phobia.

Why is the particular content of this phobia the fear of horses? Perhaps, reasoned Freud, the fear of horses prevents Hans from bringing to consciousness the real but repressed source of his anxiety. Horses, then, through some chain of association in Hans' experience, represent a class of displaceable objects, convenient targets on which to focus one's fear while distracting oneself from the true target. A feared horse thus serves in the ego's defensive strategy of preventing recognition of

---

the real object of anxiety, and, unlike the true object, it is easily avoidable. But two questions arise: What is the true object of fear, and how has it come to pass that horses, symbolically or otherwise, substitute for this true object?

> We shall make no further progress so long as we fail to take into account the entire psychic situation of the little patient as this is revealed to us during analysis. He finds himself in *the jealous and hostile oedipus attitude to his father,* whom, however, in so far as his *mother* does not enter into the picture, as the cause of dissension, he loves, devotedly. Thus we have a *conflict* springing from ambivalence—a firmly founded love and a not less justified hatred, both directed to the same person [the father]. His [Hans'] phobia must be an attempt to resolve this conflict. . . .
>
> *The instinctual impulse which succumbs to repression is a hostile impulse against the father.* The analysis furnished the evidence of this in tracing the origin of the idea of the biting horse. Hans saw a horse fall down; he saw too a playmate with whom he had played 'horsie' fall and hurt himself. *The analytic material has given us the right to construe a wish on Hans' part to the effect that his father should fall and hurt himself as had the horse and Hans' playmate. . . . Such a wish, however, is equivalent to the intention of doing away with him* [the father] *himself, or the murderous impulse of the oedipus complex.* [Italics added.]
>
> (Freud, [1926], 1963, Strachey translation)

Thus Freud's analysis revealed the true object of anxiety: Hans' father.

Hans' Stage of Psychosexual Development

Hans is at the stage of development that is described by Freud as *phallic* and that is marked by the child's budding interest in pleasurable stimulation of his genitals. (Cf. Freud, 1905 in 1965; 1940 in 1949, and 1923 in 1960.) The phallic stage occurs approximately around the ages of three to six years, and it is the time when the child begins bodily self-exploration of the genital area and develops an interest in the sexual equipment of those around him. Serving as a kind of midpoint between two earlier stages of *oral* and *anal* development and two later stages of *latency* and *genital* maturation, the phallic stage focuses on the controversial notion of childhood sexuality. Freud postulated that, prior to the phallic stage, children develop through oral and anal sequences of maturation, marked by a dominant orientation to the world through the mouth (birth to age two) during the oral phase, and a sense of the importance of the eliminative function (age two to three years) during the anal stage. During this second, anal stage, the parent-child interaction of significance shifts from feeding to toilet training, and it often involves for the child novel and intense experiences with self-discipline and parental authority. The phallic stage (three to five or six years) follows the anal, and it is marked not only by the above-mentioned interest in sexual organs and activity, but also by a longing to possess the mother since she has been the primary source of most pleasurable gratifications up to this time. In some diffuse and vaguely understood way, the pleasurable sensation produced by self-manipulation of the sexual organs is perceived by the child as connected with his relationship to mother, displacing his earlier oral and anal interests.

At this point in the developmental sequence, the child senses that his mother's attention and her warmly soothing ministrations are not exclusively his. Besides troublesome siblings, mother must be shared with father, and the child soon comes to resent and to be jealous of this interloper. Freud assumed that with increasing sophistication the child develops a belief that his father knows, or at least suspects, how much he would like to be rid of him. Anxiety-stricken and guilty, the young boy feels certain that his intense anger and avid pleasure-seeking are impossible to conceal. His submissive and overtly loving behavior, he feels, is but a transparent façade to an all-knowing, all-powerful father. What more appropriate retribution could father plan to exact than the removal of that organ that provides the most pleasure at this stage? Castration by the father becomes the overwhelming fear for the child's burgeoning ego, and this imagined outrage must be dealt with by the mechanisms of defense. Most notable of these is the mechanism of repression. This entire emotional constellation of desire, jealousy, and fear was termed by Freud the "Oedipus complex" after Sophocles' tragedy, *Oedipus Rex,* in which Oedipus unwittingly kills his father and marries his mother.

Following the phallic stage, there ensues a period of time marked by the submergence and dormancy of sexual behavior, until the time of puberty, around twelve or thirteen years of age. This period, during which the sex drive remains hidden, is called *latency.* Probably a cultural phenomenon, latency is instigated by parental reactions to the child's emerging sexuality.* At puberty, when the culture deems it appropriate, the sex drive reemerges and the individual is said to be in the *genital stage.* The young man now evidences a new interest in the opposite sex and he possesses the biological capacity to procreate.

---

* Freud was firmly convinced that the sexual strivings of the child remain biologically active during latency. However, through the impact of parental censure and the displeasure of other authority figures (e.g., school teachers), the social taboos against sexual activity soon exert a powerful redirecting influence on the form the child's sexual behavior may take. Only later, at puberty, will the sex drive be allowed to re-emerge in undisguised, sexual form as interest in the opposite sex. Thus latency is a complex phenomenon compounded of physiological and cultural trends.

These five stages of psychosexual development, as Freud called them, may be summarized as follows, keeping in mind that the age limits are approximations:

1. *Oral Stage:* birth to two years
2. *Anal Stage:* two years to three years
3. *Phallic Stage:* three years to six years (Hans' stage)
4. *Latency:* six to twelve or thirteen years
5. *Genital:* puberty

Hans' Unsuccessful Repression

Little Hans, caught in the throes of the Oedipus conflict, has had to repress his hostile and murderous wish against his father to protect his ego from the anxiety that resulted. After all, harboring such a wish against so powerful a person as a father is no joke. Furthermore, Hans experiences an irreconcilable conflict over his contradictory feelings of hate for a person whom he simultaneously loves. This double conflict is the cause of the ambivalence about which Freud speaks: love and hate; the desire to attack and the fear of retaliation. Hans' unconscious desires seek satisfaction of the sexual urge. The object of these desires is his mother. However, Hans' conscious ego perceives his father as an obstacle and a threat. Guilt feelings produced by the reaction of his conscience (superego, in Freudian terms) to the unethical demands of the unconscious for sex and aggression add to Hans' psychic pain. Hans' conscious mind protects itself from the perceived threat, and from his conscience's censure, by repressing the sources of the conflict: obliterating through repression the memory of his desire for mother and his hatred for father.

But, as we already might suspect, repression is sometimes only partially successful. The energy of the repressed urges must be given expression in disguised, symbolic form, for it is only in this way that the conscious ego remains protected (fooled), and the unconscious urges receive gratification. A phobia for horses develops out of Hans' experiences and symbolizes in miniature the conflict over the father, displacing him as the object of fear.

Freud's creative genius is apparent.

Little Hans and the Accuracy of Explanation

Despite the fertility of the Freudian system in its clinical applications, it is extremely difficult to generate empirical hypotheses from cases like Hans' repression because of a crucial issue: Can a Freudian explanation be subjected to test? If such explanations cannot be tested, they cannot be admitted to the status of a scientific theory. Note that it is not the truth or falsity of a concept as such that is important for scientific status, but rather the concept's susceptibility to test—its refutability—that counts.

As we can see from the case history, and from our own experiences of forgetting unpleasant incidents and other things such as the name of someone we dislike, motivated forgetting does exist. The problem is whether the Freudian formulation of this phenomenon can be empirically tested.

Given the Freudian explanation, we seem to know a great deal about how Hans' motivated forgetting took place and about the corresponding development of the horse phobia. But this knowledge is of the *post hoc,* speculative variety. Given that Hans has a phobia for horses, which we observe; given that he exhibits behavior from which we infer a hostility to the father and a desire for the mother: Can we now use the mechanism of repression to explain Hans' fear of horses as a camouflage of his true fear of his father's reprisal for his hostile wishes? Could we not, instead, explain the same observations along different theoretical lines and be just as correct? The answer is yes, *if* we don't test any of our proposed explanations.*

The orthodox Freudian explanation is plausible once we have observed all of Hans' symptoms, but with this type of explanation we could not *predict before* the onset of the phobia either its occurrence or its content. Just like the Monday morning quarterback, who in recounting Sunday's game, knows where, when, and how every player on the losing team made mistakes, a Freudian explanation accounts for the observed behavior and the inferred motivation *after* the symptoms appear.

This variety of *post*-diction raises some problems. First, against what

---

* An alternative theoretical explanation of phobic reactions that makes no recourse to mechanisms like displacement or repression might be drawn from learning theory. Employing the principles of stimulus generalization and higher-order conditioning, Hans' fear of horses may be explained as a conditioned adversive reaction. We might suppose that either a real horse or perhaps just the idea of horses was present when Hans experienced some traumatic or fearful incident involving his father. Horses as such represent a cue or signal for the recall of the unpleasant incident. Hans' response of avoiding horses and stimuli associated with horses is now seen as a clear case of reinforcement. Avoidance of these stimuli reduces the unpleasant sensation of anxiety, and thus reinforces the behavior that accomplishes separation. In essence, Hans can make the response of "not thinking" about the unpleasant incident by avoiding cues and stimuli that might provoke the memory. (Cf. Dollard and Miller, 1950; Wolpe and Rachman 1960 where evidence for a conditioning interpretation of Hans is presented.)

The advantage of an explanation of Hans' phobia in terms of learning principles is that we confine our explanation to *observable behavioral* events, rather than internal, unobservable mechanisms. As such, we can both confirm and disconfirm the operation of these learning variables because we know what conditions must exist for them to operate, and what conditions must exist if they are not to operate.

criterion do we test the validity or accuracy of the explanation if it seems plausible and if it accounts for all the known facts? If, indeed, it is plausible and comprehensive, does it not, therefore, perform adequately the function assigned to theory? Perhaps it does. But, again, how are we ever to know that a completely different explanation, equally creative in accounting for all of the facts, is not just as tenable? The point is, such an analysis can never be inconsistent with the facts since it is applied only where the facts are already known.

Secondly, there will be occasions when the Freudian explanation *is* an accurate statement of what has taken place, just as there will be instances when the Freudian explanation is *not* accurate, but simply accounts logically for the tally of known facts. How do we distinguish between these two situations: when the theory is accurate versus times when it is merely consistent? The answer, of course, is to predict behavior before the event, and then see how your theoretical prediction fares after the event. (Cf. Eysenck, 1953, Ch. 12, where a similar criticism of psychoanalysis is made.)

Clinical Prediction of Behavior

Freudian therapists counter these arguments by pointing to cases where it is possible, seemingly, for the therapist to intuitively predict series of correlated behavior patterns for a patient before these patterns are actually observed. For example, Jacob Arlow offers the following case:

> The fact is that analysts are always making predictions, which they submit to confirmation or invalidation by the further study of their data. . . .
> During an initial interview I asked a patient how long he had been married. He answered, "Sixteen months, three weeks." The overly exact quality of this response aroused in me the suspicion that I was dealing with a person whose character structure was colored by obsessional thinking and compulsive traits. To confirm my suspicion I asked further, "How long did you know your wife before you married her?" He answered, "Two years, three months." At this point, inwardly, I made a further set of predictions concerning this individual's mental traits. I guessed that he would be especially concerned with money, that he would have a passion for accumulating it, keeping meticulous records of his financial transactions, and that he would be most reluctant to spend it. A further set of predictions concerned his relationship to cleanliness. I could guess that he would be excessively neat regarding his person and his clothes, tidy in his surroundings, orderly in his manner, and vigorously punctual regarding appointments and fulfillment of financial obligations. Questioning confirmed each of these predictions in minute detail.
>
> (Arlow, in Hook, 1967, p. 207)

Arlow's characterization of the obsessive-compulsive personality in all of his nit-picking behavior and in his excruciating attention to the ritual of detail seems to sorely miss the point of *scientific* prediction. What Arlow seems to be referring to is the *detection* of *correlations* among traits, not the *prediction* of one pattern of behavior from another. Association or relationship between clusters of traits is far different from the forecast of behavior on theoretical grounds.

To observe a man who is bald as an egg, and then to "predict" that he does not carry a comb is not likely to be classed as a record-breaking forecast. No doubt such correlational observation as Arlow reports is highly useful in therapy and probably provides the skilled clinician with some measure of satisfaction in those instances of successful observation. But in no way does such correlational detection serve as a validation of, or a potential test for, Freudian theory.

Repression and the Criterion of Refutability

A second difficulty with the Freudian formulation, besides its inability to predict behavior, involves more directly the criterion of refutability. For instance, the way in which Freud formulated the concept of repression, as an unconscious and automatic defense of the ego, excludes any and all statements of what is necessary for repression (or the Oedipus conflict) *not* to be operating in a given instance of behavior. The intensity of the anxiety or threat sufficient to trigger repression is not specified in any quantitative way, nor is the magnitude of repression to be expected for any given memory or impulse susceptible of any manner of calculation. Repression seems to be an all-or-none, blanket phenomenon. Obviously, this is not exactly what Freud had in mind, but he was unable to specify more exactly the parameters or conditions under which repression could be the expected outcome. Therefore, there are no conditions that could be specified that would count as disproof of an explanation employing the concept of repression as a defense against threat in a given case. If Hans *were* engrossed in Oedipal strivings and *not* phobic for horses, and he *did* recognize consciously his hostility toward his father, this series of events would not be taken as evidence against the operation of repression in this instance. In such a case, the theory simply would be said not to apply. Thus events that can seemingly contradict the theory cannot disprove it; they are simply classed as exceptions that do not come under its inclusion. Likewise, the theory can never be wrong (or tested, for that matter) since the only conceivable events to which it applies are confirmatory events.

Another point bearing on the same issue is the ability to derive from the theory a method of setting up the appropriate conditions to produce the phenomenon. No one has yet been able to produce a Freudian re-

KEY CONCEPTS

The Nonrefutability of a Freudian Concept: Repression

Psychoanalytic Definition. "[Repression] . . . consists of an unconsciously purposeful forgetting or not becoming aware of internal impulses or external events which . . . represent possible temptations or punishments for, or mere allusions to, objectionable instinctual demands" (Fenichel, 1945, p. 148).

Implication. "All the defensive measures of the ego against the id [unconscious urges] are carried out silently and invisibly. The most we can ever do is to reconstruct them in retrospect: we can never really witness them in operation. This statement applies, for instance, to successful repression. . . . we are aware of it only subsequently, when it becomes apparent that something is missing" (A. Freud, 1946, p. 8).

Example. Little Hans, in the phase of psychosexual development called "phallic," is struggling against his Oedipal wishes to possess his mother and be rid of his father. He represses these objectionable instinctual demands, but succumbs to the anxiety of a horse phobia. Horses now serve as a camouflage of his true fear of his father's potential retaliation for Hans' murderous intentions.

Problem. How can we be sure that the psychoanalytic interpretation of Hans' phobia is valid? Repression itself cannot be observed. Its only evidence in this case is the presumed substitute of the horse phobia: Fear of horses conceals the true fear of father. But are we sure that this piece of evidence on which the existence of repression rests is correct?

Testing the Theory. Suppose Hans were hostile to his father and desired to possess his mother but did not develop a phobia. In fact, Hans remains aware of his hostility and desire and engages in no motivated forgetting. Could this outcome serve as evidence against the Freudian prediction of repression? The answer is *no*, because:

1. Repression as a psychoanalytic concept makes no predictions.

2. This case would be classed as an exception to the rule, but not as a disproof.

3. Repression can only be applied as an interpretation *after* the fact, in a *post*-dictive way. Thus it is applied only in cases where a presumed motivated forgetting already exists.

pression at will, under controlled conditions, in the laboratory (cf. MacKinnon and Dukes' critical review of the experimental literature on repression in Postman, 1962, Ch. 11). The reason is, to repeat, that the specific conditions for the operation of repression are not specified by the theory. To be sure, some research has been done on the issue of repression, but in all such research the concept of repression had to be redefined and translated into concrete experimental operations that often resemble only vaguely the dynamic Freudian concept. Some of this research proceeds the other way around, investigating already existing repressions in subjects who show evidence of traumatic memory loss, but in this approach the same difficulty of *post-* versus *pre-*diction prevails. The production and removal of repression under controlled, measurable conditions has not yet been demonstrated.

Summary: Houdini Revisited

Repression (motivated forgetting) does exist. The problem of defining the concept *scientifically* (operationally, empirically) so that experimental tests can be designed has not been solved within the framework of Freudian theory. Such experimental tests would involve a precise statement of both the conditions under which repression operates and the conditions under which repression may be expected *not* to function. Much like Houdini's fictional phone call, the Freudian definition of repression is compatible with, and confirmed by, any and all outcomes.

To return to our original analogy, the situation as it stands now under orthodox Freudian theory is not much different from—nor any the more testable than—the Houdini phone-call situation. "If there is life after death, I won't call." Certainly, if a call is never made, we count this as evidence that Houdini is residing comfortably in the spirit world. The prediction is confirmed. If, on the other hand, we do receive from the deceased Houdini a phone call transcending the grave, the prediction is again confirmed. No outcome can be postulated that would disprove Houdini's statement. (No one, it seems safe to say, would be more surprised by the phone call than Houdini himself.) There is another explanation to the first alternative (no call) that is equally possible: no call is forthcoming because there is no life after death.

Compare this reasoning to the Freudian scheme. Inability to recall an emotionally threatening event or impulse is taken as evidence of repression. Repression, in turn, implies the presence of a motive or self-protective urge to forget. But an alternative situation in which an emotionally threatening event or impulse is *not* forgotten is *not* counted as evidence against the existence of the mechanism of repression. It is simply classed as an exceptional case in which repression has failed to operate. This is perfectly legitimate as long as the theory tells you *why* these particular circumstances prevent the occurrence of repression. It is not legitimate for the theory to assert: "Repression exists where you find it, and does not exist where you cannot find it." Any situation of emotionally loaded forgetting counts as evidence *for* repression. No conditions are stated as having to exist if repression is not the cause of the forgetting behavior we observe. It is very much a case of Houdini's phone call. No conceivable test situation can count against repression or Houdini.

To summarize, we must conclude that the Freudian formulation of repression is scientifically deficient in at least two ways:

1. We cannot predict the occurrence of a repression before it has taken place because we do not know the conditions specific to its operation.
2. The concept of repression as defined in Freudian theory is not refutable; it provides no conditions for a test of its validity.

IMPLICATIONS

1. In terms of Freud's explanation of Hans' phobia, what would a Freudian therapist do to "cure" Hans? (What does Freud's theory suggest is the cause? HINT: How would unconscious conflicts be made conscious?)

2. In terms of the alternative explanation of Hans' phobia given in footnote on p. 102, what would a learning theorist attempt to do to cure Hans' phobia?

3. Suppose that the Freudian therapy was successful and the learning therapy was not. Which of the following statements would be accurate and scientifically correct?

    a. Freud's theory is correct; learning theory is incorrect.
    b. Freud's theory is either correct or incorrect, but learning theory is incorrect.
    c. Freud's theory is either correct or incorrect, and learning theory is correct or incorrect.

Only one of the above statements is true. Which is it? Why are the other statements false?

The Paradox of the Ravens: The Logic of Refutability

We can translate the concrete argument of refutability of scientific theory into the more abstract form of logic in order to understand what refutability actually requires.

A stronger test of a statement's validity can be made by trying to discover circumstances that would prove it false than by attempting to discover instances that conform to the statement. The "paradox of the ravens," usually associated with the philosopher Carl G. Hempel

(1965; see also Theobald, 1968, p. 80; and W. Salmon, 1973) is an illustration of this principle.

If someone were to assert, "All ravens are black," we could easily *confirm* the assertion by simply seeking out some black ravens, a relatively easy observation to make. If someone else were to assert, "All *non*-black things are *non*-ravens," he would have uttered precisely the same assertion as the first person in a logically equivalent form. But note the difference that the change in form makes when we set out to confirm the statements. To confirm the first, remember, all we had to do was observe black ravens, but to confirm that all non-black things are non-ravens, we are compelled to seek out all objects that are not ravens *and* are not black.

Although the two statements are logically equivalent, one statement's form requires only a small class of observations while the other's form

IMPLICATIONS

The following is an abstract of an experiment designed to test whether repression was the cause of forgetting:

Two groups of subjects are trained to memorize paired nonsense syllables (e.g., *krl-vid*). Several days later, both groups of subjects are asked to relearn the same material and the results indicate that there is no significant difference at this point in their learning. Immediately after the relearning task, they are given a task in which they must solve some long addition problems. The experimental group is led to believe that they did very poorly on this task and are therefore very stupid. The control group is given no indication of their performance. Now, both groups are retested on the nonsense syllable task. The experimental (ego-threatened) group performs significantly *less* well than the control group on measures of retention and relearning. The results are interpreted as due to repression in the experimental subjects, who were insulted and threatened on the task.

1. Is this the only possible interpretation? If not, what else could account for the ego-threatened group's performance?

2. Suppose that three days after the above procedures, both groups are again brought into the lab and given another task of math problems, and this time the ego-threat group is led to believe that they did very well (threat removed). When tested on the nonsense syllables, there is no difference now between the experimental group's retention and the control group's retention. Can this result be interpreted as showing that once the threat is removed, repression is lifted (implying that repression had been the cause in the first place)?

3. There is some evidence that emotionally upset subjects learn poorly when compared to emotionally unaroused subjects. Can this be a methodological flaw in the foregoing experiment? How might it explain the "lifting" of repression?

requires a seemingly endless list of observations like white shoes, yellow bananas, brown cows, *ad infinitum* in order to *confirm* it. But suppose that we change our strategy from trying to confirm the statements to trying to disconfirm them. Life gets simpler.

Both statements require only *one* type of observation to prove them *false*: a non-black raven. A non-black raven should not exist according to the first statement—all ravens are black—and an object that is a raven should not come in any color but black according to the second— all non-black things are non-ravens. In other words, confirmation is a wasteful strategy. Disconfirmation is remarkable for its efficiency. But this is true only if a statement (or a scientific theory) is formulated in such a way that it makes clear what it would take to disconfirm it. These "raven statements" are explicit in that respect: they are, in principle, refutable, though it is unlikely anyone will find a yellow raven.

With psychoanalysis as our conceptual framework, we can easily confirm the existence of repression in some cases where it appears to be operating, but, for the present, we would find it next to impossible to decide what it would take to disconfirm or refute the operation of repression. Therefore, we can return to the conclusion previously reached, that a scientific theory must be stated in a form that makes it refutable, or to put it another way, a form that provides the possibility of making fair tests of the theory's assertions.

The essential point is that, like the raven statements, some theories may pass the rigorous testing scientists will attempt. But in all cases refutability is a safeguard that scientists try to build into their theories. This generalization does not mean that Freud's conception of repression is worthless. It does mean that we will have to be ever more ingenious in devising laboratory procedures to tackle the problem because the entire scientific endeavor is focused on the construction of theories as a tool for acquiring reliable understanding. Early man, you will recall, was motivated by the same urgent need to understand his world.

Theory: The Tool of Scientific Understanding

Before ending our discussion of how scientists proceed to make discoveries, formulate explanations, and test their adequacy, it would be well to examine more closely the motive underlying the scientific endeavor. This motive, as we have seen, has not changed appreciably since early man's attempts to understand his crop failures, diseases, deaths, and natural catastrophes. Paradoxically, the motive to understand the material universe may itself become a significant problem. It may be that, in our attempt to develop methods to achieve the goal of understanding, we have neglected to develop an appreciation of what "understanding" itself may mean.

The scientific psychologist, perhaps more than other scientists, is still at the beginning of his attempts to establish reliable, useful, and general theories of human and animal behavior. Because of the very nature of his object of study, the behavior of organisms in all of its biological and psychological complexity, he relies on the methods and data of several closely allied sciences to achieve understanding in his own sphere. For the psychologist with such diverse intellectual dependencies, the nature of scientific "understanding," the very goal of his endeavor, is likely to be particularly elusive. There may be a further complication in the knowledge that the psychological, cognitive process of "understanding" is itself part of the behavioral subject matter that psychologists seek to elucidate. The irony of this realization has escaped many a contemporary investigator in psychology.

Some Meanings of Understanding

To say that we *understand* some concept does not mean the same thing in all instances. The experience of understanding may have several varieties of meanings and several levels of completeness. Mary Henle, a Gestalt psychologist, has outlined four possible, but by no means separate, meanings of *understanding* (1968):

1. Clarifying the structure of the material under consideration.
2. Making explicit what is only implicit in the material.
3. Stripping away unessential details.
4. Placing of an item into an appropriate context.

After exploring each of these meanings, we will be in a position to explore the relationship between the meanings of the experience of *understanding* and the functions of a scientific theory.

Understanding, in its most widely used context, without any necessary reference to scientific understanding, can refer to the ability *to clarify the structure of the material under consideration*. Essentially, clarification of the structure involves reducing the material to a less complex form. As Henle puts it, when understanding is based on attempts to clarify structure, we are engaged in "penetrating the disguise" of the material. A simple example might be drawn from Freud's work.

When Freud was able to discern that, in most cases, slips of the tongue revealed the true feelings of a patient, he had penetrated the disguise of the presented observation by going beyond the commonsense belief that errors of speech are only simple accidents of language (cf. Freud, 1938a). Or, to take another psychoanalytic illustration, when Freud was able to see through the apparently bizarre and meaningless surface structure of remembered dream stories, he had once again penetrated the disguise of a psychological problem. Freud then carried the process of clarification further with his realization that this latent dream content always represents an attempt by the dreamer's unconscious to provide hallucinatory satisfaction for frustrated and sometimes forbidden urges. Freud now understood dreams to be meaningful, though disguised, fulfillments of wishes (cf. *The Interpretation of Dreams*, 1938).

This process of penetrating beyond the surface of a problem, through to its inner structure, is one meaning of what we experience when we understand. But in some situations, simply clarifying the structure of the problem does not lead to the experience of understanding. So, too, with scientific understanding where simple analysis is not always sufficient.

For understanding to occur, we may have to carry the clarification a step further by *making explicit what is only implicit in the material or observation*. In fact, the ability to deduce new ideas from those already formulated is one of the most important functions of a theory for the scientist. It is not that we have "created" new ideas from old ones, but rather that we have brought to the surface what was only implied by our already-held notions. To illustrate this process of explication we can turn to the notable and elegant experiments of Gregor Mendel.

When, in 1865, this pioneering biologist presented a paper summarizing his breeding experiments with pea plants and other organisms to an Austrian society of natural science, he introduced the world to the first systematic discoveries in genetics. For some thirty-five years his work went unnoticed beyond the simple publication of his paper. Few scientists saw the significance of Mendel's deductions. Although many experimenters had obtained similar breeding results some time before Mendel began his work, Mendel's real contribution lay in his ability to see what these results implied.

Taking pea plants that had bred true (no change in their observable traits) for several generations, Mendel cross-pollinated tall plants with short plants (i.e., plants that were phenotypically* tall or short). The resulting offspring of the first filial (F_1) generation were all phenotypically tall (appeared tall to direct observation).

Questioning the disappearance of the short plants in this generation,

---

* *Phenotype* is the biological term indicating the directly observable and readily apparent structural characteristics of an organism. For example, with respect to eye color, a given individual with brown eyes is said to be "phenotypically brown-eyed." A phenotypically brown-eyed man may nonetheless carry a gene for blue eyes on his chromosomes. Thus, while his phenotype is still brown eyes, his *genotype* is mixed (heterozygous). Of course it is equally possible for a man to be phenotypically *and* genotypically brown-eyed. In this case he would be a pure type (homozygous). But the important point to remember is that an organism's *phenotype* by itself does not indicate the specific genes he may possess. Only through observation of an organism's offspring may the exact genetic constitution be determined.

Mendel sought the answer by further breeding of the plants. This time he allowed the hybrid F_1 tall plants (produced, remember, by crossing tall and short) to interbreed among themselves in order to determine whether they would continue to produce only tall offspring, or perhaps reverse, and produce only short offspring, or perhaps some combination of the two. The well-known result was 787 tall and 277 short plants, or an approximate ratio of 3:1 (actually a ratio of 2.84 to 1). From these results, the mathematically talented Mendel, unlike his predecessors, was able to make a number of deductions that brought to light what is implied by these ratios. He reasoned that tallness is dominant over shortness as a trait so that, as a result of fertilization, only the dominant trait of tallness appears phenotypically. Such reasoning accounts for the disappearance of short plants in the F_1 generation. But more importantly, Mendel went on to deduce from the F_2 generation (obtained, remember, by crossing plants of F_1 with each other) that the reason the trait of shortness makes its reappearance and the reason that the tall plants outnumber the short plants 3:1 is that more than one "factor" for the trait of tallness is carried by the original tall parent plants. Likewise, more than one "factor" (what we now call genes) for the trait of shortness is also carried by the parental short plants. During fertilization (what we have called "breeding" up to now), each parent must contribute only one half of the genetic factors that will become part of the offspring's genetic makeup; each parent, therefore, contributes only one factor for a trait to a particular offspring plant. If the parent is a pure tall (homozygous) plant, both of the factors it *could* contribute are tallness factors; if the parent is a pure short plant, both of the factors it *could* contribute are shortness factors. Each pure parent thus contributes *one* of its factors, a tall factor from the pure tall and a short factor from the pure short. The resulting offspring has the genotype or genetic makeup of Tt (one Tall factor and one short t factor). Whether this offspring plant will *be* tall phenotypically is determined by the factor that is dominant, in this case T. If, however, the offspring inherits two recessive factors for shortness, tt, the plant will be phenotypically short. Such a result would occur from the pairing of two pure-short parent plants, or from the pairing of a parent that was carrying the factor for shortness with a pure-short parent, or another parent carrying one factor for shortness. Such was the case when Mendel crossed the hybrid F_1 generations and obtained the small percentage of short plants.

Mendel's ability to reason from his observed results to a tentative explanation of his results is a real achievement. He made explicit what had been only implicit in his results. He, of course, knew nothing of DNA or chromosomes, nor had he ever observed the process of cell division in sex cells. Yet, calling them "factors," he was able to hypothesize that such things exist, and, further, how such factors must behave in sex cells—a process we now call *meiosis*. He had achieved a genuine understanding, subject to test, of the genetics of pea plants. Of course, he went on to examine further the behavior of his "factors" in more complex instances of intercrossing, but again, understanding was achieved only by elucidating the implications of his results.

Mendel's work also illustrates another meaning that the term "understanding" may have. Understanding often involves *stripping away unessential details* and the capacity to see through irrelevant complications. Mendel chose the pea plant as his experimental organism for precisely these reasons. Pea plants, he knew, are capable of both self-pollination and cross-pollination, allowing the experimenter to manipulate and to control the desired variable at will. Pea plants are also ideal genetic subjects in that they occur in widely differing varieties bearing easily detectable differential traits, such as variations in height, color, and texture. These traits appeared to be inherited independently of each other, and thus one trait at a time could be observed in the genetic process, reserving the study of the more complex case of multiple trait inheritance until the basic "rules" of genetics had been worked out. In almost every experimental investigation, the scientist attempts to strip away unessential details to achieve understanding. This procedure, in part, is what is meant by experimental control.

The last of the varieties of meaning that the experience of understanding may involve is *the placing of an item in a context*. Often, the meaning of an idea that may lead to understanding is changed by the context in which it is found or in which it may be placed. Henle uses the example of the word "dig," which has widely different meanings to a young person and to an archaeologist. More importantly for our purposes, the context in which the scientist thinks often determines when and how a solution to a problem is discovered. Almost every introductory psychology student is familiar with the concept of "set" or *einstellung* effect. To illustrate, Maier (1931) conducted experiments on what has come to be called the two-rope problem. Simply, it consists of two ropes hanging from a ceiling and placed so far apart that a person standing between the ropes cannot reach them both simultaneously, even with outstretched arms. Also present in the room is some third object of a certain weight, something like a pair of pliers or a door knob. The subject is told that his task is to tie the two ends of the rope together even though holding one rope prevents him from reaching the other. The solution involves tying the weighted object (pliers) to one of the ropes and swinging it like a pendulum while holding the other rope and waiting for the pendulum to reach you. The point is that, unless the subject is able to see the ropes and pliers in the new context of "weight and pendulum," he is unable to solve the problem.

Some subjects are not able to achieve what the Gestalt psychologists call a "reorganization of the perceptual field." That is to say, some subjects cannot escape the concreteness of the situation before them and they see only two ropes and a pair of pliers. Even more dramatically, Birch and Rabinowitz (1951), using the same problem situation with different weighted objects, found that prior experience immediately before attempting to solve the two-rope problem greatly affected the subject's ability to reorganize his thinking. Subjects were given different pre-rope problem tasks to perform involving the objects that would be part of the two-rope problem solution. The objects to be used were an electrical switch and an electrical-relay device. In the pre-rope problem task, one group of subjects had to complete an electrical circuit on a wiring board using the switch, and one group had to do the same thing but they employed the electrical-relay device instead. Following this task, both groups were tested on the two-rope problem with switches and electrical relays available for use as weights. Subjects who had been given prior experience using the switch or the relay in their *customary* functions of completing electrical circuits had greater difficulty in solving the two-rope problem than control subjects not given prior experience with the devices. Birch and Rabinowitz conclude that subjects without this critical prior experience were better able to reorganize their thinking and to see the switch and relay devices as something other than "electrical" in function. These subjects could transcend the context of normal use for these objects and were able to see them in the new and needed context of "pendulum weights."

This ability to remove oneself from preconceptions and established set, and the capacity to see new relations and functions for familiar phenomena, characterize the truly productive variety of scientific thinking. The scientist must be able to avoid the "functional fixedness" that characterized the subjects of the Birch-Rabinowitz study. In being able to accomplish alternations in context, or in being able to see beyond established contexts, the productive scientist may be able to formulate a theory that leads to understanding (Kuhn, 1970; and Toulmin, 1961, Ch. 6).

As we look over this short listing of the various meanings understanding may have—and there are probably other variations—we should bear foremost in mind that understanding is the goal of the scientific endeavor. Understanding is achieved by employing the prime tool of the scientist: namely, theory. As we have seen, a theory provides the scientist with an increased facility in summarizing individual chunks of data in a conceptual whole, which then has the capacity to explain the phenomenon under study. Once a theory is logically organized in this

KEY CONCEPTS

The Meanings of Understanding

1. Understanding is . . .

Clarifying the structure of the problem; reducing it to a less complex form. "Penetrate the disguise of the material."

Example: Can you find the number 5 in this figure?

2. Understanding is . . .

Making explicit what is only implicit in the problem.

Example: Extremely anti-Semitic persons are likely to express agreement with the following item from an attitude inventory, even though the item apparently says nothing nasty about Jews. Can you understand why?

"The trouble with letting Jews into a nice neighborhood is that they gradually give it a typically Jewish atmosphere."

(Adorno *et al.*, 1969)

3. Understanding is . . .

Stripping away the unessential details.

Example: The following verbiage contains a simple sentence.

The dog who kicked over the oil lamp that set fire to the haystack which burned down the barn that spread the flames to the woods where the forest animals ran to the stream in which swim the salmon who spawn upstream had puppies.

4. Understanding is . . .

Placing an item into context, or escaping an established context.

Example: Note the case of the young lady who read the following sign on the highway:

25¢ CARS ONLY 25¢

and demonstrated that she was a prisoner of context by asking her driving companion to explain why a 25¢ car that is only 25¢ is such a bargain.

way, it allows the scientist to deduce and to predict new phenomena not already observed. Thus the scientist can transcend the immediate empirical fact to look ahead for potentially new observations. This variety of foresight or prediction is a second function of theory; it is also a way of testing the validity and generality of theories. Predictions from theory that are not borne out in observation weaken the theory.

The Meanings of Understanding and the Functions of Theory: An Intimate Relationship

Perhaps not so surprising is the fact that the meanings of understanding that we have discussed are almost in perfect correspondence to the functions of theory. (Cf. Toulmin, 1961, for a somewhat parallel view.)

Clarifying the structure of the material and stripping away unessential details of the problem under study correspond perfectly to function number one: the capacity of a theory to *summarize data in a conceptual whole that allows explanation.*

Similarly, the capacity to *make explicit what is only implicit in the data* often involves the ability to *transcend previous thinking* and previous contexts, to *discover new ways of thinking.* These two meanings of understanding correspond nearly exactly to a theory's capability to deduce and to predict new phenomena that have not already been observed (Table 2). In short, theory is the scientist's tool for reaching the goal of science: namely, understanding. In its functions of predicting and summarizing, a theory *is* the scientist's understanding.

TABLE 2
Meanings of Understanding and Corresponding Functions of Theory

Meanings of Understanding	Functions of Theory	
1. Clarifying the structure of material and . . .	. . . SUMMARIZE DATA IN	1.
2. Stripping away unessential details . . .	. . . A CONCEPTUAL, EXPLANATORY WHOLE	
3. Making explicit what is only implicit . . .	. . . DEDUCE AND PREDICT	2.
4. Placing data into appropriate context or transcending inappropriate contexts . . .	. . . NEW DATA NCT ALREADY OBSERVED	

IMPLICATIONS

1. Classify each of the following as:

   clarifying the structure of the material (CS)
   stripping away unessential details   (SD)
   making explicit what is implicit   (MEI)
   placing data into appropriate context (PDC)

   Each statement may fit more than one scheme.

   a. Snow is just a special case of rain.
   b. If an individual is highly anxious, he will not learn as well as he would if he were only moderately anxious.
   c. When we know how cells repair themselves, we will control the aging process.
   d. DNA is what Mendel meant by "factors."
   e. Cancers are caused by virus infection.
   f. Reinforcers are drive reducers.
   g. Reinforcers are drive inducers.

2. Reclassify the above statements as:
   summarizing data into a conceptual whole
   predicting new observations

3. How does your original classification correspond with your second set?

The Limitations of Theory

Although theories are tools for understanding reality, this should not be taken to mean that theories lead inevitably to comprehension. Early man has provided us with ample demonstration of this fact. It is often the case in science that a theory that has come to be relied upon becomes a stumbling block to progress by preventing rather than facilitating new ways of seeing problems. Rigidly adhered to, a theory can blind a scientist to alternative and perhaps more useful explanations of phenomena. Much as the subjects in the two-rope problem were "functionally fixated," a theory can prevent the scientist from seeing new problems simply because it *appears* to be an adequate explanation and solution to any and all difficulties.

Francis Bacon's Idols

It is perhaps surprising that the limitations of theory have been recognized for a relatively long time. One example of outspoken criticism of theory in science is Francis Bacon's essay, *Novum Organum* (1620), written, as the title indicates, in Latin. Bacon was attempting to describe some of the stumbling blocks to the discovery of truth in science. Bacon was not a scientist in the modern sense of that term, and he is often criticized for having proposed a purely inductive, observational method for science. He distrusted theory because he felt that it leads to premature explanation and faulty understanding. It is instructive, however, that the four false notions that affect reasoning, or Idols, as Bacon called them, can be viewed today as the limitations of theory, and as warning signs to be observed when constructing theory. We do not have to accept Bacon's argument that theory, all theory, is useless and confusing. We can, instead, accept Bacon's criticisms as constructive helps and guides to realistic caution in our use of theory in science.

Using the word "Idol" in the same sense that we use the word "illusion" today, Bacon wrote of four such errors in thinking. *The Idols of the Tribe* are founded in human nature itself. Man has a tendency to evaluate the things around him in terms of himself. For example, we ascribe human traits and characteristics to pet animals when they behave in certain ways. As Bacon pointed out, "The human understanding is like a false mirror, which receiving rays irregularly, distorts and discolors the nature of things by mingling its own nature with it."

It is interesting that this same notion—that of judging things in terms of human feelings—and its limitations became the basis of a cautionary principle taken over from philosophy into animal psychology by Conwy Lloyd Morgan, *Lloyd Morgan's canon:* "In no case may we interpret an action as the outcome of the exercise of a higher psychical faculty if it can be interpreted as the outcome of the exercise of one which stands lower in the psychological scale" (Morgan, 1894, reproduced in Herrnstein and Boring, 1966). Morgan's canon (really "Occam's razor," in the literature of philosophy) enjoins us to avoid attributing human complexity to animal behavior if we can interpret the same behavior in simpler terms. Another early psychologist-physiologist, Jacques Loeb, went to the opposite extreme in interpreting all animal behavior in terms of automatic, forced reflex-like activity, similar to plant tropisms. For Loeb, consciousness, even in humans, was to be regarded as merely associations between and among past behaviors. (For a good illustration of how human interpretation may distort facts, reread the quotation from Simpson that introduces this chapter.) Bacon, like Morgan and Loeb, was very skeptical of our ability to disentangle ourselves from feelings and beliefs that would color our reasoning.

Closely related to the Idols of the Tribe are the *Idols of the Cave,* which, less poetically than their name, refer to the influence of the individual's personality and perception on thinking: ". . . owing either to his own proper and peculiar nature; or to his education and conversation with others; or to the reading of books, and the authority of those

IMPLICATIONS

Max Wertheimer, the founder of Gestalt psychology (1959, pp. 79–84) used the following tasks in an attempt to discover the limits of a retarded child's intellectual impairment:

> In dealing with these children I first tried a method which I will report in outline.
>
> Sitting at a table with one of the children, I take three blocks [from a pile of assorted sizes] and build a bridge.

> Then I tear it down. Most of the children, after such a demonstration, begin to build a bridge. . . . All this they can do. But what is it they are actually doing? Are they simply repeating what I did, or do they grasp something?

1. How would you test to see if the child grasps the concept that two blocks of equal size are needed for the uprights to make a stable bridge on a flat surface?

   Wertheimer arranged the following test in attempting to solve the problem. He built a stairway of blocks that required the child to build a bridge that was stable on the non-flat surface of the ascending side of the staircase:

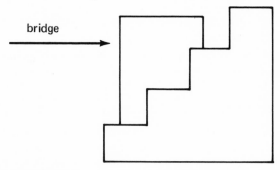

bridge

Wertheimer concludes:
> Is the equality of size of the vertical blocks decisive [in building a stable bridge]? . . . this time [I] indicate that I want them [the retarded children] to build a bridge on the steps of the staircase. They do. . . . This shows that equality itself is not decisive, but rather the inner connection between being horizontal and stable, and that the role of the part [block] is determined secondarily out of this."

2. How would you classify the performances of these children with respect to the depth of their understanding? Do they make use of prediction?

3. Is Wertheimer's conclusion justified? Explain.

whom he esteems and admires; or to the differences of impressions, accordingly as they take place in a mind preoccupied and predisposed or in a mind indifferent and settled."

Bacon also realized that language itself may obscure understanding. The ways in which ideas are communicated between men strongly in-

---

IMPLICATIONS: B. F. Skinner—a Modern Baconian?

B. F. Skinner, widely recognized as the most influential psychologist in recent history, has objected strongly to the use of theory in developing a scientific understanding of behavior. Skinner's objection to theory might be summarized in three statements.

In the first place, Skinner feels that a science of behavior is removed from the very data it seeks to study by employing theories to abstractly explain observables:

> A science of behavior must eventually deal with behavior in its relation to certain manipulable variables. Theories—whether neural, mental, or conceptual—talk about intervening steps in these relationships. . . . When we attribute behavior to a neural or mental event, real or conceptual, we are likely to forget that we still have the task of accounting for the neural or mental event.

Secondly, Skinner feels that theories may provide the scientist with a false sense of security, deceiving him into believing he has a full explanation of a phenomenon:

> We are likely to close our eyes to . . . [further explanation] and to use the theory to give us answers in place of the answers we might find through further study. It might be argued that the principal function of learning theory to date has been, not to suggest appropriate research, but to create a false sense of security, an unwarranted satisfaction with the status quo.

Thirdly,

> Research designed with respect to theory is also likely to be wasteful. That a theory generates research does not prove its value unless the research is valuable. Much useless experimentation results from theories, and much energy and skill are absorbed by them. Most theories are eventually overthrown, and the greater part of the associated research is discarded.

(1950, pp. 193–216)

Question: We might succinctly summarize Skinner's three criticisms of theory as: (1) overabstraction; (2) premature explanation; and (3) nonproductive experimentation. Are Skinner's views similar to Bacon's? If so, how? Which man's objections are more comprehensive in scope? Is Skinner completely opposed to all theory in psychology?

fluences understanding of them. "The ill and unfit choice of words [that] wonderfully obstructs the understanding" is given the name *Idols of the Marketplace*. Contemporary scientists have just begun to react to the difficulties of language, and attempts are being made to propose mathematically precise statements of theory in the behavioral sciences.

KEY CONCEPTS

Objections to Theory: Francis Bacon and B. F. Skinner

SIR FRANCIS BACON

1. Idols of the Tribe: a thinking error founded in man's tendency to be anthropomorphic—that is, to interpret the things around him in terms of his own feelings and attitudes. Scientific theory can sometimes be anthropomorphic.

2. Idols of the Cave: a thinking error that may be fostered by a theory that is based on a misconception or a peculiar quirk of an individual personality that perceives reality in its own idiosyncratic way.

3. Idols of the Marketplace: imprecise and misleading language or the vague and equivocal use of terms that can prevent a theory from being specific enough to test.

4. Idols of the Theater: principles or explanations that have been accepted for a long time and that can blind a scientist to new explanations. The scientist can be trapped by his own theory when it acts like a set of conceptual blinders to prevent new discovery.

B. F. SKINNER

1. Theories tend to over-abstract the phenomena they seek to explain and thus become removed from the empirical facts.

2. Once a scientist is in possession of a theory, he rests content that he has a full explanation of some part of nature. In fact, he may be blinded to new discoveries by his old theory.

3. Theories are inefficient and wasteful with respect to the research they generate. When a theory is overthrown, most of the experimental data on which it rests and which it inspired will be discarded with it. Good, solid research can be conducted without a theory, or in spite of it.

(Skinner, 1950)

Unfortunately, no matter how precise statements of theory become, the users of theory are still likely to succumb to what Bacon calls the *Idols of the Theater:* principles, axioms, and systems that by tradition, belief, and negligence have come to be accepted, are to be avoided at all costs. As far as Bacon was concerned, philosophy and science had all too readily abandoned observation in favor of explanatory principles that have only as much in common with reality as does a stage play.

We could summarize Bacon's objections to theories by translating them into contemporary terms:

1. Anthropomorphism (Idols of the Tribe)
2. Invalidly held preconceptions (Idols of the Cave)
3. Vague and imprecise language (Idols of the Marketplace)
4. Untested and unfounded beliefs (Idols of the Theater)

With all that can go wrong in the construction and use of theory, it would seem remarkable that anyone bothers to construct one.

The important point, as we have seen, is that theories must be testable. Given testability as a criterion for theory construction, the benefits of theory outweigh its limitations. Moreover, an awareness of the limitations involved provides scientists with a measure of healthy skepticism with which to temper their conclusions.

Overview of the Chapter

In reviewing what we have discussed in this chapter, we can list seven important concepts.

First, the traditional description of scientific method as consisting of five consecutive steps does not necessarily characterize the working scientist's behavior.

Secondly, a scientist often begins, not with a simple or direct observation, but with the discovery of a problem or the formulation of a question that arises out of the surprise he experiences when his expectations are not met. Drive-reduction theory, for example, underwent this critical test and continues to do so.

Third, once faced with a problem, a scientist attempts to offer an explanation. Such explanation is tentative and must be susceptible of test. The theory must specify what conditions are expected to exist and what conditions are expected not to exist. Thus a theory specifies what must occur and what must not occur. This criterion of refutability has not been met by many theories in psychology, as was seen in our examination of psychoanalysis. But it is equally important to remember that though Freud's theory may lie beyond the scope of scientific testability, it has nonetheless proved invaluable in clinical practice.

Fourth, the entire process by which scientists proceed in their examination of the material universe might best be described, in Popper's view, as problem—theory—criticism. Therefore, as a rule of thumb, science is defined as an attempt to explore the material universe in search of orderly relationships among observed phenomena. Science's explanations must bear the hallmark of testability.

Fifth, the reason that scientists "do" science—perform observations, conduct experiments, construct and test theories—can be found in the ageless desire to understand the world. Understanding may have several meanings, but the essence of understanding may be reduced for our purposes to the two functions of theory: (1) summarizing data into conceptual, explanatory wholes, and (2) deducing and predicting new data not already observed.

Sixth, we must be cautious in our enthusiasm for theory, because there are occasions when theory may hinder our attempts at understanding. Bacon's Idols suggest some of the restrictions and limitations of theory. Keeping these limitations in mind is a partial solution to the problems associated with theory.

Seventh, and last, the theory that is stated in such a way that it is susceptible of test provides an important tool, despite its limitations, in the search for understanding. Early man discovered this truth in his attempts to understand his world.

In the next chapter we will try to come to an understanding of how theories change. Cultural and scientific readiness, the human relevancy of the science, and failures to perform adequately the functions of summary and prediction all play a part in the modification of scientific theories.

Recommended Further Reading

The literature on the drive-reduction hypothesis is somewhat scattered throughout the professional journals, along with a series of proposed modifications of and alternatives to this formulation of motivation. Perhaps one of the best and most readily available reviews of the relevant literature is to be found in Alexander K. Bartoshuk's chapter on "Motivation" in the third edition of *Woodworth and Schlosberg's Experimental Psychology,* edited by J. W. Kling and Lorrin A. Riggs (New York: Holt, Rinehart & Winston, 1971; Ch. 18). Equally valuable in presenting some of the classic papers on drive theory and its alternatives is the comprehensive selection to be had in R. N. Haber's *Current Research in Motivation* (New York: Holt, Rinehart & Winston, 1966; Chs. 2, 5, and 6).

Karl Popper's presentation of the criterion of refutability will repay the careful reader of his *Conjectures and Refutations* (New York: Basic Books, 1963), and of his earlier classic, *The Logic of Scientific Discovery* (New York: Basic Books, 1959). Neither of the Popper books is light reading, but both volumes are considered landmarks in the philosophy of science. The second of the two books contains Popper's formulation of how he thinks scientific method really works. An entertaining but mind-boggling discussion of logical paradoxes like the raven statements is provided by Wesley C. Salmon in his article "Confirmation" (*Scientific American,* May, 1973, pp. 75–83).

Most exacting and stringently scientific of the criticisms leveled at Freudian theory is Hans J. Eysenck and Glenn D. Wilson's *The Experimental Study of Freudian Theories* (New York: Harper & Row, 1973; originally published in England by Methuen). In their review of the experimental literature associated with psychoanalysis, Eysenck and Wilson find very little support for Freudian explanations. Paul Kline, in *Fact and Fantasy in Freudian Theory* (New York: Harper and Row, 1972; originally published in England by Methuen), on the other hand, finds at least some experimental support for selected Freudian tenets. A rather comprehensive collection of papers devoted to the scientific claims and rationale of psychoanalysis may be found in S. G. M. Lee and Martin Herbert's anthology, *Freud and Psychology* (Baltimore: Penguin Books, 1970).

Students interested in reading firsthand what Freud had to say have several choices among Freud's own writings. Perhaps the most readable, lucid, and concise introduction is Freud's *Five Lectures on Psychoanalysis,* which has been published as a paperback under the title *The Origin and Development of Psychoanalysis* (Chicago: Henry Regnery Co., 1965) and is also to be found in the *Standard Edition of the Complete Psychological Works of Sigmund Freud,* Vol. 6 (London: Hogarth Press, 1957). Where the *Five Lectures* are conversational in tone, Freud's *A General Introduction to Psychoanalysis,* while no less lucid, and certainly more comprehensive, is also significantly more formal and precise in style. This volume is available in a variety of paperback editions (e.g., Washington Square Press, New York, 1960; or W. W. Norton). The Standard Edition version of this work is called *Introductory Lectures on Psychoanalysis,* Volumes XV and XVI.

Secondary sources on Freud and psychoanalysis abound, but a rather comprehensive, recent one is Raymond E. Fancher's *Psychoanalytic Psychology* (New York: W. W. Norton, 1973). Fancher's volume has the virtue of presenting Freud's thought in chronological sequence of development so that the reader may follow the logic of his attempts to establish a scientific theory.

Max Wertheimer's *Productive Thinking* (New York: Harper & Row,

1959; also available in paperback) is a gestalt-psychology classic on the nature of cognitive processes, fruitful problem-solving, and the experience of understanding. Mary Henle's distinctions among the varieties of understanding may be found in "On Understanding" (in Frazier [ed.], *The New Elementary School,* Assoc. for Supervision and Curriculum, NEA, 1968).

A picture of contrasting viewpoints on methodology and philosophy within psychology can be gleaned from the selection of papers in T. W. Wann (ed.), *Behaviorism and Phenomenology* (Chicago: University of Chicago Press, 1964); see especially the papers by Koch, Malcolm and Rogers.

Skinner's objections to formal theory in psychology can be read in his early paper "Are Theories of Learning Necessary?" (*Psychological Review,* 1950, *57,* 193–216). His more recent opinions on theory and the role of behavioristic methodology in the development of psychology may be found in "Behaviorism at Fifty" (*Science,* 1963, *140,* 951–958; this paper is reprinted in the Wann volume cited above).

4
How Theories Change: The Quiet Revolution

It was on a bitterly cold night and frosty morning, towards
the end of the winter of '97, that I was awakened by a
tugging at my shoulder. It was Holmes. The candle in his
hand shone upon his eager, stooping face, and told me
at a glance that something was amiss.
"Come, Watson, come!" he cried. "The game is afoot.
Not a word. Into your clothes and come!"
ARTHUR CONAN DOYLE
"The Adventure of the Abbey Grange"

A man may be attracted to science for all sorts of reasons.
Among them are the desire to be useful, the excitement
of exploring new territory, the hope of finding order, and
the drive to test established knowledge. . . .
Nevertheless, *the individual* engaged on a normal
research problem *is almost never doing any one of these
things*. Once engaged, his motivation is of a rather different
sort. What then challenges him is the conviction that, if
only he is skillful enough, he will succeed in solving a
puzzle that no one before has solved or solved so well.
T. S. KUHN
The Structure of Scientific Revolutions

Prospectus

A language devoid of the capacity to ask "Why?", or "What for?", or
"How?" would be marvelously efficient in preventing thought. Such a
language would, no doubt, place inescapable obstacles in the path of
such diverse and time-honored institutions as marriage, war, poetry, sex,
encyclopedias, Sherlock Holmes and, unmistakably, science.

Consider an alternative language, which consists entirely of three ut-
terances: *"Not," "Why,"* and *"Oh, yeah."* Such memorable, if limited,
interchanges as these are possible:

126

Person A: "Why?"
Person B: "Why not?"
Person A: "Not: 'why not'—*why?*"
Person B: "Oh, yeah!"
Person A: "Oh! Why not?"

In each of our two imaginary languages the problem is not the lack of words to express meaning, but the lack of meaning to express in words. Scientific progress in many ways is comparable to our languages: It must develop not only techniques of expressing the meaning it construes in nature's events, but also methods of uncovering events that might never be construed as meaningful. Science must be capable of asking not only "Why?" "How?" and "What for?", but also of asking "Why not?"

Sherlock Holmes was adamant in his refusal to devise theories to explain facts until all of the facts were at hand, lest he be led astray by speculation. T. S. Kuhn, philosopher-historian of science, suggests that scientists follow a path similar to that of Holmes, but that, once in possession of a theory, they find it difficult to play the game by any other rules. When new rules are finally devised, scientific revolution is the outcome.

Psychology's own "mini-revolution" has begun to take shape in the recognition that experimenters and subjects share a common bond: they reflect upon and interpret experiences that are thrust upon them. A discussion of the signal-detection theory, the species-identity theorem, and Pygmalion will enlarge upon these concepts.

"The Game Is Afoot!": Detective as Puzzle-Solver

Breakfast at 221B Baker Street, in the gas-lit period of late 1880-ish London, must have been a trying affair for the mundane but stalwart Dr. Watson. His fellow lodger, ignoring both his breakfast and the good doctor, is absorbed this morning in a coded message received from a henchman of the arch villain, Professor Moriarty. Watson prods Holmes to reveal the subject of his intense concentration, and he is shown the following abstruse message:*

```
534    C2   13   127   36   31   4    17   21   41
DOUGLAS   109   293   5   37   BIRLSTONE
       26   BIRLSTONE   9   47   171
```

* The following scenario is adapted from Conan Doyle's *The Valley of Fear* (New York: Garden City Press [Doubleday], 1930), and is reprinted by permission of Jonathan Cape Ltd./John Murray (Publishers) Ltd., and Baskervilles Investments, Ltd.

The mind of Sherlock Holmes is already at work deducing instructive clues from this enigmatic communication while Watson is still rooted at the level of the obvious:

> "What do you make of it, Holmes?"
> "It is obviously an attempt to convey secret information."
> "But what is the use of a cipher message without the cipher?"
> "In this instance, none at all."
> "Why do you say 'in this instance?' "
> "Because there are many ciphers which I would read as easily as I do the apocrypha of the agony column: such crude devices amuse the intelligence without fatiguing it. But this is different. It is clearly a reference to the words in a page of some book. Until I am told which page and which book I am powerless."

These last statements reveal the essential difference between the Watsons and the Holmeses of this world. To the one, the enigma is a frustrating obstacle, while to Holmes it is a beckoning mystery, an engagement of the intellect, a form of puzzle-solving raised to the level of an art. Notice that Holmes has already matter-of-factly concluded that the message refers to words in some book. (*Deduction 1*)

Inevitably, relentlessly, Watson's mind grapples with the concept:

> "But why 'Douglas' and 'Birlstone'?"

To Holmes, the question touches on the merely trivial:

> "Clearly because those are words which were not contained in the page in question." [*Deduction 2*]

"How obvious!" we feel prompted to say. But at the same time we must grudgingly admit these deductions did not escape Watson alone. With Watson, we hesitatingly ask Holmes why the sender of the message has not included the cipher or key to the code.

> "Your native shrewdness, my dear Watson, that innate cunning which is the delight of your friends, would surely prevent you from inclosing cipher and message in the same envelope. Should it miscarry, you are undone. As it is, both have to go wrong before any harm comes from it. [*Deduction 3*] Our second post is now overdue, and I shall be surprised if it does not bring us either a further letter of explanation, or, as is more probable, the very volume to which these figures refer."

The mail, we are relieved to discover, does indeed contain a further communication from the code sender, but our relief is premature. Panic-stricken, the code writer informs Holmes that he has changed his mind, will not send the cipher to uncode the previous message, and fears for his life lest Holmes pursue the matter. He concludes by saying:

"Please burn the cipher message, which can now be of no use to you."

Is it possible that we are stymied? Watson voices our desperation:

"It's pretty maddening to think that an important secret may lie here on this slip of paper, and that it is beyond human power to penetrate it."

Sherlock Holmes has pushed away his untasted breakfast and lit the unsavoury pipe which was the companion of his deepest meditations.

"I wonder!" said he, leaning back and staring at the ceiling. "Perhaps there are points which have escaped your Machiavellian intellect. Let us consider the problem in the light of pure reason. This man's reference is to a book. That is our point of departure. . . . Let us see if we can narrow it down. As I focus my mind on it, it seems rather less impenetrable. What indications have we as to this book?"

Watson, as ever, forthrightly voices our imaginative blandness:

"None."

"Well, well, it is surely not quite so bad as that. The cipher message begins with a large 534, does it not? We may take it as a working hypothesis that 534 is the particular page to which the cipher refers. So our book has already become a *large* book, which is surely something gained. [*Deduction 4*] What other indications have we as to the nature of this large book? The next sign is C2. What do you make of that, Watson?"

"Chapter the second, no doubt."

"Hardly that, Watson. You will, I am sure, agree with me that if the page be given, the number of the chapter is immaterial. [*Deduction 5A*] Also that if page 534 finds us only in the second chapter, the length of the first one must have been really intolerable." [*Deduction 5B*]

"Then it must be Column," we cry with Watson, once again led to appreciate the not-so-obvious obvious. (*Deduction* 6) Holmes continues, already far ahead of us, but enjoying the step-by-step process of our intellectual enrichment.

"So now, you see, we begin to visualize a large book, printed in double columns, which are each of considerable length, since one of the words is numbered in the document as the two hundred and ninety-third. [*Deduction 7*] Have we reached the limits of what reason can supply?"

At this point we are unwilling to admit to anything, but Watson plunges ahead, counter-foil to the last:

"I fear that we have."
"Surely you do yourself an injustice. . . . Had the volume been an unusual one, he would have sent it to me. Instead of that, he had intended, before his plans were nipped, to send me the clue in this envelope. He says so in his note. This would seem to indicate that the book is one which he thought I would have no difficulty in finding for myself. He had it—and he imagined that I would have it, too. In short, Watson, it is a very common book." [*Deduction 8*]

The deductions have been flying fast and furiously. Holmes, the master gamesman, summarizes:

"So we have contracted our field of search to a large book, printed in double columns and in common use."

Astonishingly, we Watsons find the answer almost bursting from our lips: "The Bible!" we cry triumphantly.

"Good Watson, good! But not, if I may say so, quite good enough! Even if I accepted the compliment for myself, I could hardly name any volume which would be less likely to lie at the elbow of one of Moriarty's associates. Besides the editions of Holy Writ are so numerous that he could hardly suppose that two copies would have the same pagination. . . . He knows for certain that his page 534 will exactly agree with my page 534." [*Deduction 9*]
"But," we interject with Watson, the light of day slowly dawning, "very few books would correspond with that."
"Exactly. Therein lies our salvation. Our search is narrowed down to standardized books which anyone may be supposed to possess."
"An almanac!" we shout, the idea seemingly flooding into our minds of its own accord." (*Hypothesis 1*)
"Excellent, Watson! I am very much mistaken if you have not touched the spot."

We wait patiently while Holmes thumbs through the volume in question, the heady taste of success, tinged with no small measure of admiration for ourselves, and for Holmes, rising in our consciousness.

"Here is page 534, column two, a substantial block of print dealing, I perceive, with the trade and resources of British India. Jot down the words, Watson! Number thirteen is 'Mahratta.' Not, I fear, a very auspicious beginning. Number one hundred and twenty-seven is 'Government'; which at least makes sense, though somewhat irrelevant to ourselves and Professor Moriarty. Now let us try again. What does the Mahratta government do? Alas! the next word is 'pig's bristles.' " (*Hypothesis disconfirmation 1*)

Who was it who said, "Beautiful theories are often destroyed by such ugly facts?" Holmes has sunk into a long silence. We Watsons, with so much less than Holmes invested in this exercise, are ready to dismiss the incident as one more annoyance in a lifelong chain of dimly perceived petty irritations. The long silence is broken by the sudden exclamation from Holmes, who dashes at a cupboard, from which he emerges with a second book in his hand.

"We pay the price, Watson, for being too up-to-date! . . . . Being the seventh of January, we have very properly laid in the new almanac. It is more than likely that Porlock [the code writer] took his message from the old one. No doubt he would have told us so had his letter of explanation been written. Now let us see what page 534 has in store for us. (*Hypothesis 2*) Number thirteen is 'There', which is much more promising. Number one hundred and twenty-seven is 'is'—'There is' "—Holmes' eyes were gleaming with excitement and his thin, nervous fingers twitched as he counted the words—" 'danger.' Ha! Ha! Capital! . . . . 'There is danger—may—come—very—soon—one.' Then we have the name of 'Douglas'—'rich—country—now—at—Birlstone—House —Birlstone—confidence—is—pressing.' There, Watson! What do you think of pure reason and its fruit?" (Hypothesis confirmation)

We sit back, our faith in Holmes vindicated. Even more so, as an unexpected caller to 221B Baker Street, Inspector Macdonald of Scotland Yard, reveals in an astonished tone at the sight of the deciphered message: "That Mr. Douglas of Birlstone Manor House was horribly murdered last night." (*Further Hypothesis Confirmation*)

The question that we must inevitably ask ourselves after reading a Holmes adventure is: "Could we, given the same information as Holmes, and no more than the same, rise to the occasion, set about playing the game, and arrive at the same successful conclusion?" Glance once again at the starting point, the original message on the first page of this chapter, before attempting an answer. Somehow the enigmatic numbers and the esoteric words seem to be more of a reasonable challenge, a puzzle engaging the intellect for the anticipated sheer pleasure of unlocking its intricate workings.

"The Game Is Afoot!": Scientist as Puzzle-Solver

Sherlock Holmes disdained the commonplace, petty crime. He revered the imaginative, bizarre, creative criminal's activities. Holmes particularly enjoyed tackling puzzles that confounded his colleagues of the Yard. This seemingly perverse whimsey was not motivated by a need for personal aggrandizement, or by a compulsion for relentless justice. Holmes was a gamesman in the finest sense of the term. The intellectual excitement of matching wits with opponents, of employing reason to unravel unreasonable mysteries, the connoisseur's desire to solve puzzles unsolvable by anyone else—these are the motives of a Sherlock Holmes. We Watsons admire these qualities, but we find them difficult to emulate. And so for the scientist. His motivations are largely the same as Holmes', and his activities, according to the widely respected views of Thomas Kuhn, are directly comparable to Holmes'. In other words, the scientist is a puzzle-solver.

In his monograph on scientific revolutions, Kuhn paints this intriguing portrait of the scientist-as-puzzle-solver. Pointing out that no scientist spends years simply improving standard pieces of apparatus, or in refining already developed solutions to traditional problems simply because of the importance of the outcome, Kuhn goes on to say:

> Bringing a normal research problem to a conclusion is *achieving the anticipated in a new way,* and it requires the solution of all sorts of complex instrumental, conceptual, and mathematical puzzles. The man who succeeds proves himself an expert puzzle-solver, and the *challenge of the puzzle is an important part of what usually drives him on.* [Italics added.]
>
> (1970, p. 36)

Kuhn is using the term "puzzle" in its ordinary meaning of a "special category of problems that can serve to test ingenuity or skill in solution" (1970, p. 36). The essential characteristic of the puzzle for the scientist's motivation is the test of skill:

> It is no criterion of goodness in a puzzle that its outcome be intrinsically interesting or important. On the contrary, the really pressing problems, e.g. a cure for cancer or the design of a lasting peace, are often not puzzles at all, largely because they may not have any solution. Consider the jigsaw puzzle whose pieces are selected at random from each of two different puzzle boxes. Since that problem is likely to defy (though it might not) even the most ingenious of men, *it cannot serve as a test of skill in solution. In any usual sense, it is not a puzzle at all.* Though intrinsic value is no criterion for a puzzle, *the assured existence of a solution is.* [Italics added.]
>
> (1970, pp. 36–37)

Puzzles Scientists Seek

Like Holmes, the scientist is a selective puzzle-solver. Each carefully chooses the problems he will attack in terms of the degree of elegance required in their solution. To qualify as an acceptable or worthy puzzle, the problem must be more than simply solvable, that is, it must have more than just a predictable outcome. It must be solvable within certain "rules." These rules of the game must limit the nature of the acceptable solutions and the steps by which such solutions are to be obtained (Kuhn, 1970, p. 38). Kuhn put the matter most forcibly:

> To solve a jigsaw puzzle is not, for example, merely "to make a picture." Either a child or a contemporary artist could do that by scattering selected pieces, as abstract shapes, upon some neutral ground. The picture thus produced might be far better, and would certainly be more original, than the one from which the puzzle had been made. *Nevertheless, such a picture would not be a solution.* To achieve that all the pieces must be used, their plain sides must be turned down, and they must be interlocked without forcing until no holes remain. [Italics added.]
>
> (1970, p. 38)

Scientific puzzles therefore are not to be conceptualized as merely difficult obstacles to information gathering. A normal science puzzle is, rather, to be thought of as an intricate network of observations and inferences that requires *reweaving* to some specified, but as yet unachieved, pattern.

To return to our earlier example, Holmes' encoded message becomes a tantalizing problem only when the key is lost. If the key had been at hand, the code puzzle would have been a largely routine and uninteresting translation chore. But when circumstances necessitated the deduction of the rules by which the code was originally constructed, Holmes' fascination and intellectual motivation were engaged. This transformation of a routine and boring translation problem into an extraordinary and exciting logical problem in no way changed the ultimate outcome: the code had still to be broken to reveal the *one message* that the cryptographer had embedded in it. However, the solution now required creativity: "The anticipated had to be achieved in a new way." Thus the real puzzle was not the embedded message, but the problem of deducing the manner in which the code was constructed so that the proper key could be sought and applied. This ever more subtle puzzle also called for, and would have yielded to, only *one solution*. Deciphering the message was trivial when compared to this requisite first step: to discover *how* this eminently solvable puzzle was constructed.

The Rules of the Game: "Normal Science"

Motivated to test his skill in the solution of puzzles that challenge current thinking of members of his discipline, the puzzle-solving scientist is engaged in what Kuhn terms "normal science." Normal science is practiced by a group of like-minded thinkers who share an intellectual commitment to a particular explanation or theory of some part of nature. This shared explanation is called a "paradigm." Practitioners of normal science, once in possession of an acceptable paradigm, proceed according to certain rules of the game dictated by the paradigm.

"Rules of the game" is not meant as a demeaning description of normal scientific activity, but rather is meant to extend the puzzle-solving metaphor to include a statement of the cultural-social variables that shape the scientist's perceptions of his field. Among the most fundamental commitments characterizing the scientist is his concern to understand the world. (Cf. Chapter 1 of this book.) He is thus led to scrutinize some aspect of nature, "and if that scrutiny displays pockets of apparent disorder, then these must challenge him to new refinement of his observational techniques or to a further articulation of his theories" (Kuhn, 1970, p. 42). Understanding the world in terms of his scientific community's shared paradigm is thus the key rule of the game.

However, as we have seen, a theory or paradigm can often become a set of conceptual blinders. The theory or paradigm now prevents the discovery of new problems, new observations, or new solutions to redefined old problems. (Cf. Bacon's and Skinner's objections to theory and the effects of the subject's set on solutions to the two-rope problem in Chapter 3.) Scientists who adhere to the conceptions of a given intellectual community of thinkers, and who fully accept the shared explanation of nature that binds this community, are encouraged to tackle only problems that make sense in terms of their paradigm. Problems which hold no immediate hope of solution *in terms of the paradigm* are excluded from consideration—or simply not *seen* as problems (1970, p. 37 ff). This rule of the game is largely responsible for the apparent rapid progress of normal science. Practitioners of normal science "concentrate on problems that only their own lack of ingenuity should keep them from solving" (1970, p. 37).

At a much less abstract level, there is a rule of normal science that regulates the types of apparatus that scientists will employ. Preferences extend not only to the actual apparatus that will be seen as most useful, but to the manner in which that apparatus will be most successfully employed. Although a variety of other subtle rules or commitments may be discerned in normal science, the three we have briefly discussed point up the essentially conservative character of normal science.

The existence of the strong network of commitments—conceptual, theoretical, instrumental and methodological—is a principal source of the metaphor that relates normal science to puzzle solving. Because it provides rules that tell the practitioner of a mature speciality what both the world and his science are like, he can concentrate with assurance upon the esoteric problems that these rules and existing knowledge define for him.

(Kuhn, 1970, p. 42)

KEY CONCEPTS

The Scientist's Rules of the Game

In normal science, according to T. S. Kuhn, the scientist is bound by his paradigm to perceive nature in a particular way and to approach the solutions to problems dictated by the paradigm according to certain unwritten "rules."

Rule 1: The most fundamental commitment for the scientist is the overriding concern to understand nature. The appearance of disorder or unexplained phenomena challenges him to discover a *method* of understanding, but only in terms dictated by his theory.

Rule 2: Only *problems* that can be stated meaningfully in terms of his scientific community's shared paradigm are acceptable for investigation.

Rule 3: The importance of the solution is not the most significant aspect of choosing problems to solve. Rather, Rule 2 comes into play again, compelling the scientist to seek problems that have a foreseeable solution. It makes no sense to tackle problems which the theory says are not solvable.

Rule 4: The paradigm dictates what type and in what ways apparatus will be employed. Actually, this is a logical extension of Rules 3 and 2, in that order.

Normal science thus provides rules that tell the scientist what the world is expected to be like.

Pre-Paradigm Scientific Achievement

Developmentally, normal science is a kind of midpoint in the history of a science's achievements. Normal science's possession of a full-blown paradigm implies an earlier "pre-paradigm" stage, and a later, "post-paradigm" phase. We are, therefore, prompted to ask two obvious questions:

1. How does science proceed *before* the development and articulation of a paradigm?
2. How does science proceed *after* the accepted paradigm is weakened, blurred, or discarded?

The first question need not occupy us at length since the chief concern of the present chapter is the nature of paradigm *change,* post-normal scientific achievement.

Paradigms spring from previous scientific achievements that some particular scientific community accepts as the basis for further investigation (Kuhn, 1970, p. 10). Some of these past accomplishments are dismissed as myths, or superstitions, and it is probable that most of them were gathered without guidance from an organizing theory. The absence of a unifying theory or paradigm in this phase of scientific development is what chiefly characterizes "pre-paradigm science." Nonetheless, Kuhn argues, these achievements are no less "scientific" than currently prevailing theory. They are simply in conceptual conflict with what is presently held to be "true."

Thus, in this pre-paradigmatic phase of science, it is possible for a variety of divergent opinions and research traditions to exist side by side. "Schools of thought," in which some ranges of phenomena are interpreted differently by different men, are the result. (Psychology's own early history was characterized by divergent schools such as structuralism, functionalism, gestalt, and behavioristic psychology. In fact, contemporary psychology is only slightly less diversified into competing schools. See, for example, Murphy, 1949; or Watson, 1963.) As the science progresses, these competing schools gradually cease to exist. "When in the development of a natural science, an individual or group first produces a synthesis [of competing ideas] able to attract most of the next generation's practitioners, the older schools gradually disappear." (Kuhn 1970, p. 8). Most of the members of these schools convert to the new and unifying synthesis. Those individuals unwilling or unable to accept the change in viewpoint proceed in isolation. Consequently, the growth of a science proceeds gradually from the pre-paradigmatic, multiple-viewpoint phase, to the paradigm stage.

As we have seen, the chief activity of the paradigm stage is normal science, "which is predicated on the assumption that the scientific community knows what the world is like" (1970, p. 5).

IMPLICATIONS: The Rules of the Game

Central figures in the early history of experimental psychology, men such as E. B. Titchener and Wilhelm Wundt, molded scientific method toward what they thought was the only proper study for the new science: the states of consciousness that undergo change in response to changing stimulation. "Mind" was understood by Titchener to mean the sum total of mental processes experienced by the individual during his lifetime (Marx, and Hillix, 1963). So for Titchener, psychology's goal was to analyze mental experience into its simplest parts, discover how the elements combine, and discover their bodily connections.

To do this Titchener employed the introspective method. Trained observers were exposed to various stimuli—say, colored geometrical shapes. Having been taught to avoid reporting the characteristics of the stimulus, they verbally described how the stimulus affected them, how it looked, how long the sensation lasted, its aftereffects, and so on. As you can imagine, introspection as a method gave rise to much controversy. One figure in the ballyhoo was John B. Watson, founder of the school of behaviorism. To grasp the flavor of Watson's rejection of introspectionism, read his introduction to the paper he wrote founding behavioristic psychology:

> Psychology as the behaviorist views it is a purely experimental branch of natural science. Its theoretical goal is the prediction and control of behavior. Introspection forms no essential part of its methods, nor is the scientific value of its data dependent upon the readiness with which they lend themselves to interpretation in terms of consciousness. The behaviorist, in his efforts to get a unitary scheme of animal response, recognizes no dividing line between man and brute.
>
> (Watson, 1913)

Thus Watson's behaviorism was focused only on observables, only on those aspects of behavior that could be objectively manipulated. In effect, Watson was out to change the face of psychology, and he nearly succeeded.

Problems:
1. Using Kuhn's concept of rules of the game, compare introspectionism and behaviorism in terms of the following:
   a. subject matter
   b. conception of mind
   c. proper problems to investigate

2. What criticisms do you think the introspective method elicited from Watson?

3. Is psychology returning to the concept of mind? In what ways is the "new mind" of psychology likely to be different from introspectionism and similar to behaviorism?

Anomaly: Blurring of the Paradigm

The outstanding goal at which normal science does *not* aim is the discovery of new phenomena. Likewise, scientists do *not* normally aim to invent new theories (Kuhn, 1970, p. 24). Although we might feel that such characteristics reduce the range and restrict the usefulness of science, Kuhn demonstrates that it is precisely these qualities of normal science that are essential to the advancement of the scientific enterprise as a whole.

By focusing attention upon a small range of relatively esoteric problems, the paradigm forces scientists to investigate some part of nature in detail and depth that otherwise would be unimaginable. *And normal science possesses a built-in mechanism that ensures the relaxation of the restrictions that bound research whenever the paradigm from which they derive ceases to function effectively.* At that point scientists begin to behave differently, and the nature of their research problems changes. In the interim, however, during the period when the paradigm is successful, the profession will have solved problems that its members could scarcely have imagined and would never have undertaken without commitment to the paradigm. *And at least a part of that achievement always proves to be permanent.* [Italics added.]

(1970, pp. 24–25)

The italicized part of this quotation from Kuhn contains the answer to our second question: "How does science proceed *after* the accepted paradigm is weakened or blurred?" When normal science is successful, it does not uncover novelties, or violations of expectation. All activity is directed toward applying orthodox paradigm-explanations to phenomena. But, during the articulation of normal science's paradigm, a variety of surprises are produced inadvertently. "Produced . . . by a game played under one set of rules, their assimilation requires elaboration of another set" (1970, p. 52). In other words, the paradigm is found to be wanting or incapable of incorporating some novelties of fact. We have seen an example of this violation of expectation in Chapter 3 in our discussion of drive-reduction theory. Where Karl Popper used the phrase "violation of expectation," Kuhn prefers the term "anomaly" (literally: a deviation from a rule; anything abnormal).

Discovery commences with the awareness of anomaly, i.e., with the recognition that nature has somehow violated the paradigm-induced expectations that govern normal science. It [discovery] then continues with a more or less extended exploration of the area of anomaly. And *it closes only when the paradigm theory has been adjusted so that the anomalous has become the expected.* [Italics added.]

(1970, pp. 52–53)

The adjustment of the anomaly-shaken paradigm requires that the scientist learn to "see nature in a different way" from the way he has customarily viewed it within the previous rules of the game.

Reconsider, for a moment, our discussion of the *einstellung* effect (perceptual set) and its relationship to the two-rope problem. Subjects were required to see the ropes and the weight in a new perspective, an entirely novel context. Successful problem solvers were able to escape their own preconceptions and to view the rope as a pendulum. Such a change of "set" is what is required in adjusting the paradigm to assimilate the anomalous discovery. Kuhn hints that such reorganization of conceptual categories is part of the human perceptual process, and he cites some evidence from the cognitive psychology of Jerome Bruner (see "Implications" section following). In a sense, scientists in the Normal Science period are hampered by their conceptual paradigm as were subjects who had previously used the electrical switch in its customary capacity (see two-rope problem described in Chapter 3). Conceptual readiness is therefore the hallmark of scientific change.

Crisis: Extraordinary Science

An anomaly can appear only when there is a background of carefully constructed, interlocking expectancies. Expect nothing, and nothing will surprise you. In this sense, the paradigm is the instigator *par excellence* of discovery since it provides the normative framework an anomaly violates. "Failure of existing rules is a prelude to search for new ones" (1970, p. 68). When the puzzles of normal science persistently fail to come out as they are expected to, the groundwork for scientific crisis is laid.

The most immediate result of such failures is the proliferation of varieties of theory to account for one or several of the anomalies. Difficulties arise, however, when each newly proposed theory conflicts with other versions. Such conflict almost constitutes a return to the earlier pre-paradigm phase of multi-school viewpoints. Though the resulting intellectual insecurity is a potent motivator, scientists will not abandon the failing paradigm unless a new comprehensive candidate is available to take its place.

Declarations of the invalidity of the beleaguered old paradigm are thus delayed until substantial comparisons can be made between it and the new alternative, and between both of these and nature (1970, p. 70). Kuhn, unlike Popper, rejects the idea that anomaly or violation of expectancies *alone* is sufficient to cause the adoption of a new strategy. "The decision to reject one paradigm is always simultaneously the decision to accept another" (1970, p. 77). Men who are unable to tolerate the crisis, "the essential tension of science," are likely to abandon science in favor of another occupation. "To reject one paradigm without simultaneously substituting another is to reject science itself. That act reflects not on the paradigm but on the man. Inevitably he will be seen by his colleagues as 'the carpenter who blames his tools' " (1970, p. 79).

Once the anomaly has come to be recognized as significant by the general community of professional scientists, their concerted attempts to deal with the difficulty inevitably leads to a loosening or revision of the rules of the game. The crisis thus provides the needed latitude for a new paradigm to emerge. New rules mean new ways of conceptualizing nature's puzzles. Science, as conducted under the new game rules, is no longer "normal." We can begin to speak of "extraordinary science."

During the phase of extraordinary science, the resistant anomalous puzzle may come to be seen as *the* sole subject matter of the science. The entire field undergoes change as the focus of scientific scrutiny contracts around the anomaly. Though the paradigm is still said to exist, few practitioners agree on its fundamentals. Moreover, since the rules of investigation and conceptualization have been loosened, more wide-ranging discoveries (and anomalies) are likely to emerge.

Blurring of the paradigm began this crisis. It can end in one of three ways:

Sometimes normal science ultimately proves able to handle the crisis-provoking problem. . . . On other occasions the problem resists even apparently radical new approaches. Then scientists may conclude that no solution will be forthcoming in the present state of their field. The problem is labelled and set aside for a future generation with more developed tools. Or, finally, . . . a crisis may end with the emergence of a new candidate for a paradigm and with the ensuing battle over its acceptance.
(Kuhn, 1970, p. 84)

This last possibility—a transition to a new paradigm—is scientific revolution.

Scientific Revolution: Living in the New World

By fostering a new conception of nature, the new paradigm eases the sense of intellectual malfunction engendered by its incompatible predecessor. The new paradigm also serves to harmonize the efforts of the crisis-induced, competitive factions within the prerevolution scientific community (Kuhn, 1970, pp. 92–95). In essence, "after a revolution scientists are responding to a different world."

. . . the historian of science may be tempted to exclaim that when paradigms change the world itself changes with them. Led by a new paradigm, scientists adopt new instruments and look in new places. Even more important, during revolutions scientists see new and different things when looking with familiar instruments in places they have looked before. It is rather as if the professional community had been suddenly transported to another planet where familiar objects are seen in a different light and are joined by unfamiliar ones as well.

(1970, p. 111)

Kuhn goes on to compare this change in the scientist's world-view to the familiar classroom demonstration of reversals in visual gestalt. In the most widely used demonstration, subjects are shown a figure that can be seen as either a vase or as a pair of human faces because the contours of the ambiguous drawing are reversible (see Figure 2). Once seen as a vase, the identical pattern of lines suddenly shifts to the image of two faces. A perceptual revolution!

The postrevolution scientist experiences just such a perceptual shift in the way he views once familiar segments of nature. Whole new segments of experience begin to emerge for him from what was previously a confusing flux of background events.

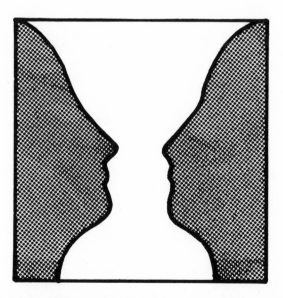

Figure 2. A widely used example of an ambiguous drawing. Fixate the center of the unshaded area for thirty seconds. Reversal of the image should occur.

Thus, for Kuhn, scientific progress is not a linear, cumulative, and gradual evolutionary effort. It is, rather, in some instances, a sudden, dramatic, and "revolutionary" reorganization of the conceptual rules of the most compelling game that the human mind has undertaken.

IMPLICATIONS

Jerome S. Bruner, a cognitive psychologist at Harvard University, has devoted much of his theorizing and research to understanding how people process information. Like T. S. Kuhn, Bruner seems to believe that basic perceptual processes are the prototype for such higher mental processes of thought as memory and problem-solving.

Stimuli, in Bruner's thinking, never impinge on a passive organism. "The organism in perception is one way or another in a state of expectancy about the environment" (Bruner and Postman, 1949, in Bruner, 1973). A second axiom of perception is that the organism possesses directive tendencies to maximize perception of stimuli relevant to current needs and to minimize irrelevant, and, for the moment, distracting stimuli (Bruner and Postman, 1949). It follows from these two statements about the nature of the perceptual process that the organism will attempt to ward off or to prevent the perception of incongruity or any perception that violates what it expects.

For example, Bruner and Postman (1949) showed Harvard and Radcliffe undergraduates a series of playing cards. Within the series of normal cards there were interspersed some incongruous cards, cards printed in an incorrect color; e.g., three of hearts was printed in black, two of spades in red, and so on. When viewing three series of cards in tachistocopic presentation, a method that controls the amount of time a stimulus may be seen, incongruous cards required on average, 114 milliseconds, while normal cards required only 28 seconds to be recognized. (See also Kuhn, 1970, who cites this experiment.)

Problem:
1. Noting the reference to Kuhn above, answer the following:

   a. If you were Kuhn, how would you use Bruner and Postman's research in supporting your description of the development of science?
   b. Are there any similarities between this experiment and the two-rope problem discussed in Chapter 3?
   c. Which experiment—the two-rope problem or the card experiment— provides the best support for Kuhn's thesis? Why?

2. What conditions could the experimenter employ to increase the subject's efficiency in perceiving the incongruous cards?

3. Generalize from your answer to the preceding question to speculate on how scientists might improve their chances of discovering and understanding incongruities.

Progress—Regress—Distress—Redress: An Overview of Scientific Change

Following Kuhn's thesis, scientific progress, as well as changes in scientific outlook, may be conceptualized as three overlapping stages and one discontinuous phase:

Pre-Paradigm Science—Normal Science—Anomaly—Revolution

In the first stage, pre-paradigm science, the diverse viewpoints *progress* toward the accumulation of data and explanation to the point where a unifying and useful synthesis is possible. Steady *progress,* with some discord, is the rule.

Possession of a paradigm, in the second stage of normal science, characterizes the nature of this stage's conduct of the scientific enterprise. The emphasis of normal science is on the articulation of the valued paradigm; hence the flavor of this period is conservative and *regressive.* Regressive is an adequate description only in the sense that contradictory and disconfirming instances are ignored in favor of problems that have a predictable solution in terms of the normal-science paradigm.

Distress characterizes the third stage, in which the cumulative effects of counter-paradigm instances—anomalies—result in professional insecurity within the scientific community. The treasured paradigm is now seen as wanting, but only when an alternative paradigm is available will the distress be relieved. Thus the emergence of crisis colors the main feeling of this period: *distress.*

Finally, acceptance of a new paradigm and the transition period during which its implications are articulated cause a widespread reorganization of world view among members of the discipline. Scientists are now living in a different conceptual world. This fourth phase is scientific revolution, and its chief characteristic is the success with which it has *redressed* the intellectual dilemma caused by recognition of the anomaly in the previous stage. In short, scientific change can be conceptualized as:

Progress—Regress—Distress—Redress

Scientific Revolution in Psychology

Psychology is a long way from the kind of scientific revolution that characterized the physics of Einstein or the biology of Darwin. To some small extent, however, psychology shared in the Darwinian revolution (cf. Chapter 2) in such areas as learning and physiological psychology, developmental psychology, and psychological testing. To a much lesser degree, psychology shared in or, more precisely, was affected by, developments in physics in such areas as sensory psychology and psychophysics. It is unclear as yet to what extent the "Chomsky revolution" in linguistics will affect psychology, but Noam Chomsky's work in linguistics (cf. Chapter 2) will be most likely to have its immediate effects in the areas of learning, perception, psycholinguistics, and developmental psychology. (See John Lyons' brief introduction (1970) to Chomsky's theory for a good historical overview, in nontechnical language, of the impact on psychology.)

Within psychology itself, however, a full-blown and radical revolution of method and theory has not occurred. Some psychologists would

KEY CONCEPTS

The Structure of Scientific Revolution

According to T. S. Kuhn (1970), scientific progress is not necessarily a gradual and linear process. It proceeds in four stages, of which the last phase is seen as a total break with the cumulative tradition that preceded it.

1. Pre-Paradigm Science (Progress)

Multiple schools of thought develop to account for observed phenomena.

2. Normal or Paradigm Science (Regress)

One of the schools achieves an elegant and successful synthesis of available explanations; diverse opinion drops out as adherents of various schools convert to the unifying paradigm. Normal science is carried on as paradigm is extended and articulated to solve puzzles set for it by paradigm. Radically new phenomena are ignored or deferred.

3. The Crisis of Anomaly (Distress)

As more and more of the puzzles of normal science fail to be solved in the way the paradigm dictates, the rules of the game are loosened. The paradigm becomes blurred and is less able to function as an effective guide to research and to normal puzzle solving. Diverse opinion returns, and the major effort of the scientific community is directed to developing an explanation of the anomaly.

4. Revolution (Redress)

Scientists will reject the old paradigm only when a new theory is available to take its place. The new paradigm not only solves the problem set by the anomaly but causes a change in the world view of the scientist. Ultimately, acceptance of the new paradigm necessitates a return to a new period of normal science.

argue that the innovative research and theory of Sigmund Freud into the nature of the unconscious, the studies of Ivan Pavlov (in physiology) into the nature of the conditioned reflex, and the investigations of Jean Piaget into the sequence and quality of cognitive development constitute revolutions in psychology. Certainly one would be hard put to deny that these men wrought significant and startling changes in the discipline. However, taken in the aggregate, none of these contributions (and many others could be named) serve to unify the diverse traditions within psychology in the way that Darwin's natural selection theory unified biology, or Einstein's relativity theory unified physics. In many ways, therefore, psychology remains at the pre-paradigmatic stage of development, characterized by a variety of subdisciplines, and controversies within and between disciplines.

Thus, each of the men we have named revolutionized a segment of psychology's endeavor to be scientific without creating the "new world" of a comprehensive psychological revolution. One of the readers of this book may some day be credited with that honor, or villainy (depending upon which side of the revolution you happen to be) by members of the profession. That event will, hopefully, not be long in coming, and certainly it will depend most profoundly on those who have gone before.

Happily, it is possible to discern several shifts in method and theory within contemporary psychology that, while not radical in Kuhn's sense, are substantial, hard-won achievements. We shall briefly examine such a "mini-revolution" in order to capture some of the flavor of conceptual change in psychology, and then we shall move on to a beginning revolution in psychology's methodology.

An Illustrative Case: Classical Versus Contemporary Psychophysics

It is possible for an individual to detect the wing of a bee as it falls on his cheek from a distance of one centimeter; or to hear the tick of a watch under quiet conditions at twenty feet; or to see a candle flame at thirty miles on a dark, clear night (Galanter, 1962). These seemingly astounding feats of sensory sensitivity are rather crude but concrete ways of conceptualizing one of the key problems of classical phychophysics: *What is the minimum amount of physical energy a stimulus must possess to be capable of detection by a given sensory system (eye, ear, skin, etc.)*?

Put another way, the detection problem can be viewed as the question of how much sound (light, odor, or pressure) is needed in order for a person to be able to say, "I heard (saw, smelled, or felt) something"

(Galanter, 1962). The classical psychophysical name for this lower limit of sensitivity is "absolute threshold."

Theoretically, the notion of absolute threshold asserts that there is a point reached in the continuum of stimulus intensity where the energy of a stimulus is so small in quantity that a person reports that nothing is present. Above this point, the subject is able to detect the stimulus. The problem of detection is thus conceived to be an "all-or-none" proposition. In practice, however, subjects fluctuate in their judgments of stimulus intensity, sometimes reporting a stimulus present when in fact the stimulus is not. At other times, subjects fail to detect a stimulus present at an intensity that, for them, is usually detectable.

This problem of the fluctuating judgments of subjects was treated by classical psychophysics as a form of experimental error, and procedures were devised to bring this variability under control. Many presentations of the stimulus were employed above and below the hypothetical absolute-threshold intensity of the subject, and an average value was calculated as indicative of the real-threshold point. The intensity at which the subject says he detects the stimulus on one half of the presentations (therefore the intensity at which one half of the time he fails to detect the stimulus's presence) is taken as his absolute threshold. The technique used is called the method of limits, and it represents only one of the methods devised to answer questions about the nature of sensory functioning. (Cf. D'Amato, 1970, Ch. 5, and Engen, 1971, for a comprehensive survey of psychophysics.)

In all cases, the variability of the subject's report is conceived of as the result of certain biases. For example, some subjects commit the error of habituation in making judgments about a series of stimuli that decrease in intensity so that they continue to say "Yes, I hear it (or see it, etc.)," beyond the point where they really can detect the sound. They are caught up in the momentum of the situation, so to speak. Other subjects commit the error of anticipation by which they begin to expect that constantly reporting "I don't hear it yet," in a long series of increasingly intense stimuli has got to change *soon,* and so they report detecting the sound before, in fact, they do hear it.

The classical psychophysicist conceived his task to be the invention and employment of ingenious methods to control or to bypass biases and momentary fluctuations of the subject's judgment. By so eliminating "error," the most accurate measurements of sensitivity could be made.

Contemporary Psychophysics

A minor revolution in psychophysics was heralded by the development of a statistical decision model of sensory sensitivity called the theory of signal detectability (Tanner and Swets, 1954; and Swets *et. al.,* 1961).

With signal-detection analysis as his conceptual paradigm, the experimenter's focus of attention and the rules by which he plays the psychophysics game are greatly altered. The psychophysicist now devotes more of his attention to the nature of the subject's cognitive and emotional judgmental processes affecting his decisions to report "yes, I hear it," or "no, I do not." Signal-detection theory (SDT) is thus markedly different from the attempts at "pure" sensory measurement of classical psychophysics, which conceived of such motivational influences as experimental error to be "controlled out" (Engen, 1971). SDT conceptual rules of the game dictate that stimuli are *not* discrete and not all-or-none in their effect, but are, instead, continuous in their impact on the organism. Thus, for SDT, subject judgment variability is a product of both biological sensitivity *and* motivational decision processes. Consequently, in contrast to the assumption of classical phychophysics, the notion of an absolute threshold is abandoned. A mathematical model of the *relative probability* that a given stimulus will capture the subject's attention on a given trial is substituted for the rigid all-or-none threshold concept.

The probability that a signal (stimulus) will be detected by a subject is a function of three factors (based on Engen, 1971, p. 35):

1. *The effect of the signal relative to the random background stimulation called "noise."* Noise is a technical term referring not simply to auditory stimulation, but to any random, spontaneous stimulation that competes with the intended signal. In the present discussion it is best to think of "noise" as the spontaneous firing of neurons which provide continual background activity within the nervous system.

2. *What the subject expects in the experimental situation.* Subject expectations are those cognitive and emotional factors referred to above which affect (bias) his decisions about the presence or absence of the signal, in short, how often he has been led to expect that the signal will be present.

3. *The potential consequences of his decisions,* the risk and payoff factors associated with correct and erroneous reports of *yes* and *no.*

Although only the most nontechnical discussion of signal-detection theory is appropriate here, some basic concepts and an example will serve to clarify the differences between classical and contemporary psychophysics. SDT will also lay the groundwork for our later discussion of scientific revolution in psychology's treatment of experimental subjects.

The Basics of Signal-Detection Theory

Consider the experimental situation in which the typical psychophysics subject finds himself. He is required to indicate by a *yes* or *no* on each of many trials whether the stimulus was present. The most basic assumption is that the subject's experience of the stimulus varies over time in a way that can be mathematically represented by a bell-shaped (normal) curve (Figure 3). Background stimulation present on each occasion that the signal is present also varies over time and is represented by a similar bell-shaped curve. Thus we have two curves representing the distribution of noise events and the distribution of signal events. However, since the signal is always superimposed on the background of noise, the distribution for the signal is properly represented as signal-plus-noise. Thus the distribution of sensory events represented by the signal-plus-noise curve has a mean or average value that is always greater than the average or mean value of the noise distribution alone.

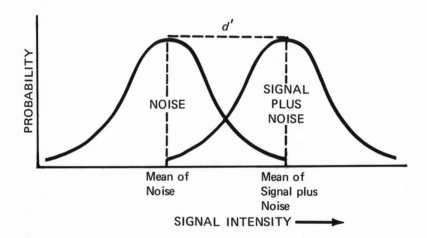

Figure 3. N and S+N Distributions of Signal-Detection Theory. Two bell-shaped distributions represent the events of a psychophysics detection experiment as experienced by the subject. The *Noise* distribution overlaps with the *Signal-plus-Noise* distribution, but the average intensity of *Signal* events is always greater than the average intensity of the distribution of *Noise* events. When a subject decides that what he experienced was no more intense than what he customarily experiences when no signal is present, he replies: "No, I did not see the signal." In theoretical terms, the subject has decided that this trial was a *"Noise* trial." If the subject decides that his experience on this trial was more intense than if no signal had been present, he replies: "Yes, I did see the signal." In this latter instance, the subject has decided that his experience was sampled from the *Signal-plus-Noise* distribution.

In the graph, the distribution of background stimulation or noise is represented in the left-hand curve, which overlaps with the distribution of events that the subject experiences as signal-plus-noise. For all practical purposes, the subject is being asked on each trial to make a decision about what he has just experienced. "Did this event I just experienced come from the noise distribution, or was it intense enough to have come from the signal-plus-noise distribution?" When he believes it came from the noise distribution, he reports, "No, I did not hear the signal." When he believes (decides) that the event he experienced on a given trial was of sufficient intensity to belong to the signal-plus-noise distribution, he reports, "Yes, I did hear the signal."

As the intensity of the signal becomes stronger, the distance between the two distributions is greater and the possibility of correct detection is increased. Look at Figure 4.

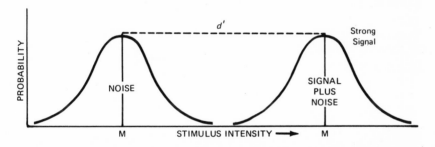

Figure 4. Hypothetical Distributions for a Strong Signal Trial. Note distance between the means of the curves. When a strong signal (intense light or loud sound) is presented to a subject, he will have very little difficulty in detecting that signal's presence. *SDT* represents this fact by depicting the *Noise* distribution and the *Signal-plus-Noise* distribution as widely separated along the stimulus intensity axis. In short, with an intense stimulus, the two distributions no longer overlap and the subject has little difficulty in discriminating noise from signal.

With *decreases* in signal strength (intensity of stimulus) the overlap between the two distributions increases, and the probability of a correct detection is diminished. See Figure 5.

This critical distance between the mean of the noise distribution and the mean of the signal-plus-noise distribution is designated d'. Without attention to the mathematical details, d' can be considered to represent a subject's sensory sensitivity with respect only to signal strength and his own biological sensitivity.

However, if a subject's report of the presence or absence of a signal were dependent only on signal strength and his sensitivity, the concept

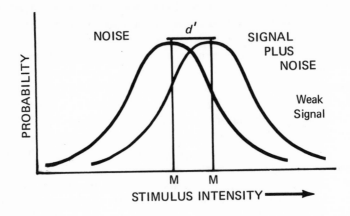

Figure 5. Hypothetical Distributions for Weak Signal Trial. Note distance (d') between the means of the curves. A weak signal (low intensity light, barely audible sound) is difficult for a subject to detect. *SDT* represents this situation by depicting the *Noise* distribution and the *Signal-plus-Noise* distribution with considerable overlap along the stimulus intensity axis. Compare to Figure 4.

of d' would represent only a small improvement over classical absolute-threshold concepts. But, as we already know, the subject's motivational state influences his decisions about what to report. In effect, under some conditions some subjects are very cautious and unwilling to attribute a trial to the signal-plus-noise distribution unless they are absolutely sure, and they report *no*. Under different motivational conditions, the same-strength signal may cause the subject to loosen his cautious criterion so that he is willing to assign that event to the signal-plus-noise distribution, and he reports *yes*.

The key question is: "What affects his criterion, assuming that signal strength and his sensory capacity remain relatively constant?" For the answer to this question, a question which most clearly distinguishes between the classical and contemporary paradigms of psychophysical measurement, we must turn to an example.

Payoff Matrices: Examples of Risk and Conservatism in Decision-Making

In the simple *yes–no* experimental situation similar to the classical method of limits discussed above, the subject reports the presence or absence of a light of various intensities. Objectively, there are two events: *light-on* and *light-off*. From the subject's point of view there are two responses: "Yes, I see it," or "No, I don't." The ideal subject with perfect sensitivity, under ideal conditions, should perfectly match his responses of yes and no to the conditions of on and off. However, in an experiment in which the light is objectively present in some relatively large number of trials, we might expect perfection on the subject's part, but we soon learn to temper our expectations and to tolerate some percentage of error with even the most ideal subject. Thus, the subject's pattern of responses against external conditions might look like the pattern in Table 3.

TABLE 3: Theoretically Expected Response Pattern

		RESPONSE		
		Yes	No	
STIMULUS	On	86%	14%	←Error$_1$
	Off	0%	100%	

(After Galanter, 1962)

In Table 3 the subject is correctly reporting the presence of the light (signal) in *almost* perfect correspondence with external reality. He makes only one kind of error, and he errs in that one way only a small percentage of the time. He *misses* the signal (light) when it is present about 14 per cent of the time, while he correctly detects the light's presence on 86 per cent of the occasions when it *is* present. In actuality, however, a real experimental result differs from these somewhat idealized findings.

TABLE 4: Actual Experimental Result

		RESPONSE		
		Yes	No	
	On	86% (Hits)	14% (Miss)	Error$_1$
STIMULUS				
	Off	8% (False Alarms)	92% (Correct Rejections)	
Error$_2$ →				

(After Galanter, 1962)

Table 4 shows the response pattern of a subject who reports signals present and absent in the same pattern as our idealized subject, but who, additionally, errs in another way. He reports the presence of a signal when, in reality, there is no signal present. This new contingency (8 per cent) is called a "false alarm." If the subject, on the other hand, reports no signal when, in reality, there *is* a signal present, that response (14 per cent), as we have seen, is called a "miss." Correct responses (*yes* for signal when it is present, and *no* when it is not present) are called "hits" and "correct rejections," respectively. We can conceptualize this terminology and its operational meaning by referring to Table 5 and Figure 6.

RESPONSE

		Yes	No
S T I M U L U S	On	Hit	Miss
	Off	False Alarm	Correct Rejection

Table 5. Signal-detection terminology.

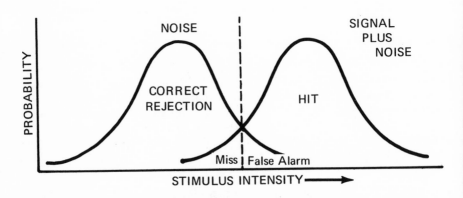

NOISE

SIGNAL
PLUS
NOISE

PROBABILITY

CORRECT
REJECTION

HIT

Miss | False Alarm

STIMULUS INTENSITY ➔

Figure 6. Signal-Detection Terminology. Read through the table of terminology (Table 3) first, then scan the distributions. The two kinds of error
that a subject may make—Misses and False Alarms—are depicted by *SDT*
as belonging to the areas of overlap between the *Noise* and the *Signal-plus-
Noise* distributions. Thus, a subject *misses* a signal when it is present because
he decides wrongly that a given trial belonged to the *Noise* distribution when,
in fact, it was a sample from the left tail of the *Signal-plus-Noise* distribution. Similarly, a subject gives a *False Alarm* when he again decides wrongly
that a given trial belonged to the *Signal* distribution when, in fact, that trial
was sampled from the lower right tail of the *Noise* distribution. The reasons
for such errors are discussed in the text.

Read over Table 5 first. Then, reading the curves from left to right,
compare the placement of hits, misses, etc., to the table. A clear conception of the meanings of these terms should emerge.

Figure 6 is adapted and reproduced from Gregory A. Kimble and Norman
Garmezy, *Principles of General Psychology*, Third Edition, copyright © 1968 by
The Ronald Press Company, New York. Used by permission.

KEY CONCEPTS

Signal-Detection Theory Terminology

1. **correct rejection** occurs when there is no signal present and the perceiving subject correctly decides that the experience is from the noise distribution. He correctly says *no*.

2. **miss** is scored when the perceiving subject erroneously reports that this experience is from the noise distribution when in fact there is a signal present. He should have said *yes*.

3. **false alarm** occurs when the subject reports "Yes, there is a signal," when there was none.

4. **hit** occurs when the subject reports the presence of a signal and a signal is present.

high-risk criterion: Subject behaves as if he is willing to accept any event as having come from the signal-plus-noise distribution. He therefore reports *yes* on every trial.

cautious criterion: Subject is willing only to accept the most intense signals as strong enough to warrant a report of "Yes, I hear it." This strategy maximizes the number of misses.

d′ (d-prime): A measurement of the subject's biological sensitivity in relation to a given signal intensity. It can be conceived of as the distance separating the mean of the noise distribution from the mean of the signal-plus-noise distribution on a given trial. Weak signals imply that the means are very close, making discrimination difficult. Strong signals imply that the means are distant, making discrimination easier.

THE HIGH-RISK STRATEGY

The problem for the experimenter is to discover what conditions affect the subject's probability of hits, misses, correct rejections, and false alarms. Suppose we tell a subject that we will *not* penalize him for false alarms (saying there is a signal, when there is none), and that we will pay him 25 cents for each hit. Since false alarms cost him nothing, the ingenious subject will simply settle on a strategy of saying yes all the time. He will maximize his gain, though he simultaneously raises the level of erroneous responses in the form of false alarms. *It is as if the subject were setting an internal decision criterion so low in terms of acceptable stimulus intensity that he is willing to interpret any event as intense enough to qualify as signal-plus-noise.* At least, this is how the process is conceptualized in the signal-detection paradigm. This high-risk strategy on the subject's part is pictured in Figure 7.

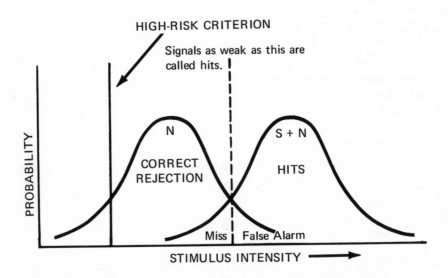

Figure 7. High Risk Criterion to Maximize the Probability of Hits Without Regard to Errors. (After Kimble and Garmezy, 1968, p. 204) Subject behaves in a detection experiment as if *any* event he experiences is intense enough to be called "Signal." *SDT* depicts this situation in the above figure by indicating this subject's high-risk strategy with a vertical line shifted to the extreme low end of the stimulus intensity axis. The vertical line represents the subject's decision criterion, or point in the stimulus intensity continuum, at which he is willing to interpret a given event as a signal event. In the case illustrated above, the subject's decision criterion is set at an extremely low point so that, in effect, he calls every trial a signal trial, and reports, "Yes, I see it," on every trial.

By moving his criterion to the left so that it encompasses most of the noise distribution, the subject minimizes the probability of bypassing a signal when it occurs. But the probability of false alarms is greatly increased.

THE CAUTIOUS STRATEGY

If we again change the rules of the game so that a high-risk strategy incurs penalties, we change the decision processes of the subject. Consider the following payoff matrix:

	RESPONSE	
	Yes	No
On	Hit 10¢	Miss −5¢
STIMULUS	False Alarm −5¢	Correct Rejection 10¢
Off		

(After Galanter, 1962)

Penalties are now assigned in the form of losses of 5 cents for misses (saying *no* when signal *is* present), and to false alarms (saying *yes* when signal is *not* present). The subject must now change his strategy to accommodate the change in rules and to minimize the penalties he might incur. In extreme form, *the subject behaves as if he has pushed his criterion far to the right, so that the probability of false alarms is very low, while the probability of detecting a weak signal is decreased. Thus he increases his chances of avoiding false alarms, but he increases his chances of misses.* The observant reader will also notice that this strategy has another characteristic: the equally high-paying correct rejection response (10¢) is maximized. To visualize this conservative criterion consider Figure 8: Because subject is penalized for false

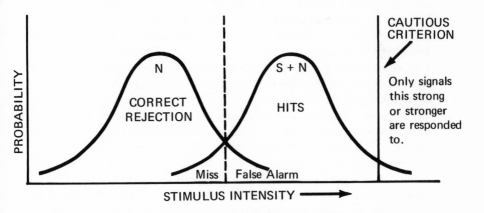

Figure 8. Cautious Criterion to Increase Probability of Hits. (After Kimble and Garmezy, 1968, p. 204) Because subject is penalized for *False Alarms*, he moves his decision criterion far to the right along the stimulus intensity continuum. Now, in effect, only strong signals, about whose presence little doubt exists, elicit from the subject the response, "Yes, I see it." This cautious decision criterion eliminates *False Alarms*, but greatly increases the chances of missing a weak signal when it is present.

alarms, he moves his decision criterion far to the right along the stimulus intensity continuum. Now, in effect, only strong signals, about whose presence little doubt exists, elicit from the subject the response, "Yes, I see it." This cautious decision criterion eliminates false alarms, but greatly increases the chances of missing a weak signal when it is present.

THE RATIONAL STRATEGY

Obviously neither the high risk nor the cautious strategy results in perfect responding. The most rational game plan would be to set one's criterion midway between the distributions of noise and signal-plus-noise where they intersect. In this way, the number of hits would be maximized while the possibility of error in the form of misses and false alarms would rise only slightly. Humans, however, do not always behave as rationally as our theories say they should.

Thus the value of a signal-detection analysis of perceptual behavior takes on more meaning when we consider that these payoff matrices used in the laboratory are only models of the payoff matrices subjects bring to the laboratory with them. In other words, the apparently nonrational behavior of subjects in the decision task is the result of motivational variables that are enduring characteristics of a subject's personality. Experimental participants are not ideal, inert, nonreactive bundles of yes-no responses (Orne, 1969). Subjects are human beings who bring to the experiment their characteristic expectations of success and failure, their differing emotional dispositions to risk-taking, and their past histories of interpersonal relations that may affect their momentary decision values, motivations, apprehensions, and desires (Galanter, 1962, p. 110; and Rosenberg, 1969). This conceptualization of *human* responders in the laboratory constitutes the genuinely radical change of contemporary psychophysics over classical methodology. The influence of personality variables, once considered the bane of the experimentalist, has become a significant phenomenon in its own right. In a very real sense, this shift in experimental method, from treating subjects as *passive* organisms to regarding them as dynamic, motivated, ideational beings, as illustrated here by signal-detection theory, is comparable to Kuhn's notion of scientific revolution through paradigm change. The implications of SDT have already begun to have impact on other areas of psychology, including a reconceptualization of the unconscious.

KEY CONCEPTS

Classical Versus Contemporary Psychophysics

Assumptions of Classical Psychophysics: The classical psychophysicist set out to measure the *limits* of sensory sensitivity. In short, he assumed that there was an absolute threshold, that is, a point in the sensory continuum above which a given stimulus intensity is always perceived, and below which a stimulus is too weak ever to be perceived. The classical conception may be pictured by reference to the graph below of a hypothetical absolute function.

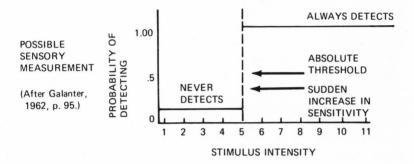

POSSIBLE
SENSORY
MEASUREMENT

(After Galanter,
1962, p. 95.)

As the graph above shows, the assumption was that there would be a definite point in intensity where the subject would shift his report of not detecting the stimulus to always reporting that he detects it 100% of the time. In fact, when an actual subject's sensory sensitivity is measured, the resulting graph looks more like the one below:

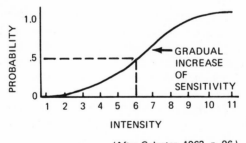

(After Galanter, 1962, p. 96.)

Where is the precise point of the absolute threshold in the curve above? There is none. The best that can be done is to pick some arbitrary point. That point is the intensity at which the probability of saying *yes* is 50% and the probability of saying *no* is 50%.

Signal-detection theory asserts that the subject's probability of saying *yes* is a function of internal motivational variables that affect his perception about the consequences of his yes-no responses.

Summary and Implications of SDT: The Unconscious Threshold

Signal-detection theory distinguishes between a subject's biological sensory sensitivity and his response decisions. Although his willingness to make specific responses is a motivational matter, his biological sensitivity to stimuli should, in principle, remain relatively constant. Moreover, d' has the mathematical property of accurately representing this stable sensory sensitivity while remaining unaffected by the subject's response bias. Thus SDT provides for a relatively "pure" measure of sensory functioning and a way of monitoring the effects of personality variables.

The concept of an absolute threshold, below which stimuli are not experienced and above which all stimuli are perceived, had to be abandoned. Furthermore, as a result of the distinction between sensitivity and decision-making, psychologists have begun to look at other areas of behavioral research that involve analogous absolute threshold concepts to see if the distinction will shed new light on these areas.

Reconsider for a moment Freud's notion of the unconscious and its contents of repressed impulses and ideas. (Cf. Chapter 3 for a discussion of repression and its associated research problems.) In his series of lectures designed to introduce students to the basics of psychoanalysis, Freud employed the analogy of a series of interconnecting rooms to depict the relations between consciousness and the unconscious. Looking at it from the viewpoint of signal-detection theory, the analogy sounds similar to the absolute-threshold concept of classical psychophysics:

> The unconscious system may . . . be compared to a large ante-room, in which the various mental excitations are crowding upon one another, like individual beings. Adjoining this is a second, smaller apartment, a sort of reception room, in which consciousness resides. But on the threshold between the two there stands a personage with the office of doorkeeper, who examines the various mental excitations, censors them, and denies them admittance to the reception room when he disapproves of them. . . .
>
> Now this metaphor may be employed to widen our terminology. The excitations in the unconscious, in the ante-chamber, are not visible to consciousness, which is of course in the other room, so to begin with they remain unconscious. When they have pressed forward to the threshold and been turned back by the doorkeeper, they are *"incapable of becoming conscious"*; we call them then *repressed*. But even those excitations which are allowed over the threshold do not necessarily become conscious; they can only become so if they succeed in attracting the eye of consciousness. This second chamber, therefore, may be suitably called *the preconscious system*.

(1962, Riviere translation, p. 305–6)

It would seem, then, that in Freud's thinking repressed contents remain below the absolute threshold of consciousness. Because such repressed material is beyond the reach of observational, laboratory techniques of investigation, the Freudian concept of the unconscious and the repressed has defied a great many experimenters' efforts to study them (cf. Chapter 3). Supposing the paradigm change wrought by SDT in psychophysics could be applied to investigations of the unconscious, would a corresponding "revolution" in conceptualization occur?

One attempt to apply SDT to the analysis of unconscious internal states follows the paradigm in abandoning the absolute threshold conception in favor of a probability model (Brody, 1972, pp. 282–83). Thus, any stimulus that can be observed must also be in awareness to some degree, but may not be responded to appropriately. In short, though a stimulus may be experienced, it may not be labeled a "hit." *Unconscious phenomena are not below some absolute threshold in this view; they are simply treated in the subject's decision-making as misses.* This represents a radical shift in interpretation of Freud's original notion of a threshold between consciousness and unconsciousness, but it remains to be seen whether this reinterpretation will aid in the experimental investigation of the phenomenon. The difficulty may lie in the fact that Freud was focusing on the even more complex problem of *internal* stimulation, which may not customarily be verbally labeled in an individual's lifetime.

In any event, such attempts at reanalysis of an old-paradigm phenomenon demonstrate the significance of SDT, not only for psychophysics, but for psychology in general.

Conclusions

Three important conclusions seem evident from our brief survey of SDT:

1. Classical psychophysics discovered this anomaly: an absolute threshold implies that there is a precise point in an organism's sensory sensitivity at which low intensity stimuli are not perceived. Measurements reveal human subjects do not react in the all-or-none fashion demanded by the absolute threshold paradigm.
2. Signal-detection theory may be viewed as a "mini-revolution" in psychophysics because it radically changes the rules of the game in its adoption of a probability model of sensory events.
3. Most important of all, SDT indicates a shift in experimental procedure for psychologists. Behavioral investigators have begun to realize that the organisms with which they deal are not passive

bundles of responses, easily, reliably and perpetually triggered to action by known stimuli.

Homo sapiens is a peculiar creature: he can think and have his own ideas about experiments: he knows that the experimenter knows that he knows the experimenter wants to know something about him. There's the rub.

IMPLICATIONS

1. Employing the concept of refutability developed in Chapter 3, analyze the signal-detection interpretation of Freud's notion of the unconscious with respect to:

   a. the increase or decrease in its refutability;
   b. its value for initiating new research;
   c. a comparison of the original orthodox interpretation and the SDT interpretation for providing an explanation of repressed ideas.

2. Using the signal-detection model, design an experiment to test the validity of repression as an explanation of motivated forgetting.

Experimenter-Subject Dyads: The Quiet Revolution

Much like the experimenter and his subject, Peter and Paul lack a sense of fundamental mutual trust. A series of mismatched expectations and interpretations is the result. Ponder this cognitive-emotional spiral (modified from Laing, Phillipson and Lee, 1966, pp. 21–22):

PETER (thinks)	PAUL (thinks)
1. I am upset.	1. Peter is upset.
2. Paul is acting very calm and dispassionate.	2. I'll try to help him by remaining calm and just listening.
3. If Paul cared about me and wanted to help he would get involved and show some emotion also.	3. He is getting even more upset. I must be even more calm.
4. Paul knows that this upsets me.	4. He is accusing me of hurting him.
5. If Paul knows that his behavior upsets me, he must be intending to hurt me.	5. I'm really trying to help.
6. He must be cruel, sadistic. Maybe he gets pleasure out of it.	6. He must be projecting (his cruel, sadistic tendencies onto me.)

Peter's and Paul's conflicting interpretation of each other's behavior is a relatively straightforward example of the impact individuals' expectations can have in a one-to-one interaction or dyad. Mismatched not only in cognitive perspective, Peter and Paul trigger an escalating series of equally mismatched and inappropriate *emotional* reactions. A spiraling set of even more profoundly mismatched expectations is triggered in turn. Ultimately, a tangled network of values, attitudes, expectations, and strivings—all based in misinterpretation—emerges.

At best, further interaction is misleading for the partners of the dyad, and, at worst, leads to an emotional stalemate which culminates in breaking off the relationship. Laing, Phillipson, and Lee spell out some of the possible patterns in detail:

> What happens when two people do not agree on the meaning to be assigned to a particular act? A very complicated process ensues. If communication is optimum, they *understand* that they differ on the interpretation of the act, and also *realize that they both understand* that they differ in its interpretation. Once this is established they may get into a struggle over whether or not to change the act under consideration in the future. This struggle may take various forms:
> Threat—Do this or else.
> Coaxing—Please do this.
> Bribery—If you do this I will do that in return.
> Persuasion—I believe it is a good idea for you to do this because, etc.
>
> (1966, pp. 12–13)

Threat, coaxing, bribery and persuasion, as forms of behavioral choice, are in many ways comparable to the cognitive-emotional decision processes that signal-detection theory so admirably brought into experimental focus. Think of the relationship between the subject in an experimental investigation and the experimenter with whom he has primary contact as a dyadic, interactive, and inter-experiential event. When the experimenter's attitude toward his subjects is authoritarian and "supercompetent professional," does he not subtly threaten them and alter their behavior? In effect, his prestige and the prestige of his discipline imply either the threatening: "Do this or else" attitude of authority, or the persuasive "I think it is good for you to do this . . . " approach of the equally authoritarian, knowing "scientist."

Coaxing and bribery, no doubt, are also to be found in the unwitting repertoire of the experimenter who finds himself deeply committed to his research (cf. Rosenberg, 1969, and Rosenthal, 1969). Totally without the intention of doing so, his general demeanor may communicate to the subjects the importance he attaches to success in this experiment.

Equally without direct intention, subjects unwittingly respond to this surreptitious emotional tug with behavior biased in the direction of confirming the experimenter's hypothesis. A subject knows that he is taking part in this research because his responses are important and count.

> Inevitably he will wish to produce "good" data; that is, data characteristic of a "good" subject. To be a "good" subject may mean many things: to give the right responses, i.e., to give the kind of response characteristic of intelligent subjects; to give the normal response, i.e., characteristic of healthy subjects; to give a response in keeping with the individual's self-perception, etc., etc.
>
> (Orne, 1969, p. 145)

It is thus possible for psychology to reconceptualize the outcome (data) of any experimental investigation as more complex than a straightforward function of the independent variable. It is as if psychologists have taken the hint of SDT. Orne has stated this position clearly:

> . . . we do not study passive physical particles, but active, thinking human beings *like ourselves*. The fear that knowledge of the true purposes of an experiment might vitiate its results stems from a tacit recognition that the subject is not a passive responder to stimuli and experimental conditions. Instead, he is an active participant in a special form of socially defined interaction which we call "taking part in an experiment. . . ."
> Because subjects are active, sentient beings, they do not respond to the specific experimental stimuli with which they are confronted as isolated events but rather they perceive these in the total context of the experimental situation.
>
> (1969, pp. 143–44; italics added)

Experimental outcomes, then, are at least partially "contaminated," if that is the correct word, with the multiple and divergent meanings that grow out of the social nature of psychological scientific investigation.

From a variety of viewpoints, this insight is not a radically new discovery. Many traditions within psychology have acknowledged the fundamental importance of the interactive process between psychologist and subject (for example, the clinical tradition of psychotherapy). But it is only within relatively recent times that the nature of the process has been construed as important in itself, and as more than a mere (and hopefully, controllable) artifact of experimental method. Signal-detection theory is but one example of this change in viewpoint. The emphasis currently is on the attempt to pull together the scattered threads of these acknowledgements of the human side of science into a coherent and useful paradigm for psychological research. For precisely this reason—that the tradition has had a diffuse but long-term existence—we can refer to the shift in paradigm as a quiet revolution.

Species-Identity Theorem and the Participant Observer

"Everyone and anyone is much more simply human than otherwise, more like everyone else than different." With these words, Harry Stack Sullivan, psychiatrist and personality theorist, sought to organize in the form of a basic postulate his belief that humans are the most complex and unique creatures in the natural world. In doing so, he simultaneously laid the groundwork for one interpretation of the experimenter-subject interaction problem.

Originally called the "species-identity theorem" by Sullivan in a notebook dated 1944, (1962, frontispiece) the kernel of this idea was changed years later to the "one-genus postulate":

> . . . the differences between any two instances of human personality—from the lowest-grade imbecile to the highest-grade genius —are much less striking than the differences between the least-gifted human being and a member of the nearest other biological genus. *Man—however undistinguished biologically—as long as he is entitled to the term, human personality, will be very much more like every other instance of human personality than he is like anything else in the world.* [Italics added.]
> (Sullivan, 1953, pp. 32–33)

Because Sullivan's clinical attention was focused on the characteristics of the interpersonal situation, the one-genus postulate was meant to demonstrate the uniquely human quality of the relationship between psychiatrist and patient, and between patient and patient.

As a consequence of his formulation of the one-genus postulate, Sullivan emphasized that the psychiatrist is no less human, no less involved, no less of a participant, and no less changed than the patient he treats. It was his conviction that social science, and psychiatry in particular, are "concerned with the kinds of events or processes in which the psychiatrist participates while being an observant psychiatrist" (1953, p. 13). "Ivory tower observation," with its implied element of objective, uninvolved commitment to scientific truth finding is a myth, according to Sullivan.

> . . . the investigator is immersed in his investigation and participates more or less unwittingly in the data which he is assembling. This participation in the data cannot be avoided if one is to do more than count noses or other crude indices of human existence.
> (1964, p. 15)

Sullivan, therefore, was most concerned with elucidating the nature of the processes between people in the therapeutic setting, and his formulations have direct relevance to the problems of the experimentalist that we have been considering.

Because "everyone is much more simply human than otherwise," observer and observed (experimenter and subject; psychiatrist and patient) share a common ground of meaning that cannot help but be an intrinsic part of the scientific process. In fact, it was Sullivan's feeling that an observer could not make sense of his observations of another unless he shared some common background of experience, expectation, and circumstance: "Without this past background, the observer cannot deduce, by sheer intellectual operations, the meaning of the staggering array of human facts" (1954, p. 19). Thus a picture of *mutual* influence begins to emerge, in which the observer and the observed play equal roles.

The theme of concordant (or conflicting) expectations and interpretations which stem from observer-observed dyads was present to the clinical tradition in a form clearly similar to the present concern of the experimentalist for the validity of his approach. Sullivan recognized the prime importance of this participatory interaction for the beneficial outcome of the therapeutic process from the patient's viewpoint, and, from the observer's viewpoint, for the development of an adequate scientific explanation of psychotherapy.

Additional examples from personality, clinical, and developmental psychology could be cited from psychology's recent past to illustrate the concern of these disciplines for the significance of experimenter effects on data collection. However, the important point is not the multiplication of illustrations, but the fact that psychology has now begun to systematize these independent but strongly similar recognitions of the unique problems of a science that employs human subjects and human observers to understand human behavior.

The Importance of Being Earnest: "Psychologists Always Lie"

One fact has clearly emerged in our discussion so far: experimenters and subjects view participation in an investigation quite differently and see each other's role differently from the way each sees it himself.

The knowledge that he is taking part in a *psychological* study is sufficient to arouse even the mildest subject's suspicions that the psychologist is concealing the true purpose of the experiment, or, worse, has perpetrated an outright falsehood: "As one subject pithily put it, 'Psychologists always lie!' " (Orne, 1962).

To some degree, the suspicious subject approaches the experimental task as the problem of uncovering the real hypothesis or expectation of the experimenter (cf. Rosenberg, 1969, pp. 279 ff.). He then becomes sensitive to cues-of-the-setting and to cues-of-experimenter's-behavior, which may reveal a discrepancy between what he is forthrightly told and what he is able to figure out. As Laing wrote in another context, we might imagine the subject thinking: "They are playing a game. They are playing at not playing a game. If I show them I see they are, I shall break the rules and they will punish me. I must play their game, of not seeing I see the game" (1969, p. 1).

The sum total of cues, which, consciously or not, the subject seeks in order to enlarge his understanding of the situation in which he finds himself, and which may significantly affect his subsequent behavior are called "demand characteristics" of the experimental situation (Orne, 1959; and 1969). Demand characteristics include such things as the scuttlebutt about the experiment, its setting, implicit and explicit instructions, the person of the experimenter, subtle cues provided by him, and the experimental procedure itself (1969, p. 146). Although those particular characteristics of the experiment that qualify as demand characteristics in a given instance vary with the sophistication of the subject, their operation in a given study will affect the likelihood that the experiment can be replicated. Consequently, it becomes extremely important to determine the kinds of demand characteristics that may be operating, and the degree to which they affect the intended independent variables.

To take an amusing illustration provided by Orne of the generality of demand characteristics, we can refer to the following informal demonstration:

> A number of casual acquaintances were asked whether they would do the experimenter a *favor;* on their acquiescence, they were asked to perform five push-ups. Their response tended to be amazement, incredulity, and the question "Why?". Another similar group of individuals were asked whether they would take part in an *experiment* of brief duration. When they agreed to do so, they too were asked to perform five push-ups. Their typical response was "Where?" [Italics added.]
>
> (1962, p. 777)

As soon as a rather meaningless task is referred to as an "experiment," subjects react cooperatively without hesitation. We must assume that they manufactured some good reason for the push-ups, since a psychologist, who is not likely to tell them the truth anyway, has asked them to commit themselves to *experimental* exertion. It is as though the authority and prestige associated with "experiment," and its verbal associate, "scientific," were enough to induce immediate compliance with anything a "scientific experimenter" might require. But, simultaneously, subjects feel hesitant about voicing their doubts, uncertainties, and justifiable puzzlement. "If he wanted me to know, he'd tell me. But if he tells me, it won't be the truth anyway. I'll have to figure it out for myself." Such is the quandary experimenter prestige and authority produce in subjects.

IMPLICATIONS

Perform the following experiments:

1. Ask several friends to do you a favor: clap their hands together five times, while you time it with your watch. If they perform this task, make note of what they say before and after.

   Next ask some other friends to do the same thing, but this time carry a notebook or clipboard and pencil and hold your wristwatch in your hand while timing. If possible, borrow a white lab coat from someone, and make sure you tell this group of friends that you are conducting an experiment for psychology class. Make note of their responses before and after the task, but explain that you are doing so. Act professionally.

   Compare the subjects' hypotheses about the nature of the task they are performing in both instances. In which instance, are the subjects' guesses about what they're doing more complicated?

2. Now tell both groups of friends several days after their participation that you were doing nothing. You just felt like playing a joke, and the task was meaningless.

   Which group requires more time to accept this explanation?
   Which group is more angered by your honesty?
   Why?

Demand Characteristic: Obedience to "Scientific" Authority

A much more compelling illustration of unhesitating compliance to perceived scientific authority is to be found in the often-cited studies of Stanley Milgram (1963, and 1965).

It is interesting to speculate, in considering the Milgram study, that it investigates as an *experimental* variable what would normally be an unintentional *demand characteristic* of an experiment. Because of the dramatic nature of these experiments, it is probably permissible to break with tradition and to report some of the experimental results before describing the experimental procedures. Milgram gave the following account of the reactions of his experimental subjects:

> Many subjects showed signs of nervousness in the experimental situation, and especially upon administering the more powerful shocks. In a large number of cases the degree of tension reached

extremes that are rarely seen in sociopsychological laboratory studies. Subjects were observed to sweat, tremble, stutter, bite their lips, groan, and dig their fingernails into their flesh. These were characteristic rather than exceptional responses to the experiment.

(1963, p. 375)

One is prompted to ask what possible experimental procedures could bring about such reactions in subjects? The experimental procedures responsible for this outcome are, incidentally, examples of the origin of psychologists' reputation for lying.

Lie Number One: Milgram recruited subjects for a study of "memory and learning" at Yale University through advertisements in local Connecticut newspapers and through direct mail solicitation. The real purpose of the study, however, was to investigate conditions of obedience to perceived authority, but such an admission would destroy any chance of studying obedience. Subjects who volunteered for the "memory study" were drawn from a wide range of blue- and white-collar occupations, and subjects ranged in age from 20 to 50 years.

Lie Number Two: Subjects were told, on arrival at the prestigious Yale laboratory, that they would work together in pairs. One member of the team would be the "learner" and the other member would be the "teacher." In truth, however, the "learner" was not a real subject; he was an accomplice of the experimenter who was prepared to fake a series of reactions to electric shock administered by the real, naive subject-teacher.

Lie Number Three: Real subjects were told a cover story to justify in a credible way the use of electric shock in a memory study. They were given some general information on the relationship between punishment and learning, and were further told that since very little was known about the effects of punishment on various ages and occupations, *this* experiment was designed to test its impact. After the bogus explanation, real and accomplice-subjects drew slips of paper to determine "randomly" who was to be learner and who the teacher. Actually, the drawing was rigged so that only naive subjects would draw teacher-slips, and only accomplices would seem to draw learner-slips.

The Experimental Situation: The accomplice-learner is strapped into a chair and wired with a wrist-electrode. Real subjects (teachers) are told that the electrode is connected to a shock generator in the next room. Actually, this is lie number four; the electrodes are totally nonfunctional. No electric shock can be given through them. But the shock generator in the next room is nonetheless a rather awesome-looking machine, consisting of thirty lever switches set in a horizontal row. Each switch is labeled with a voltage designation ranging from 15 to 450 volts, and a corresponding verbal description ranging from "slight shock" to "moderate shock" to "strong shock," and so forth, up to *"Danger: Severe Shock."* Two remaining switches after this last are labeled ominously: "XXX, 450 volts."

Appropriate buzzes and light flashes accompany depression of a given switch. To further substantiate the aura of authenticity, each naive subject is given a sample shock of 45 volts from a hidden battery wired to make it appear that the shock has come from the shock-generator machine. These real subjects are then instructed in the administration of the learning materials to the "learner." These materials consist of a list of paired words. The teacher reads one member of the pair, and the learner tries to respond with its correct mate through a signaling device from the next room. For each mistake (including no response at all) the teacher is to give a shock to the learner, increasing the intensity by one level for each successive mistake.

The learner responds—unknown to the teacher—with a predetermined pattern of mistakes, and apparently suffers the consequences of his errors quite silently until the 300-volt (intense-shock) level is reached. At this point, the learner pounds on the wall of the room in which he sits bound to his chair. Teachers, somewhat shaken at this point, usually ask for guidance from the experimenter, who, in turn, tells them to continue to the 315-volt level. The learner repeats his pounding on the wall after the 315-volt shock, but then ceases to respond altogether. If the teacher refuses to go past this level, the experimenter responds to him with preplanned, escalating prods: "Please go on," or "The experiment requires that you continue," or "You have no other choice, you *must* continue."

EXPERIMENTAL OUTCOME

The enormous emotional tension engendered in these teacher-subjects has been partially previewed. These responses, you will recall, included sweating, trembling, stuttering, biting of the lips, groaning, and digging their nails into their flesh. On occasion, even more bizarre behavior was observed:

> One sign of tension was the regular occurrence of nervous laughing fits. Fourteen of the 40 subjects showed definite signs of nervous laughter and smiling. The laughter seemed entirely out of place, even bizarre. Full-blown, uncontrollable seizures were observed for 3 subjects. On one occasion we observed a seizure so violently convulsive that it was necessary to call a halt to the experiment. The subject, a 46-year-old encyclopedia salesman, was seriously embarrassed by his untoward and uncontrollable behavior. In the post-experimental interviews subjects took pains to point out that they were not sadistic types, and that the laughter did not mean they enjoyed shocking the victim.
>
> (Milgram, 1963)

The extreme emotional reactions that had been induced in the "teachers" attest convincingly to the conflict they experienced in obeying the perceived authority of the experimenter. Nevertheless, they obeyed.

Really disturbing in its implication was the finding that each of the forty teachers continued administering shocks to the 300-volt, wallpounding level, while only fourteen of the forty defied the experimenter at some level above 300 volts. Further, of the forty subjects, twenty-six continued to obey the orders of the experimenter to proceed with shocks to the most extreme level provided in the shock generator, the ominous "XXX, 450 volts" level.

Milgram appraises his findings this way:

Subjects have learned from childhood that it is a fundamental breech of moral conduct to hurt another person against his will. Yet 26 subjects abandon this tenet in following the instructions of an authority who has no special powers to enforce his commands. To disobey would bring no material loss to the subject; no punishment would ensue.

(1963, p. 376)

Miligram's study shows the degree to which a subject's perception of the "authority" of an experimenter can control his behavior, even at the expense of enduring extreme emotional tension and violating long held personal values. Further studies by Milgram (1965) have shown that the obedience effect decreases with decreasing degrees of perceived prestige and authority. Nonetheless, in terms of the demand characteristics of the experimental situation, perceived "authority" of scientists and science must rank as one of the most potent.

Demand Characteristic: Evaluation Apprehension

Sometimes the perception of the experimenter as an "authority" induces not only compliance but intense suspicion and anxiety in subjects who comply with his demands in order to forestall his negative psychological evaluation. Subjects are suspicious when working with a psychologist because they feel he is constantly making judgments about their mental adjustment or intellectual competence. "Even when the subject is convinced that his adjustment is not being directly studied, he is likely to think that the experimenter is nevertheless bound to be sensitive to any behavior that bespeaks poor adjustment or 'immaturity' " (Rosenberg, 1965, quoted in Rosenberg, 1969, p. 281). The anxiety state thus induced motivates the subject to behave in ways that are likely to win a positive evaluation, or at least to avoid a negative one. Rosenberg (1965) has called this anxiety-toned emotional state "evaluation apprehension."

Evaluation apprehension is a two-edged sword: It prevents the subject from taking the experiment at face value, and it also, therefore, induces him to create his own hypotheses to explain what the experimenter "really wants." Subject-created hypotheses induced by evaluation apprehension can invalidate the theoretical interpretation applied to experimental results because the subject is *not* responding to the experimental variables manipulated by the experimenter, but to what he *thinks* the experimenter intends.

An illustration of the invalidating power of evaluation apprehension can be drawn from the recent debate in psychology over the correct interpretation of dissonance-motivated attitude change. The main assumption of dissonance theory is that individuals strive toward consistency within themselves (Festinger, 1962). In those unusual cases where the individual perceives that his behavior is inconsistent with his thinking, he experiences the psychological discomfort called cognitive dissonance. For example, the individual who smokes and who simultaneously knows that smoking is detrimental to health, endures a certain amount of psychological conflict (Festinger, 1962, p. 2). The resulting dissonance —the existence of nonfitting relations among cognitions—is a motivating factor (1962, p. 3).

The smoker is motivated to reduce his discomfort in a variety of ways. Generally, he can either change his *belief* ("smoking is *not* dangerous") or he can change his *behavior* (quit smoking). Since he is already committed to the behavior of smoking, it is more likely that he will alter the cognition.

Interesting theoretical questions can be derived from dissonance theory. For example, what will an individual do if he is *forced* to comply with some demand that is contrary to what he believes? How will he reduce the resulting dissonance? Dissonance theory predicts that the conflict will force him to change his true belief to correspond to the belief forced upon him by the demanded behavior. Moreover, the greater the dissonance induced in him, the greater the shift to the forced counter-attitude (cf. Brehm, 1960).

One way of forcing an individual to do something he would not normally undertake is to offer him a reward. He will then undertake the task to obtain the reward even though he still does not enjoy complying. So far, little if any dissonance is aroused. But if you offer him *insufficient* reward, and yet *still* get him committed to the task, he then experiences dissonance. (See, for example, Festinger, 1961.) In effect, the subject says to himself: "I am doing something I don't like in order to obtain this reward. But this reward is ridiculously small, yet I *am* committed and I can't back out now. This contradiction makes me uncomfortable."

Dissonance theory now predicts that the insufficiently rewarded individual will reduce his psychological discomfort by changing his troublesome belief, resulting in the conviction that he really likes what he is doing. (Festinger once remarked, tongue-in-cheek: "I sometimes like to summarize all this by saying that rats and people come to love things for which they have suffered" [1961].)

Earlier studies seemed to confirm this prediction (Festinger and Carlsmith, 1959; Brehm, 1960). For example, one study (Cohen, in Brehm and Cohen, 1962) involved paying Yale undergraduates to write brief essays supporting a position opposite to the one that they really held concerning the actions of the New Haven police in a recent campus riot. Since most undergraduates at Yale felt that the police behaved abusively, they were requested to write a counter-attitudinal essay entitled: "Why the actions of the New Haven Police were justified."

Subjects were paid either fifty cents, one dollar, five dollars, or ten dollars to comply. Because dissonance theory predicts that the lower the reward paid for this unpleasant task, the greater will be the dissonance aroused, subjects receiving only fifty cents should show greater attitude change than any other subjects in the direction of opinion expressed by the essay. Furthermore, the effect should be proportional so that subjects paid one dollar will show less shift in attitude in the pro-police direction than the fifty-cent subjects, while five-dollar receivers will show even less, in similar decreasing magnitude to the ten dollar subjects, who should evidence little or no attitude change. Being paid ten dollars to write a disagreeable essay is sufficient justification to engage in the unpleasant act without inducing dissonance. Results show that the fifty-cents and one-dollar groups shifted their attitudes most in the pro-police direction, while the five- and ten-dollar groups showed no significant change in their anti-police feelings. Thus far the cognitive-dissonance explanation seems borne out.

Suppose, however, that these changes stem *not* from the arousal of cognitive dissonance in the underpaid subjects, but result instead from the arousal of evaluation apprehension in the overpaid five and ten dollar subjects. On this assumption, Rosenberg (1965) proposed a different interpretation of the experiment. Large monetary rewards for counter-attitudinal essay writing, he reasoned, are likely to arouse the subject's suspicion. He may well feel that the experiment has little to do with his feelings about police on campus, and instead, concerns some form of *psychological* evaluation of *him*.

As a result the typical subject . . . may be aroused to a comparatively high level of evaluation apprehension; . . . he may be led to hypothesize that the experimental situation is one in which his autonomy, his honesty, his resoluteness in resisting a special kind of bribe, are being tested.

(Rosenberg, 1965, quoted in
Rosenberg, 1969, p. 286)

KEY CONCEPTS

Cognitive Dissonance

Here is a shortened account of cognitive dissonance theory by its creator, Leon Festinger.

Two elements are dissonant if, for one reason or another, they do not fit together. They may be inconsistent or contradictory, culture or group standards may dictate that they do not fit, and so on. . . .

These two elements are in a dissonant relation if, considering these two alone, the obverse of one element would follow from the other. To state it a bit more formally, x and y are dissonant—if not x follows from y. Thus, for example, if a person knew there were only friends in his vicinity and also felt afraid, there would be a dissonant relation between these two cognitive elements. Or, for another example, if a person were already in debt and also purchased a new car, the corresponding cognitive elements would be dissonant with one another. [Italics added.]

The reduction of dissonance:

The presence of dissonance gives rise to pressures to reduce or eliminate the dissonance. The strength of the pressures to reduce the dissonance is a function of the magnitude of the dissonance. In other words, dissonance acts in the same way as a state of drive or need or tension. The presence of dissonance leads to action to reduce it just as, for example, the presence of hunger leads to action to reduce the hunger. . . . if dissonance exists between two elements, this dissonance can be eliminated by changing one of those elements.

(Festinger, 1962, pp. 9–18)

Try this experiment:

There is an experiment in psychology that you can perform easily in your own home if you have a child three or four years old. Buy two toys that you are fairly sure will be equally attractive to the child. Show them both to him and say: 'Here are two nice toys. This one is for you to keep. The other must go back to the store.' You then hand the child the toy that is his to keep and ask: "Which of the two toys do you like better?" Studies have shown that in such a situation most children will tell you they prefer the toy they are to keep.*

(Festinger, 1962, in R. C. Atkinson, 1971, p. 409)

Subjects who form this hypothesis about the real nature of the experiment are likely to be only those to whom the extravagant five- and ten-dollar rewards are offered. Therefore, their suspicions aroused, and their anger triggered, they write the essay and reason as follows: "They probably want to see whether getting paid so much will affect my own attitude, whether it will influence me, whether I am the kind of person whose views can be changed by buying him off" (Rosenberg, 1969).

When any subsequent attempt is made to measure their attitudes about police, these apprehensive and angered subjects resist, and they express their resentful resistance by refusing to reveal anything but strong disapproval for the police. Evaluation apprehension, not cognitive dissonance motivation, could plausibly be the cause of these experimental results. The matter can be decided only by further experimentation. Rosenberg replicated this study with a different attitude issue, but avoided making the dissonance-arousing segment of the study seem connected to the attitude measuring procedures. When subjects thought the essay writing and its associated rewards had nothing to do with the experimenter's questions about their feelings on the issue, results came out just opposite to the dissonance prediction: the greater the reward, the *more* attitude change occurred (Rosenberg, 1965).

As a consequence, it is now customary in dissonance experiments to control for the possibility of such demand characteristics by separating dissonance-arousal and attitude measurement. The important point, however, is that evaluation apprehension may be involved in any psychological experiment, and unless control procedures appropriate to the given study are instituted, subjects are likely to respond to *their own* hypotheses.

Demand Characteristic: Pygmalion Effects

Pygmalion, a sculptor, carves an ivory statue of his ideal of womanhood. He falls desperately in love with the statue, praying, hoping, wishing that it could be brought to life. In answer to his prayers, Venus brings the statue to life. Moral of the story: If you wish strongly enough, the imagined can be realized.

The mythological story of Pygmalion is a rather apt portrayal of another form of demand characteristic in experimentation called the "self-fulfilling prophecy" by Merton (1948). If you, or an experimenter, predicts the outcome of some series of events, wishful thinking or gullible fatalism may be responsible for subtle changes in your behavior that actually make the event come to pass. For example, suppose that at a party in the presence of someone who you know dislikes you, you think: "How awful it would be if I spilled this plate of potato salad in my lap. I would look like a fool." Of course, the thought barely is through your mind when you're red-facedly scraping mayonnaise and potato chunks from your suit.

Freud dealt with a number of such unconsciously motivated acts, grouping them under the heading *Psychopathology of Everyday Life* (1938a). Freud, however, would be more likely to predict the "accidental" spilling of the potato salad into the lap of your tormentor.

Wish-fulfilling behavior, or self-fulfilling prophecies, may be subtly responsible for the outcome of investigations that, Pygmalion-like, involve strongly held convictions and expectations on the part of the experimenter. Rosenthal and Jacobson, for example, have investigated the effects of teachers' expectations on the performance of their pupils (1968; and 1971, in R. Atkinson (ed), pp. 448–52). (The heading for this section, "Pygmalion Effects," is borrowed from the title of their book: *Pygmalion in the Classroom.*) The jumping-off point for Rosenthal and Jacobson's research was the suspicion that the cliché explanation of culturally disadvantaged children's poor school performance obscured a more fundamental cause:

> The reason usually given for the poor performance of the disadvantaged child is simply that the child is a member of a disadvantaged group. There may well be another reason. It is that the child does poorly in school because that is what is expected of him.
>
> (1971, p. 448)

Using students and teachers of an elementary school, called Oak School in the study, Rosenthal and Jacobson systematically misinformed teachers about the nature of their pupils and the purposes of the study. Teachers were told that the investigators were validating a new test of intellectual development called "The Test of Inflected Acquisition." Actually, the test was a standardized measure of intelligence with which most teachers were not familiar.

In May 1964 the test was administered to all students in kindergarten and grades one through five. Oak School draws most of its students from lower-class families, and it provides a three-track system whereby each grade from first through sixth is divided into three classes: below-average, average, and above-average achievement.

Without reference to their actual performance on the test, 20 per cent of the children in the various classes of the six grade levels studied were *randomly* selected as potential academic spurters. The actual number amounted to about five children, so designated, per classroom. Nonchalantly, at the first staff meeting of the year, the names of the children were revealed to the teachers with the offhand remark: "By the way, in case you're interested in who did what in those tests we're doing for

Harvard . . . " Thus the only differences between the designated children and the remaining "control group" of children were in the minds of the teachers (1971, p. 451).

All of the children retook the test three more times: four months into the school year, at the end of the school year, and again in May of the following year.

EXPERIMENTAL RESULTS

At the end of the school year, teachers of Oak School were asked to describe the classroom behavior of their pupils. The data show that the randomly chosen "intellectual spurters" were described as

> . . . having a better chance of being successful in later life and as being happier, more curious and more interesting than the other children. There was also a tendency for the designated children to be seen as more appealing, better adjusted, and more affectionate, and as less in need of social approval. In short, the children for whom intellectual growth was expected became more alive and autonomous intellectually, or at least were so perceived by their teachers.
>
> (1971, p. 451)

Another interesting and unexpected result was the finding that undesignated children, who were not expected to gain, but who nevertheless actually showed improvement comparable to the designates, were rated *poorly* by teachers. In fact, the teacher ratings of such children who improved against expectation were even *lower* than the ratings of undesignated children who did not improve and who did not, therefore, violate teachers' preconceptions. In other words, for a child in the slow track who shows gains *against expectations,* "it is likely to be difficult . . . even if his I.Q. is rising, to be seen by his teacher as well adjusted and as a potentially successful student" (1971, p. 451).

How do Rosenthal and Jacobson account for their findings? Ruling out the possibility on the basis of their data that teachers spend more time and expend greater effort with designated children, the researchers offered the following hypothesis:

> It would seem that the explanation we are seeking lies in a subtler feature of the interaction of the teacher and her pupils. Her tone of voice, facial expression, touch and posture may be the means by which—*probably quite unwittingly—she communicates her expectations* to the pupils. Such communication might help the child by changing his conception of himself, his anticipation of his own behavior, his motivation or his cognitive skills. [Italics added.]
>
> (1971, p. 452)

IMPLICATIONS

Review the concepts of magical thinking developed in Chapter 1, with particular reference to Piaget's explanation of magico-phenomenalistic thinking.

1. Is cognitive dissonance a form of magical thinking?
2. Are the motivations for magical thinking and for the reduction of cognitive dissonance similar? Be specific.
3. Here is a facetious example of cognitive dissonance. In what way is it similar or different from magical thinking?

> Let us imagine a person who is given to pacing up and down in his living room at home. Let us further imagine that for some unknown reason he always jumps over one particular spot on the floor. The cognitive element corresponding to his jumping over that spot is undoubtedly dissonant with his knowledge that the floor at that spot is level, strong, and in no way different from any other part of the floor. If, some evening when his wife is away from home, he breaks a hole in the floor at that exact spot, he would completely eliminate the dissonance. The cognition that there is a hole in the floor would be quite consonant with the knowledge that he jumps over the place where the hole exists.
>
> (Festinger, 1962, p. 20)

This teacher expectation study is a rather good model of the demand characteristics inherent in the experimenter's attitudes, values, and aspirations which he may communicate during the course of his interaction with subjects, and which may help to fulfill his privately held prophecy. It is apparent that not only can subjects have expectations about experiments and experimenters, but the equally fallible human experimenter may harbor his own set of potentially contaminating biases: "People are more alike than they are different."

Hawthorne Effects, Volunteer Effects, and Things That Go Bump in the Night

Suspicions, apprehensions, misinterpretations, and self-fulfilling prophecies can have biasing effects on research. Although we have surveyed a variety of these artifacts, grouping them under the general title introduced by Orne of "demand characteristics," there are other forms of potential artifact-production in experimentation that deserve brief mention.

1. *The Hawthorne effect* is named for the Hawthorne plant of the Western Electric company in Chicago, in which a series of workers' performance studies was conducted some years ago (Roethlisberger and Dickson, 1939). The major aim of that series of studies was to investigate the effect on female workers of changes in such conditions as

illumination, temperature, rest periods, wages, and others. A startling result that emerged from the studies was that *any change* in conditions increased the girls' work output. Even when experimental manipulations brought about conditions that objectively make work more difficult, work output continued to increase. The reason was a simple one: the workers perceived almost any manipulation on the part of the experimenters as evidencing respect for and interest in them. Their morale was given a boost just by being part of a "scientific" investigation; the company was taking an interest in them.

In a sense, it is possible to conceive of the "Hawthorne effect" as the opposite of apprehension evaluation. Instead of arousing the distrust of the workers, the experimenters provided an inadvertent boost to self-esteem. Campbell (1957 and 1969) has coined the term "reactive arrangements" to refer to situations such as this one, where the very act of studying a behavioral phenomenon changes the nature of the event.

2. As for *volunteer effects,* Rosenthal and Rosnow (1969 and Rosnow and Rosenthal 1970) have proposed that the most ubiquitous source of artifact* in behavioral experiments is the volunteer system of securing subjects. In most experimental designs, it is assumed that the subjects engaged in the task are a representative sample of people at large. Rosenthal and Rosnow make a case for the opposite conclusion: volunteers are substantially different from people who do not volunteer.

Although we cannot summarize all of the relevant research here, these authors have provided a brief summary of some pertinent facts about the distinction between volunteers and nonvolunteers:

> On the basis of studies conducted both in the laboratory and in the field, it seemed reasonable to postulate with some confidence that the following characteristics would be found more often among people who volunteer. . . .
> 1. Higher educational level
> 2. Higher occupational status
> 3. Higher need for approval
> 4. Higher intelligence
> 5. Lower authoritarianism
>
> With less confidence we can also postulate that more often than non-volunteers, volunteers tend to be:
> 6. More sociable
> 7. More arousal seeking
> 8. More unconventional
> 9. More often firstborn
> 10. Younger

(1969, p. 111)

---

* The word *artifact* is usually used to describe some man-made object. In the present context of experimental design, artifact refers to *unintentional* man-made (experimenter or subject) effects introduced into the experimental situation.

KEY CONCEPTS

The Quiet Revolution: Varieties of Experimental Artifact

The essence of the quiet revolution is that psychologists have begun to realize that psychology is a unique science in its attempt to establish coherent explanations of human behavior using human subjects in its investigations. Human subjects, unlike the passive particles of physics or chemistry, have ideas, values, and interpretations of their own which affect their behavior in the experiment. Often, more than the independent variable is responsible for the outcome of a psychological study. In fact, the psychological experiment might best be conceived in terms of a social-psychological event, to use Orne's terms, or as a mutual interaction of two very-much-alike human beings, to use Sullivan's terms.

Varieties of Artifact

1. Experimenter-Subject Misinterpretation. Experimenter thinks the subject thinks that he is engaged on such and such a task; the subject thinks that the experimenter *really* thinks he is engaged in doing something else.

2. Demand Characteristics. Implicit and explicit cues of the experimental setting or of the experimenter's behavior are discrepant with the "forthright" explanation given to the subject. Subject now feels compelled to create his own hypothesis about the meaning of the experimental task.

3. Perceived Authority. Prestige associated with things "scientific" assures ready and unhesitant cooperation from most individuals, even when the task is meaningless or involves profound conflict with long-cherished values or personal ideals.

4. Pygmalion Effects. Experimenter expectations of the self-fulfilling prophecy type surreptitiously alter the ongoing event in the direction of fulfilling the experimenter's hypothesis.

5. Evaluation Apprehension. When working with a psychologist, most subjects are motivated to avoid expected negative evaluations. Subtle changes in their behavior unrelated to the independent variable are the result.

6. Hawthorne Effects. Subtle changes in behavior result in subjects who perceive participation in a scientific investigation as a mark of honor. Opposite to evaluation apprehension, the Hawthorne-effected subject perceives the experimental manipulation as evidencing interest or respect for them.

7. Volunteer Effects. Subjects on which most psychological research is based may not be a representative sample of people in general. I.Q., occupational, and motivational differences exist.

It thus seems possible that the subjects of experiments, individuals on whom is based the majority of psychological theorizing, may be a rather select, nonrandom, nonrepresentative group of humans.

Summary: The Life of an Artifact

A quiet revolution has been occurring in psychology. Experimenters have begun to focus on the active, dynamic, motivated aspects of the subjects with whom they work. We have seen several varieties of this influence on experimentation. Clearly the common denominator that binds these diverse artifacts together is the recognition that psychology deals with a unique creature, the thinking human.

McGuire has proposed a three-stage life history for the scientific artifact:

> At first, the researchers seem unaware of the variable producing the artifact and tend even *to deny it* when its possibility is pointed out to them. The second stage begins as its existence and possible importance become undeniable. In this *coping phase,* researchers tend to recognize and even overstress the artifact's importance. They give a great deal of attention to devising procedures which will reduce its contaminating influence and its limiting of the generalizability of experimental results. The third stage, *exploitation,* grows out of the considerable cogitation during the coping stage to understand the artifactual variable so as to eliminate it from the experimental situation. In their attempt to cope, some researchers almost inevitably become interested in the artifactual variable in its own right. It then begins to receive research attention, not as a contaminating factor to be eliminated, but as an interesting independent variable in its own right. [Italics added.]
>
> (1969, pp. 15–16)

McGuire's three stages of denial, coping, and exploitation in the life of the artifact are at least partially comparable to Kuhn's stages of scientific revolution: normal science (denial); anomaly (coping), and revolution (exploitation). It would be well not to underestimate the importance of the similarity since the virtual interchangeability of McGuire's and Kuhn's stages suggests that psychology may have reached something of a plateau in its growth to maturity.

It might be instructive to speculate briefly on the similarity of the first two stages of each theorist and to focus on their common factor of a vested interest in maintaining the status quo. Leslie White proposed the following question about science:

Generalizing broadly, we may say that the physical sciences appeared earlier and have developed farther than the biological sciences; the biological sciences took form earlier and have developed farther than the social sciences. The question naturally arises, Why has this been so?

(1947, in Fried, 1968, p. 16)

White's answer takes us back to the main concepts of Chapter 1 in which we reviewed man's progress from a magical explanation of events to a naturalistic explanation in terms of observation. With magical explanation and animistic thinking, man interprets the universe in terms of self, in terms of his own experiences. Piaget's children showed the same egocentrism. By the time he progresses to natural explanation, man is more willing to concede that things exist in their own right, subject to explainable and repeatable external causes. This progression from self-explanation to external explanation corresponds to the order of the development of the sciences:

The distinction between the self and the not-self was achieved in astronomy and physics before it was made in physiology and psychology because it was *easier* of accomplishment in the former. . . . *And it was easier because the phenomena of astronomy and physics are more remote and less significant as determinants of human behavior than are the processes of physiology and psychology.*

(White, in Fried, 1968, p. 18)

In short, White is proposing that scientific revolution comes last to sciences that deal most directly with man himself because it is these sciences that find it most difficult to externalize the self and to treat it as a natural phenomenon. This reasoning may in part account for the intellectual resistance to change shown by normal science and the denial stage of an artifact's existence.

At worst, White's reasoning is an imaginative speculation that might serve well as food for thought. He has formalized his hypothesis in the form of a law of scientific development.

Science emerges first and matures fastest in fields where the determinants of human behavior are weakest and most remote; conversely, science appears latest and matures slowest in those portions of our experience where the most intimate and powerful determinants of our behavior are found.

(1947, in 1968, p. 19)

If White is correct, psychology is one of the last sciences to mature because its practitioners find it most difficult to objectify and externalize subject matter of which they themselves are a part.

The intellectual drag that characterizes the conservative phase of normal science and the reluctance that characterizes the denial stage in the investigation of artifacts may be rooted in this emotional paradox. Consider, for example, the emotional resistance Darwin's theory of evolution and Freud's theory of infantile sexuality encountered. When the science's subject matter happens to involve people, methodological difficulties ride hand in hand with the psychological threat posed by scientists' predilection for depersonalization of their subject matter. Yet, White argues, it is just this capacity to depersonalize and to objectify phenomena that characterizes the advanced science.

Human scientific psychologists have begun to develop experimental methods for studying human subjects in ways that are consistent with the scientific goal of understanding and appropriate to the complex cognitive nature of the understood.

KEY CONCEPTS

McGuire (1969) has proposed that the discovery and course of research in the life of an artifact progresses through three stages.

The Life of an Artifact

1. Denial Stage. At first when it seems possible that some experimental results may be due to "uncontrolled" factors, or unexpected causes, scientists marshal evidence to deny the existence of the artifact. Its very possibility threatens the foundations of scientific accomplishment.

2. Coping Stage. When it becomes clear that an artifact has been discovered, scientists exert effort to bring its operation under control and to devise techniques to limit its influence.

3. Exploitation Stage. In their efforts to cope, some scientists become interested in the artifact as a phenomenon in itself. It is no longer perceived as a contaminating factor, but as an interesting independent variable.

Coping with Experimental Artifact

The quiet revolution we have been considering would be a sterile revolution if it did not motivate psychologists to develop new procedures for coping with experimental artifacts, and, indeed, to exploit their significance. Orne has sardonically commented: "It never fails to amaze me that some colleagues go to the trouble of inducing human subjects to participate in their experiments and then squander the major difference between man and animal—the ability to talk and reflect upon experience" (1969, p. 153).

Asking experimental subjects what they think, once a source of great reluctance among behaviorists, has become the cornerstone of cognitively oriented, social psychologists' strategies for dealing with artifact. We will briefly examine several of these strategies for dealing with artifact, but it is important to keep in mind that in experimental methodology, such procedures are relatively recent additions which signal the conquering of a profound investigative myopia. Spielberger and DeNike (1966) make this point very well:

> It seems reasonable to conjecture that biologists of an earlier generation who did not believe in *protozoa* probably contended at times that objects too small to be observed by the naked eye were irrelevant to *scientific* analysis (of disease, for instance). . . .
>
> Similarly, we might expect that present day psychologists who consider thoughts and hypotheses to be beyond the limits of "scientific" inquiry would not vigorously search for them in experimental subjects. Furthermore, we should not be surprised to find that such psychologists were uninterested and unskilled in evaluating cognitive phenomena which for them do not exist.

The methods devised to cope with potential artifacts are, to a degree, all techniques for monitoring the subject's and experimenter's expectations and interpretations with an eye toward controlling them.

IMPLICATIONS

Using McGuire's concepts of denial, coping, and exploitation as stages in the life of an artifact, decide:

1. What stage scientific psychology is now in. Offer evidence.
2. Which of the artifacts discussed in the text is most likely to lend itself to exploitation.

Monitoring the Subject's Interpretations

1. POSTEXPERIMENTAL INQUIRY

It is becoming a widespread practice among psychologists who work with human subjects to sit down with each individual after the experiment and *judiciously* inquire about the perceived demand characteristics of the study. Such an interview requires great skill if it is not to introduce new demand characteristics into the situation.

Orne (1969) recommends that the postexperimental inquiry be conducted by an investigator other than the psychologist who conducted the study. In such a case, it is unlikely that the interviewer would communicate the experimenter's hypotheses, or other cues, and is more likely that the subject's conversation would reveal what he actually experienced during the experiment. Perhaps the greatest danger involved in asking subjects what they thought and felt during the experiment is the "pact of ignorance":

> The subject knows that if he has "caught on" to some apparent deception and has an excess of information about the experimental procedure he may be disqualified from participation and thus have wasted his time. The experimenter is aware that the subject who knows too much or has "caught on" to his deception will have to be disqualified; disqualification means running yet another subject, still further delaying completion of his study. *Hence, neither party to the inquiry wants to dig very deeply.* [Italics added.]
>
> (Orne, 1969, p. 153)

The main requirement of the interviewer, therefore, is a genuine interest in discovering what his subjects experienced, rather than a single-minded concern for rapid data collection.

While it is important, Orne points out, that the interviewer be someone other than the experimenter, it is equally important that he not be perceived as someone checking up on the experimenter. In this case, the subject is likely to be motivated to protect the experimenter, responding with something less than an honest appraisal of his experiences.

There are other shortcomings to the postexperimental inquiry as a technique for artifact control; the following are based on Orne's views (1969):

1. Postexperimental inquiry comes at the end of a long and complex chain of experiences which the subject may not fully remember, may not be able to verbalize, or may not have perceived in the first place.
2. Subject's perceptions of the demand characteristics may have changed during the course of the experiment. His perceptions before and after he "caught on" might well be different producing different patterns of responding at various times throughout the experiment.

3. A more sophisticated version of postexperimental inquiry would involve removing subjects at various times throughout the experiment, conducting the inquiry to sample their present opinions, and dismissing them from further participation. Unfortunately, such a procedure is time consuming and expensive.

Yet another purpose of the postexperimental inquiry, besides assessing subject interpretation and expectation, is illustrated by those experiments that involve some form of deception. As in the Milgram study of obedience considered earlier, it is necessary and ethically demanded that subjects be de-hoaxed. They must be told the real purpose of the experiment, and if possible, how their performance compares to others in the experiment. Above all, they must not leave the experimental situation wondering and concerned about their own mental competence (cf. Campbell, 1969, p. 371).

Clearly, postexperimental inquiry leaves a great deal to be desired as a method of artifact control. Nonetheless, such procedures forestall the even more undesirable result of invalid data, or hopelessly confused interpretations.

2. PRE-EXPERIMENTAL INQUIRY: THE NONEXPERIMENT

A still more powerful technique for monitoring subjects' expectations and interpretations of a research study is the nonexperiment. (Ulric Neisser coined this term, cited in Orne, 1969; see also Riecken, 1962.) For the nonexperiment or pre-experimental inquiry, a group of individuals from the same population as the actual experimental subjects are asked to imagine themselves participating in the experiment. Great pains are taken to provide these nonexperimental subjects with as much exposure to information about the real experiment as possible: they are shown the equipment, taken into the experimental setting; they listen to the same instructions as will real subjects, but *they never engage in the experiment.* Now, the non-subject is asked to respond the way he thinks he would have had he actually been in the experiment. Thus, the nonexperimental subject produces data similar to real experimental-subject data, but only on the basis of what he *perceives* the experiment to be, and how he *imagines* he would act.

His responses, theoretically, are solely the result of perceived demand characteristics, not of experimental variables. Comparisons are now possible between the real experimental subjects' data and the nonexperimental subjects' responses. "If these two kinds of data are identical, it shows only that the subject population in the actual experiment could have guessed what was expected of them. It does not tell us whether such guesses were the actual determinants of their behavior" (Orne, 1969, p. 156).

An interesting example of the use of the pre-experimental type of inquiry is to be found in Orne's research (1959) into the nature of hypnotism. One of the central hypotheses of Orne's study was that "much hypnotic behavior results from the subject's conception of the role of the hypnotic as determined by past experience and learning, and by explicit and implicit cues provided by the hypnotist and situation." In other words, a good part of the behavior associated with hypnotic trance may be the result of perceived demand characteristics.

To test the validity of this possibility, two groups of subjects were presented to Orne for him to hypnotize. One of the groups was told to fake their responses and attempt to "really fool Dr. Orne." They were further instructed that Orne knew some subjects would be faking, but that he had no idea who they were. This, in fact, was the truth.

Briefly, the results show that real and faking subjects are indistinguishable to a pair of independent observers. Analgesia for pain, for instance, was inducted in all subjects by the hypnotist and it is reasonable to suppose that faking subjects would show marked differences to real subjects in their capacity to tolerate discomfort. (The experimenter forcibly flexes the tip of the subject's little finger and then presses his thumbnail into the back of the same finger.) Employment of such techniques failed to discriminate between real and faking subjects. In fact, when electric shock was employed as the pain stimulus, it was found that the faking group tolerated the discomfort better and flinched less than real subjects. Only through postexperimental inquiry were differences between real and fake subjects apparent. Other behavioral differences did emerge, but the startling finding was that demand characteristics account for a very large portion of hypnotic behavior. Nonexperimental (faking) subjects thus served a very valuable role of demonstrating, by contrast to the behavior of real subjects, those aspects of hypnotic trance that cannot be accounted for in terms of perceived demand characteristics.

It seems reasonably clear from our discussion that the pre-experimental (nonexperiment) inquiry requiring subjects to produce imaginary data serves as a useful check on demand characteristics. As Orne has pointed out:

> Only when we succeed in setting up an experiment where the results are counterexpectational in the sense that a preinquiry would yield different findings from those obtained from the subjects in the actual situation can we be relatively comfortable that these findings represent the real effects of the experimental treatment rather than being subject to alternative explanations.
>
> (1969, pp. 157–58)

3. THE DISGUISED EXPERIMENT

If it is true that the subject's knowledge that he is participating in an experiment affects his behavior, then a simple solution to the problem would seem to be some form of deception to conceal the fact.

Almost all introductory psychology students have been exposed to what Campbell (1969) calls the "gleeful reporting of deception experiments" to the extent that at least some students believe that the first step of scientific method is lying. (Recall Orne's subject: "Psychologists always lie!")

In some cases, outright deception may not be necessary. Instead, the investigator may design a nonreactive setting in which to collect his data (Campbell, 1969). Such a setting usually means that the respondents are unaware of participating in an experiment. Typically, such research is conducted in natural settings as opposed to the laboratory. For example, Campbell describes an unpublished study of Schaps on the helping behavior of shoe salesmen as a function of customer dependency. A woman with a broken heel may elicit different responses from the salesman than a customer without this handicap. Likewise, salesmen may react differently to a woman alone as compared to a woman accompanied by a companion. Such observations can be made without the salesman's awareness that he is being scrutinized. But it is important to note, as Campbell points out, that such techniques raise serious ethical and moral questions about the invasion of privacy and the matter of compensation for participation.

Unfortunately, the obvious limitation of such procedures is their dependence on the restrictions of the natural setting, and on the ingenuity of the experimenter in devising relevant and provocative hypotheses to test in such surroundings. (Cf. Chapter 2, Natural Observation.)

Monitoring the Experimenter's Expectations

We turn now to a brief consideration of some techniques of monitoring the experimenter's expectations about the outcome of an experiment and the possible effect of these expectations on the behavior of subjects.

It is possible that Pygmalion effects exist not only in the classroom, but in the animal laboratory as well, where human experimenters are the observers of rats' maze-learning performance. Rosenthal (Rosenthal and Fode, 1963, cited in Rosenthal, 1969) reports an intriguing study in which experimental psychology students were systematically misled about the maze-learning ability of their rats. Half the students were told that they were working with "maze-bright" rats, animals that had been selectively inbred for superior maze-solving ability. The remaining half of the class of student experimenters were told that they were working with "maze-dull" animals. Relatively simple in procedure, the learning task required rats to run to the darker side of a two-arm T-maze. When the animal ran to the correct side, he was rewarded with food.

From the first day of the experiment, "animals *believed* to be better performers *became* better performers. Animals believed to be brighter showed a daily improvement in their performance, while those believed to be dull improved only to the third day and then showed a worsening of performance" (Rosenthal, 1969, p. 199).

After the experiment was terminated, the student experimenters rated their own and their rats' performance. The reason for the drastic difference between the ersatz "maze-bright" and "maze-dull" rats became clear: students led to believe they were working with intelligent animals saw their animals as more pleasant and more likeable. These experimenters were thus more relaxed around their animals and handled their rats not only more often, but more gently than students who were led to expect that their rats were dummies. *Problem:* how can experimenters' attitudes be controlled and how can this experiment be redesigned to avoid the difficulty?

1. SINGLE- AND DOUBLE-BLIND TECHNIQUES

The most obvious step to be taken in controlling experimenters' expectations is to keep from them the identity of the group with which they are working and knowledge of the experimental treatment to which this group has been exposed. In this way, the lack of certain knowledge about the nature of their subjects prevents the experimenters from acting in a systematically different way toward different subjects. Such a procedure—where the experimenter remains ignorant of the characteristics of his treatment groups—is called a single blind. However, in some experiments that involve humans, a double blind is called for. A good example of the double blind is the traditional drug study in which patients in a hospital setting are given some medication designed to relieve the symptoms of a disease. In orthodox experimental manner, half the patients receive a placebo or inert substance as a control for the possibility that mere knowledge of receiving a drug for their illness makes some people feel better. (Incidentally, the word "placebo" is Latin for "I shall please.") Unfortunately this control is effective only for patient expectations; researchers who administer the drug know which patients received the real substance and who received the placebo. It is possible, therefore, that the researchers may treat differently patients who have received the real substance and patients who are placebo patients, lavishing more attention, more real concern, and more consistent medical care on these more "interesting" patients.

Any results that emerge would be contaminated with these factors so that any improvements in drug patients might be the result of the intensified medical attention rather than the curative powers of the drug. In such a situation, a double-blind procedure is necessary. Neither the patients *nor* the researchers are aware of the identity of the drug patients and placebo patients. Only independent observers who are not actively engaged in medical care with these people know who received what.

Double-blind and single-blind techniques are customary procedures not only in drug studies, but in any psychological assessment routine that involves a determination of the effect of differential treatment for various groups of individuals. Consequently, double-blind and single-blind techniques have found their way into social and personality psychological research, ranging from the evaluation of various forms of psychotherapy to the administration of preschool learning materials; from studies on retention and recall of nonsense syllables to investigations of the functioning of the nervous system.

2. MULTIPLE MEASUREMENTS

Our last example of a technique of coping with experimental artifact produced by experimenter expectation is not really a technique at all, and it is not limited to controlling experimenter expectations. It is more nearly a fundamental principle of research. In its simplest form the principle states that when any measurement is to be undertaken, there will be error from a variety of sources. Therefore, measurements should be repeated several times, using several different methods of measuring the same thing (cf. Campbell, 1969; and Mischel, 1968).

Repetition of measurement improves the reliability of the result, while variety of measurement technique increases the likelihood of discovering important interactions among variables. Within a single experimental design, therefore, it is desirable to include several variations of administration of the experimental treatment and several modes of assessing its effects (Cf. Cronbach, Gleser, Nanda, and Rajaratnam, 1972, Ch. 1). Sophisticated statistical techniques have been devised for this purpose, but without getting enmeshed in the details, we can list several advantages of multiple measurement (modified from Cronbach *et al.,* 1972, p. 2):

1. Ambiguities concealed in single measurement design may be revealed.
2. Interactions among the experimental variables can be assessed.
3. One multimeasure study can answer several questions that formerly required many single sets of data.

To take a commonsense example, suppose that a researcher were interested in the effectiveness of some form of psychotherapy. What criteria would he be willing to accept as evidencing a favorable outcome for a given patient under a given form of treatment? Does he accept the therapist's rating of the individual; does he accept the patient's rating of his own improvement? Perhaps, the researcher could turn to members of the patient's immediate family and ask them to rate his behavior before and after psychotherapy? Or an external criterion like the time required for the patient to return to work and to lead a productive existence might be the best measure.

In actuality, the outcome problem in psychotherapy is a difficult one, and the solution seems to be the use of multiple measurements. That is, all of these procedures, and more, would be attempted and compared. In this way, multiple criteria combine to provide a picture that is relatively unbiased by any one viewpoint. It also makes possible the

KEY CONCEPTS

Dealing with Artifacts: Monitoring Expectations

Monitoring Subjects' Expectations

1. Postexperimental Inquiry. Subject is asked what he felt, perceived, thought, and expected during the experiment.

2. Pre-experimental Inquiry: Nonexperimental subjects are asked to *imagine* how they would respond to the experimental variables. Comparisons are then made with subjects' responses to the real experimental variables.

3. Disguised Experiments. In nonreactive arrangements subjects are unaware that they are participating in an experiment. Limited to natural settings, or to extraordinarily successful deception.

Monitoring the Experimenter's Expectations

1. Single and Double Blind. Subjects and/or experimenters remain unaware of the treatment conditions to which subjects have been exposed.

2. Multiple Measurement. Experiment is designed to study some phenomenon from several aspects at once. Variety of measurement of same outcome is undertaken simultaneously to improve reliability of interpretation and to shed light on possible unsuspected interactions.

discovery of new relationships among variables that would not be available in a single measure design. Data might show that when the patient's therapist and family agree that he is improved but his own ratings do not, it is best to continue therapy or change its form. (Cf. Bergin, 1971, for a thorough review of the outcome problem in psychotherapy.)

Conclusion

We have come a long way from our point of departure—the nature of scientific progress and revolution. An essential point that bears reiterating is that experimental methodology is not infallible. It is, however, a close approximation to reliable observation and measurement of reality, and such refinements in technique as we have discussed are likely to improve experimental method still further. This acknowledgement of the potential fallibility of experimental method with human subjects is what we have been referring to as the quiet revolution. At least part of the revolution has been the motivation to develop control procedures to deal effectively with the possible artifacts that result from subject and experimenter cognitions.

Orne has pointed out that procedures like pre- and postexperimental inquiry and simulating subjects are really *quasi controls*. The term is meant to point out the partial similarity of these subjects to traditional control-group subjects while emphasizing the fact of their differences. Quasi-controls do not permit inference about the effects of the real experimental variables. Since they have not been exposed to the independent variable, they serve, by contrast to those who have, to suggest alternatives to the orthodox independent-variable explanation of the outcome. Quasi-controls thus clarify the demand characteristics of experimental design and permit the design of better procedures (Orne, 1969).

Overview of the Chapter

Sherlock Holmes was a master gamesman. The contrast between Holmes' fascination with intellectual puzzles and Watson's puzzlement with Holmes' fascination illustrates the unique characteristics, and the layman's attempt to comprehend them, of the puzzle-solving scientist.

For T. S. Kuhn, science proceeds through several phases of development toward major discovery and the revolution of existing thought. In the first phase of development, the pre-paradigm stage, a variety of viewpoints or schools of thought exist side by side in their attempt to account for natural phenomena.

Eventually, this diversity disappears as one of the schools achieves a synthesis of existing explanations capable of converting the members of the scientific community to a unified methodological and conceptual approach. Called "normal science," this phase is characterized chiefly by possession of a paradigm or theory that binds the scientific community into a coherent discipline, and by the intensive efforts of this community to articulate and extend the synthesizing paradigm to known natural phenomena. Guided by its paradigm, Normal Science proceeds in a relatively conservative way to select problems which have forseeable solutions and to reject those violations of paradigm expectation that are accidentally uncovered. Scientists are committed to solving puzzles dictated by the paradigm, and at first to rejecting or dismissing puzzles which fail to be solvable according to the paradigm's rules of the game.

Eventually the anomalies—exceptions to the rules—force the scientific community's attention to the failure of the paradigm to account for significant novel events. Loosening of the rules results in the anomaly assuming major importance for the discipline.

Ultimately, in the fourth and last stage, a new paradigm emerges which is able to account for the anomaly, and which provides the foundation for an entirely new world view for members of the profession. This remolding of the discipline and its rules is scientific revolution.

Thus scientific progress proceeds in four phases:

PROGRESS———REGRESS———DISTRESS———REDRESS
(Pre-Paradigm)   (Normal Science)   (Anomaly)   (Revolution)

Psychology has yet to evidence the profound form of radical intellectual change that could qualify as scientific revolution in Kuhn's sense, despite a variety of profound (but limited) novel contributions. Yet, it is still possible to discern a mini-revolution that may have wide-ranging consequences in psychology as, for example, in the changeover from classical to contemporary psychophysics.

Classical psychophysics was primarily concerned with the measurement of sensory limits—the absolute threshold. By definition, the absolute threshold is the point in the sensory continuum above which stimuli are intense enough to be detected, and below which stimuli lack the physical energy to be perceived. In actuality, however, organisms do not behave the way this all-or-none conception of sensory sensitivity says they should. There is, in fact, no one level of intensity for a given subject that could be called an *absolute* threshold. Thus the concept of a *relative,* probabilistic threshold emerged with the development of signal-detection theory.

Signal-detection theory focuses on the decision-making processes of the subject and the influences of personality variables like risk-taking on his decision making. The essential point is that SDT conceptualizes the subject in a psychophysics task as an active, dynamic, cognitive human being, *not* as the passive bundle of static responses pictured by classical psychophysics.

The notion that *human* subjects and *human* experimenters harbor expectations and interpretations of the experiments in which they participate is a relatively new conception for psychologists. Social psychologists have begun to center their attention on the sociopsychological nature of the experimental situation and to elucidate the possibility that more than just known independent variables are operating between the stimulus and the response. When, in fact, the outcome of an experiment *is* a function of unintended subject effects or equally unintended experimenter effects, we are dealing not with an experimental result but with experimental artifact.

Psychology's interest in examining the nature of experimental artifacts is the quiet revolution. Harry Stack Sullivan summed up the point well in his one-genus postulate, or species-identity theorem: "Everyone and anyone is much more simply human than otherwise, more like everyone else than different."

Several varieties of artifact have been isolated, but the common feature of all is the human, cognitive-emotional nature of the individuals involved. Procedures designed to monitor the expectations of subjects and experimenters recognize this fact and exploit the human capacity to verbalize experience.

Most fundamental of all is the simple truth: Psychology is a scientific endeavor that employs human investigators to study human behavior.

Recommended Further Reading

Thomas S. Kuhn's now classic monograph, *The Structure of Scientific Revolutions* (Chicago: University of Chicago Press, Vol. 2; No. 2 of the *International Encyclopedia of Unified Science,* 1970) is "must reading" for the serious student of scientific method. Along these same lines, Stephen Toulmin's small book, *Foresight and Understanding: An Enquiry into the Aims of Science* (New York: Harper & Row, 1961; paperback) is an attempt to conceptualize science as an intellectual commitment with social, idealistic and practical goals, yet as a discipline that continues to evolve.

The work of Jerome Bruner in characterizing cognitive development and change has been collected in *Beyond the Information Given* (edited by J. Anglin, New York: W. W. Norton, 1973; see especially the selections in sections 1 and 4.).

Discussions of classical psychophysics and contemporary psychophysics are widely available. Consult the references cited in the text.

An especially thorough account is given by M. R. D'Amato in Chapter 5 of his *Experimental Psychology: Methodology, Psychophysics and Learning* (New York: McGraw-Hill, 1970). Eugene Galanter's treatment of the changeover from classical to contemporary psychophysics is extraordinarily lucid and may be found in "Contemporary Psychophysics" (in *New Directions in Psychology*, Vol. 1; New York: Holt, Rinehart & Winston, 1962).

For a compelling account of change in conceptual viewpoint in a "hard" science by a master instigator of that revolution, consult *The Evolution of Physics* (New York: Simon and Schuster, 1938; paperback) by Albert Einstein and Leopold Infeld. Even the reader with a distaste for mathematics will find the Einstein-Infeld volume exciting and informative reading. Other examples of revolution in science can be read in Perry London's article "The End of Ideology in Behavior Modification" (*American Psychologist*, 1972, *27*), in Michael Ghiselin's article "Darwin and Evolutionary Psychology" (*Science*, 1973, *179*), and in Ernst Mayr's article "The Nature of the Darwinian Revolution" (*Science*, 1972, *176*).

A somewhat controversial proposal for social change, written in semi-popular style, is provided by B. F. Skinner in *Beyond Freedom and Dignity* (New York: Alfred A. Knopf, 1971; paperback available).

The best compendium of papers dealing with artifact in psychological research is the one edited by R. Rosenthal and R. Rosnow, entitled *Artifact in Behavioral Research* (New York: Academic Press, 1969). Martin Orne's ground-breaking paper on demand characteristics, "On the Social Psychology of the Psychological Experiment: With Particular Reference to Demand Characteristics and Their Implications," *American Psychologist*, 1962, *17*, pp. 776–83) should be consulted.

An informative and quite lively account of research techniques that do not disturb the behavior being investigated is provided by E. Webb, D. Campbell, R. Schwartz, and Lee Sechrest's *Unobtrusive Measures: Nonreactive Research in the Social Sciences* (Chicago: Rand McNally, 1966; see especially Chapters 1, 2, and 5.).

Cognitive dissonance theory is given its fullest exposition in Festinger's *A Theory of Cognitive Dissonance* (California: Stanford University Press, 1962). A selective survey of the research-testing hypotheses derived from cognitive dissonance theory is given by Eliot Aronson in his chapter, "Dissonance Theory: Progress and Problems" (in Abelson *et al., Theories of Cognitive Consistency: A Sourcebook* [Chicago: Rand McNally, 1968]).

Readers interested in learning more systematically about Harry Stack Sullivan's theory of personality should consult his most complete presentation, *The Interpersonal Theory of Psychiatry* (New York: W. W. Norton, 1953).

Bibliography

ADORNO, T. W.; FRENKEL-BRUNSWICK, ELSE; LEVINSON, DANIEL, and SAN-
FORD, R. NEVITT. *The Authoritarian Personality.* New York: W. W.
Norton, 1969.

ALLPORT, GORDON. *Personality and Social Encounter.* New York: Beacon
Press, 1960.

ALLPORT, GORDON. *Pattern and Growth in Personality.* New York: Holt,
Rinehart & Winston, 1961.

ARLOW, JACOB. "Psychoanalysis as a Scientific Method." In S. Hook (ed.),
Psychoanalysis, Scientific Method and Philosophy: A Symposium. New
York: New York University Press, 1959.

ATKINSON, JOHN W. *An Introduction to Motivation.* New York: Van Nostrand, 1964.

BACON, FRANCIS. *Novum Organum* (1620). R. Ellis and J. Spedding, trans.
In A. Witherspoon and F. Warnke (eds.), *Seventeenth-Century Prose
and Poetry* (2d ed.). New York: Harcourt, Brace, & World, 1963.

BAKER, JEFFREY, and ALLEN, GARLAND E. *The Study of Biology.* Reading,
Mass.: Addison-Wesley, 1967.

BERGIN, ALLEN E. "The Evaluation of Therapeutic Outcomes." In Allen
E. Bergin and Sol L. Garfield (eds.), *Handbook of Psychotherapy and
Behavior Change.* New York: John Wiley & Sons, 1971.

BIRCH, H. G., and RABINOWITZ, H. S. "The Negative Effect of Previous
Experience on Productive Thinking." *Journal of Experimental Psychology,* 1951, *41,* 121–25.

BREHM, JACK W. "Attitudinal Consequences of Commitment to Unpleasant
Behavior." *Journal of Abnormal and Social Psychology,* 1960, *60,* 379–
83.

BREHM, JACK W., and COHEN, A. R. *Explorations in Cognitive Dissonance.*
New York: John Wiley and Sons, 1962.

BREUER, JOSEPH, and FREUD, SIGMUND. *Studies in Hysteria* (1895). A. A.
Brill, trans. Boston: Beacon Press, 1964.

BRODY, NATHAN. *Personality: Research and Theory.* New York: Academic
Press, 1972.

BROWN, JUDSON. "Pleasure-Seeking Behavior and the Drive-Reduction Hypothesis." (Presidential address delivered at 26th annual Midwestern
Psychological Association in Columbus, Ohio, 1954.) In Ralph Haber
(ed.), *Currest Research in Motivation.* New York: Holt, Rinehart &
Winston, 1966. (Originally published: *Psychological Review,* 1955, *62,*
169–79.)

BRUNER, JEROME. The Growth of Representational Processes in Childhood"
(1966). In J. Bruner, *Beyond the Information Given.* New York: W. W.
Norton, 1973.

BRUNER, JEROME and POSTMAN, LEO. "On the Perception of Incongruity:
A Paradigm." In J. Bruner, *Beyond the Information Given.* New York:
W. W. Norton, 1973. (Originally published: *Journal of Personality,* 1949,
18, 206–23.)

CAMPBELL, DONALD T. "Factors Relevant to the Validity of Experiments in Social Settings." *Psychological Bulletin,* 1957, *54,* 297–312.

CAMPBELL, DONALD T. "Prospective: Artifact and Control." In Robert Rosenthal and Ralph Rosnow (eds.), *Artifact in Behavioral Research.* New York: Academic Press, 1969.

COLBY, KENNETH MARK. *An Introduction to Psychoanalytic Research.* New York: Basic Books, 1960.

CRONBACH, LEE J.; GLESER, GOLDINE C.; NANDA, HARINDER; and RAJARATNAM, NAGESWARI. *The Dependability of Behavioral Measurements: Theory of Generalizability for Scores and Profiles.* New York: John Wiley & Sons, 1972.

D'AMATO, M. R. *Experimental Psychology: Methodology, Psychophysics, and Learning.* New York: McGraw-Hill, 1970.

DARWIN, CHARLES. *The Voyage of the Beagle.* (1845) New York: Natural History Library (Doubleday), 1962.

DARWIN, CHARLES. *The Origin of Species.* (1859) New York: Mentor Books, 1958.

DARWIN, CHARLES. *The Descent of Man* (1871). In C. Darwin, *The Origin of Species* and *The Descent of Man.* (One-volume, unabridged edition.) New York: Random House, undated.

DE BEER, GAVIN, SIR. "Evolution by Natural Selection." In M. H. Fried (ed.), *Readings in Anthropology.* (Vol. 1, 2d ed.) New York: Thomas Y. Crowell, 1968. (Originally published: *The Darwin-Wallace Centenary,* 1958, *17,* 61–76.)

DELGADO, JOSÉ M. R. *Physical Control of the Mind: Toward a Psychocivilized Society.* New York: Harper & Row, 1969.

DOLLARD, JOHN, and MILLER, NEAL. *Personality and Psychotherapy: An Analysis in Terms of Learning, Thinking, and Culture.* New York: McGraw-Hill, 1950.

DOYLE, ARTHUR CONAN, SIR. *The Complete Sherlock Holmes.* New York: Garden City Press (Doubleday), 1930.

DUNNINGER, JOSEPH. *Complete Encyclopedia of Magic.* New York: Spring Books (Crown Publishers), undated.

ENGEL, LEONARD. "Darwin and the Beagle." Editor's introduction to Charles Darwin, *The Voyage of the Beagle.* New York: Natural History Library (Doubleday), 1962.

ENGEN, TRYGG. "Psychophysics I: Discrimination and Detection." In J. W. Kling & Lorrin A. Riggs (eds.), *Woodworth and Schlosberg's Experimental Psychology.* New York: Holt, Rinehart & Winston, 1971.

EYSENCK, HANS. *Uses and Abuses of Psychology.* Baltimore: Penguin Books, 1953.

EYSENCK, HANS. *The Biological Basis of Personality.* Springfield, Ill.: Charles Thomas, 1967.

FALK, JOHN L. "Issues Distinguishing Ideographic from Nomothetic Approaches to Personality Theory." *Psychological Review,* 1956, *63,* 53–62.

FENICHEL, OTTO. *The Psychoanalytic Theory of Neurosis.* New York: W. W. Norton, 1945.

FESTINGER, LEON. "The Psychological Effects of Insufficient Rewards," *American Psychologist,* 1961, *16,* 1–11.

FESTINGER, LEON. *A Theory of Cognitive Dissonance.* Stanford, Calif.: Stanford University Press, 1962.

FESTINGER, LEON. "Cognitive Dissonance." In R. C. Atkinson (ed.), *Con-*

temporary Psychology. San Francisco: W. H. Freeman, 1971. (Originally published: *Scientific American,* October, 1962.)

FESTINGER, LEON, and CARLSMITH, J. MERRILL. "Cognitive Consequences of Forced Compliance," *Journal of Abnormal and Social Psychology,* 1959, *58,* 203–10.

FLAVELL, JOHN H. *The Developmental Psychology of Jean Piaget.* New York: Van Nostrand, 1963.

FRAZER, JAMES GEORGE, SIR. *The Golden Bough.* New York: Macmillan, 1963.

FREUD, ANNA. *The Ego and the Mechanisms of Defense.* New York: International Universities Press, 1946.

FREUD, SIGMUND. *Three Essays on the Theory of Sexuality* (1905). James Strachey, trans. New York: Avon Books, 1965.

FREUD, SIGMUND. *The Ego and the Id* (1923). James Strachey, ed.: Joan Riviere trans. New York: W. W. Norton, 1960.

FREUD, SIGMUND. *The Problem of Anxiety* (1926). H. A. Bunker, trans. New York: W. W. Norton, 1963.

FREUD, SIGMUND. *Psychopathology of Everyday Life.* In A. A. Brill (trans.), *The Basic Writings of Sigmund Freud.* New York: Random House, 1938a.

FREUD, SIGMUND. *The History of the Psychoanalytic Movement.* In A. A. Brill (trans.), *The Basic Writings of Sigmund Freud.* New York: Random House, 1938b.

FREUD, SIGMUND. *Totem and Taboo.* In A. A. Brill (trans.), *The Basic Writings of Sigmund Freud.* New York: Random House, 1938c.

FREUD, SIGMUND. *An Outline of Psychoanalysis* (1940). James Strachey, trans. New York: W. W. Norton, 1949.

FREUD, SIGMUND. *A General Introduction to Psychoanalysis.* Joan Riviere, trans. New York: Washington Square Press, 1962.

FREUD, SIGMUND. "Analysis of a Phobia in a Five-Year-Old Boy." In Phillip Rieff (ed.), *The Sexual Enlightenment of Children.* New York: Collier Books, 1963.

GALANTER, EUGENE. *Contemporary Psychophysics.* In Theodore Newcomb (ed.), *New Directions in Psychology,* Vol. 1. New York: Holt, Rinehart & Winston, 1962.

GUROWITZ, EDWARD M. *The Molecular Basis of Memory.* Englewood Cliffs, N.J.. Prentice-Hall, 1969.

HALL, CALVIN S., and NORDBY, VERNON J. *A Primer of Jungian Psychology.* New York: Mentor Books, 1973.

HARTMANN, HEINZ. "Comments on Scientific Aspects of Psychoanalysis." In H. Hartmann, *Essays on Ego Psychology.* New York: International Universities Press, 1964.

HEMPEL, CARL G. *Aspects of Scientific Explanation.* New York: Free Press, 1965.

HENLE, MARY. "On Understanding." In Frazier (ed.), *The New Elementary School.* Association for Supervision and Curriculum Development, *NEA,* 1968.

HILGARD, ERNEST R., ATKINSON, RICHARD, C., and ATKINSON, RITA. *Introduction to Psychology* (5th ed.). New York: Harcourt Brace Jovanovich, 1971.

HOOK, SIDNEY. (ed.) *Psychoanalysis, Scientific Method and Philosophy: A Symposium.* New York: New York University Press, 1959.

HOOK, SIDNEY. "Science and Mythology in Psychoanalysis." In Sidney Hook (ed.), *Psychoanalysis, Scientific Method and Philosophy: A Symposium.* New York: New York University Press, 1959.

HULL, CLARK. *A Behavior System.* New York: John Wiley & Sons, 1952.

HULL, CLARK L. *Principles of Behavior.* New York: Appleton-Century, 1943.

HUME, DAVID. *An Inquiry Concerning Human Understanding.* Indianapolis, Indiana: Bobbs-Merrill, 1955.

HUNT, J. McV. *Intelligence and Experience.* New York: Ronald Press, 1961.

JAHODA, GUSTAV. *The Psychology of Superstition.* Harmondsworth, Middlesex, England: Penguin, 1970.

JUNG, CARL G. *Archetypes of the Collective Unconscious.* In Violet de Laszlo (ed.), *The Basic Writings of C. G. Jung.* New York: Random House, 1959.

JUNG, CARL G. "Synchronicity: An Acausal Connecting Principle." In C. G. Jung, *The Collected Works,* Vol. 8, *The Structure and Dynamics of the Psyche.* Princeton, N.J.: Princeton University Press, 1969. (See also: C. G. Jung, "On Synchronicity." In C. G. Jung, *The Collected Works,* Vol. 8. Princeton, N.J.: Princeton University Press, 1969.)

KANT, IMMANUEL. *Prolegomena to Any Future Metaphysics.* Indianapolis, Indiana: Bobbs-Merrill, 1950.

KETTLEWELL, H. B. D. "Darwin's Missing Evidence." *Scientific American,* March, 1959.

KIMBLE, GREGORY A., and GARMEZY, NORMAN. *Principles of General Psychology* (3d ed.). New York: Ronald Press, 1968.

KÖHLER, WOLFGANG. *The Mentality of Apes.* New York: Vintage Books, 1959.

KÖHLER, WOLFGANG. *The Task of Gestalt Psychology.* Princeton, N.J.: Princeton University Press, 1969.

KUBIE, LAURENCE S. "Psychoanalysis and Scientific Method." In Sidney Hook (ed.), *Psychoanalysis, Scientific Method and Philosophy: A Symposium.* New York: New York University Press, 1959.

KUHN, THOMAS S. *The Structure of Scientific Revolutions* (2d ed.). Chicago: University of Chicago Press, 1970.

LAING, R. D. *Knots.* New York: Random House (Vintage Books), 1969.

LAING, R. D.; PHILLIPSON, H.; and LEE, A. R. *Interpersonal Perception: A Theory and a Method of Research.* New York: Springer Publishing Co., 1966.

LEWIN, KURT. *A Dynamic Theory of Personality: The Selected Papers of Kurt Lewin.* New York: McGraw-Hill, 1935.

LORENZ, KONRAD. *King Solomon's Ring.* New York: Thomas Y. Crowell, 1952.

LYONS, JOHN. *Noam Chomsky.* New York: Viking Press, 1970.

McGUIRE, WILLIAM J. "Suspiciousness of Experimenter's Intent." In Robert Rosenthal and Ralph Rosnow (eds.), *Artifact in Behavioral Research.* New York: Academic Press, 1969.

MacKINNON, D. W., and DUKES, W. F. "Repression." In L. Postman (ed.), *Psychology in the Making: Histories of Selected Research Problems.* New York: Alfred A. Knopf, 1962.

MAIER, NORMAN R. F. "Reasoning in Humans II. The Solution of a Problem and Its Appearance in Consciousness," *Journal of Comparative Psychology,* 1931, *12,* 181–94.

MALINOWSKI, BRONISLAW. *Magic, Science and Religion.* New York: Doubleday, 1954.

MARX, MELVIN, H. and HILLIX, WILLIAM A. *Systems and Theories in Psychology.* New York: McGraw-Hill, 1963.

MERTON, ROBERT K. "The Self-Fulfilling Prophecy." *Antioch Review,* 1948, *8,* 193–210.

MICHENER, JAMES A. *The Source.* Greenwich, Conn.: Fawcett Publications, 1965.

MILGRAM, STANLEY. "Behavioral Studies of Obedience." *Journal of Abnormal and Social Psychology,* 1963, *67,* 371–78.

MILGRAM, STANLEY. "Some Conditions of Obedience and Disobedience to Authority." *Human Relations,* 1965, *18,* 57–76.

MISCHEL, WALTER. *Personality and Assessment.* New York: John Wiley & Sons, 1968.

MORGAN, CONWAY L. "On Lloyd Morgan's Canon," (1894). In Richard Herrnstein and Edwin Boring (eds.), *A Source Book in the History of Psychology.* Cambridge, Mass.: Harvard University Press, 1966. (Originally published: *An Introducton to Comparative Psychology.* London, 1894.)

MURPHY, GARDNER. *Historical Introduction to Modern Psychology.* New York: Harcourt, Brace & World, 1949.

NIETZSCHE, FRIEDRICH. *The Joyful Wisdom.* New York: Frederick Ungar, 1964.

OLDS, JAMES. "Pleasure Centers in the Brain." *Scientific American,* October, 1956.

OLDS, JAMES, and MILNER, PETER. "Positive Reinforcement Produced by Electrical Stimulation of Septal Area and other Regions of Rat Brain." *Journal of Comparative and Physiological Psychology,* 1954, *47,* 419–27.

OLDS, JAMES, and OLDS, MARIANNE. "Drives, Rewards, and the Brain." In Theodore M. Newcomb (ed.), *New Directions in Psychology,* Vol. 2. New York: Holt, Rinehart, & Winston, 1965.

ORNE, MARTIN T. "The Nature of Hypnosis: Artifact and Essence." *Journal of Abnormal and Social Psychology,* 1959, *58,* 277–99.

ORNE, MARTIN T. "On the Social Psychology of the Psychological Experiment: With Particular Reference to Demand Characteristics and Their Implications." *American Psychologist,* 1962, *17,* 776–83.

ORNE, MARTIN T. "Demand Characteristics and the Concept of Quasi-controls." In Robert Rosenthal and Ralph Rosnow (eds.), *Artifact in Behavioral Research.* New York: Academic Press, 1969.

PIAGET, JEAN. *The Child's Conception of the World.* London: Kegan Paul, 1929.

PIAGET, JEAN. *The Origins of Intelligence in Children.* New York: International Universities Press, 1952.

PIAGET, JEAN. *The Construction of Reality in the Child.* New York: Basic Books, 1954.

PIAGET, JEAN, and INHELDER, BÄRBEL. *The Psychology of the Child.* New York: Basic Books, 1969.

PLATO. *The Republic.* (Jowett translation.) New York: Random House, undated.

POPPER, KARL. *The Logic of Scientific Discovery.* New York: Basic Books, 1959.

POPPER, KARL. *Conjectures and Refutations.* New York: Basic Books, 1963.

POPPER, KARL. "Science: Problems, Aims, Responsibilities." (Paper presented at 47th annual meeting of Federation of American Societies for Experimental Biology, Atlantic City, N.J., April 17, 1963.) In John M. Foley, Russell A. Lockhart, and David Messick (eds.), *Contemporary Readings in Psychology*. New York: Harper & Row, 1970.

PREMACK, DAVID. "Reversibility of the Reinforcement Relation." *Science*, 1962, *136*, 255–57.

RIECKEN, H. W. "A Program for Research on Experiments in Social Psychology." In N. F. Washburne (ed.), *Decisions, Values and Groups*, Vol. 2. New York: Pergamon Press, 1962.

ROETHLISBERGER, F. J., and DICKSON, W. J. *Management and the Worker*. Cambridge, Mass.: Harvard University Press, 1939.

ROSENBERG, MILTON J. "When Dissonance Fails: On Eliminating Evaluation Apprehension from Attitude Measurement." *Journal of Personality and Social Psychology*, 1965, *1*, 18–42.

ROSENBERG, MILTON J. "The Conditions and Consequences of Evaluation Apprehension." In Robert Rosenthal and Ralph Rosnow (eds.), *Artifact in Behavioral Research*. New York: Academic Press, 1969.

ROSENTHAL, ROBERT. "Interpersonal Expectations: Effects of the Experimenter's Hypothesis." In Robert Rosenthal and Ralph Rosnow (eds.), *Artifact in Behavioral Research*. New York: Academic Press, 1969.

ROSENTHAL, ROBERT, and JACOBSON, LEONORE F. *Pygmalion in the Classroom: Teacher Expectations and Pupils' Intellectual Development*. New York: Holt, Rinehart and Winston, 1968.

ROSENTHAL, ROBERT, and JACOBSON, LEONORE F. "Teacher Expectations for the Disadvantaged." In Richard C. Atkinson (ed.), *Contemporary Psychology*. San Francisco: W. H. Freeman, 1971. (Originally published: *Scientific American*, April, 1968.)

ROSENTHAL, ROBERT, and ROSNOW, RALPH. "The Volunteer Subject." In Robert Rosenthal and Ralph Rosnow (eds.), *Artifact in Behavioral Research*. New York: Academic Press, 1969.

ROSNOW, RALPH, and ROSENTHAL, ROBERT. "Volunteer Effects in Behavioral Research." In Theodore Newcomb (ed.), *New Directions in Psychology*, Vol. 4. New York: Holt, Rinehart & Winston, 1970.

SALMON, WESLEY C. "Confirmation." *Scientific American*, May, 1973.

SALTER, ANDREW. *The Case Against Psychoanalysis* (rev. ed.). New York: Citadel Press, 1963.

SCHACTER, STANLEY, and SINGER, JEROME E. "Cognitive, Social, and Psychological Determinants of Emotional State." *Psychological Review*, 1962, *69*, 379–99.

SHEFFIELD, FRED. "A Drive-Induction Theory of Reinforcement." (Paper read at Psychology Colloquium, Brown University, November, 1954.) In Ralph Haber (ed.), *Current Research in Motivation*. New York: Holt, Rinehart & Winston, 1966.

SHEFFIELD, FRED. "New Evidence on the Drive-Induction Theory of Reinforcement." (Revised version of paper read at the Stanford Psychology Colloquium, November, 1960.) In Ralph Haber (ed.), *Current Research In Motivation*. New York: Holt, Rinehart & Winston, 1966.

SIMPSON, GEORGE G. "Biology and the Nature of Science." *Science*, 1963, *139*, 81–88.

SIMPSON, GEORGE G., and BECK, WILLIAM S. *Life: An Introduction to Biology* (2d ed.). New York: Harcourt, Brace & World, 1965.

SKINNER, B. F. " 'Superstition' in the Pigeon." *Journal of Experimental Psychology,* 1948, *38,* 168–72.

SKINNER, B. F. "Are Theories of Learning Necessary?" *Psychological Review,* 1950, *57,* 193–216.

SKINNER, B. F. *Science and Human Behavior.* New York: Free Press, 1953.

SKINNER, B. F. "Critique of Psychoanalytic Concepts and Theories." *In Minnesota Studies in the philosophy of science,* Vol. 1. Minneapolis: University of Minnesota Press, 1956.

SKINNER, B. F. "Behaviorism at Fifty." *Science,* 1963, *140,* 951–58.

SPIELBERGER, CHARLES D., and DENIKE, L. DOUGLAS. "Descriptive Behaviorism Versus Cognitive Theory in Verbal Operant Conditioning." *Psychological Review,* 1966, *73,* 306–26.

SULLIVAN, HARRY STACK. *The Interpersonal Theory of Psychiatry.* New York: W. W. Norton, 1953.

SULLIVAN, HARRY STACK. *The Psychiatric Interview.* New York: W. W. Norton, 1954.

SULLIVAN, HARRY STACK. *Schizophrenia as a Human Process.* H. S. Perry, ed. New York: W. W. Norton, 1962.

SULLIVAN, HARRY STACK. *The Fusion of Psychiatry and Social Science.* New York: W. W. Norton, 1964.

SWETS, J. A., TANNER, W. P., JR., and BIRDSALL, T. G. "Decision Processes in Perception." *Psychological Review,* 1961, *68,* 301–40.

TANNER, W. P., JR., and SWETS, J. A. "A Decision-Making Theory of Visual Detection." *Psychological Review,* 1954, *61,* 401–9.

THEOBALD, D. W. *An Introduction to the Philosophy of Science.* London: Methuen & Co., 1968.

TOULMIN, STEPHEN. *The Philosophy of Science.* New York: Harper & Row, 1960.

TOULMIN, STEPHEN. *Foresight and Understanding.* New York: Harper & Row, 1961.

VAN LAWICK-GOODALL, JANE. *In the Shadow of Man.* New York: Dell, 1971.

WATSON, JOHN B. "Psychology as the Behaviorist Views It." *Psychological Review,* 1913, *20,* 158–77.

WATSON, ROBERT I. *The Great Psychologists.* Philadelphia: J. B. Lippincott, 1963.

WEISZ, PAUL. *The Science of Biology* (3d ed.). New York: McGraw-Hill, 1967.

WERTHEIMER, MAX. *Productive Thinking* (enlarged ed.). New York: Harper & Row, 1959.

WHITE, LESLIE. "The Expansion and Scope of Science." In Morton H. Fried (ed.), *Readings in Anthropology* (Vol. 1, 2d ed.). New York: Thomas Y. Crowell, 1968. (Originally published: *Journal of the Washington Academy of Sciences,* 1947, *37,* 181–210.)

WOLPE, JOSEPH, and RACHMAN, STANLEY. "Psychoanalytic 'Evidence': A Critique Based on Freud's Case of Little Hans." *Journal of Nervous and Mental Diseases,* 1960, *130,* 135–48.

Index